# The Man Who Tried
# to Buy the World

# The Man Who Tried to Buy the World

✦ ✦ ✦

JEAN-MARIE MESSIER AND
VIVENDI UNIVERSAL

Jo Johnson

AND

Martine Orange

PORTFOLIO

PORTFOLIO
Published by the Penguin Group
Penguin Group (USA) Inc., 375 Hudson Street, New York, New York 10014, U.S.A.
Penguin Books Ltd, 80 Strand, London WC2R 0RL, England
Penguin Books Australia Ltd, 250 Camberwell Road, Camberwell, Victoria 3124, Australia
Penguin Books Canada Ltd, 10 Alcorn Avenue, Toronto, Ontario, Canada M4V 3B2
Penguin Books India (P) Ltd, 11 Community Centre, Panchsheel Park,
New Delhi - 110 017, India
Penguin Books (N.Z.) Ltd, Cnr Rosedale and Airborne Roads, Albany, Auckland, New Zealand
Penguin Books (South Africa) (Pty) Ltd, 24 Sturdee Avenue, Rosebank,
Johnnesburg 2196, South Africa

Penguin Books Ltd, Registered Offices: 80 Strand, London WC2R 0RL, England

First American edition
Published in 2003 by Portfolio, a member of Penguin Group (USA) Inc.

1   3   5   7   9   10   8   6   4   2

Excerpts from an article by Peter Bart, *Variety,* June 19, 2000. Used with permission of and copyrighted by © Variety Magazine, owned and published by Cahners Business Information, a division of Reed Elsevier, Inc.; excerpt from "There's Bad News Folks, I'm French" by Bruno Graccio, *Time,* April 22, 2002. © 2002 Time Inc. Reprinted by permission; excerpts from "The Big Fix" by Michael Woolf, *New York Magazine,* May 13, 2002 and "Meet Barry Buffet" by Michael Woolf, *New York Magazine,* September 30, 2002. Copyright © Michael Woolf, 2002. Reprinted by permission of the author.

LIBRARY OF CONGRESS CATALOGING IN PUBLICATION DATA
Johnson, Jo.
The man who tried to buy the world : Jean-Marie Messier and Vivendi Universal /
Jo Johnson and Martine Orange.
p. cm.
Includes bibliographical references and index.
ISBN 1-59184-018-X (alk. paper)
1. Messier, Jean-Marie, 1956–   2. Business—France—Biography.   3. Vivendi (Firm)—History.
4. Universal Pictures (Firm)   5. Seagram Company—History.   6. Bronfman family.
7. Businessmen—Canada—Biography.   8. Conglomerate corporations—France.
9. Conglomerate corporations—Canada.   10. Consolidation and merger of corporations—
France—Case studies.   11. Consolidation and merger of corporations—Canada—Case studies.
12. Consolidation and merger of corporations—United States—Case studies.
I. Orange, Martine.   II. Title.
HC272.5.M48J64 2003
338.8'092—dc21       2003043643
[B]

This book is printed on acid-free paper. ∞

Printed in the United States of America

To Milly

# CONTENTS

*Introduction*                                           *ix*

PROLOGUE: Where Egos Dare                                  1

CHAPTER ONE: A Perfect Frenchman                           7

CHAPTER TWO: In Medias Res                                26

CHAPTER THREE: Hurry Up Please, It's Time                 47

CHAPTER FOUR: Bonjour Hollywood!                          70

CHAPTER FIVE: Maître du Monde                             90

CHAPTER SIX: Vivendi Frères                              105

CHAPTER SEVEN: The French Exception                      125

CHAPTER EIGHT: Speeding Up                               143

CHAPTER NINE: Claude and the Boys                        169

CHAPTER TEN: Vivendi vs. Universal                       195

CHAPTER ELEVEN: The Last Days of J6M                     215

EPILOGUE                                                 233

*Acknowledgments*                                        249

*Notes*                                                  251

*Index*                                                  255

# INTRODUCTION

The first raids came at dawn in the weeks leading up to Christmas. On Thursday, December 12, 2002, fifteen police officers from the fraud squad swooped down on the headquarters of Vivendi Universal to seize computer files, documents, and e-mails. Anything that would help explain the sudden financial collapse that summer of France's best-known company was bundled into boxes and loaded into the unmarked cars lining avenue Friedland. Other units fanned out across the capital to search the two homes of Jean-Marie Messier—long familiar to readers of *Paris Match*—in the chic neighborhood near the parc de Monceau and in the Forest of Rambouillet, southwest of Paris.

Over the following days, in scenes that echoed events at Enron, Tyco, and WorldCom earlier in the year, the fraud squad descended on the homes and offices of some of the most illustrious figures of French capitalism, among them Marc Viénot, the seventy-four-year-old honorary chairman of Société Générale, France's second largest bank, and onetime emblem of the French business establishment. Vivendi Universal's board members, including Bernard Arnault, the billionaire founder of the Moët Hennessy–Louis Vuitton luxury goods group, and Serge Tchuruk, chairman of Alcatel, the telecommunications equipment manufacturer, all nervously anticipated the indignity of the domestic raid. The criminal investigations had started.

It seemed that with this dawn raid the crisis of corporate America had finally crossed the Atlantic. For several months after the collapse of the world's second largest media group, it appeared that the Parisian business world had successfully buried the Vivendi Universal affair. "There is no doubt in my mind that the French will do everything in their power to attempt a cover-up. The French establishment does not eat its own," cautioned Edgar Bronfman Jr., whose family lost over $5 billion when Vivendi Universal plunged into crisis in 2002. But the sudden flurry of criminal investigations and regulatory probes suggested that shareholders and employees might eventually receive a full explanation for the incredible collapse of the company.

Not since the failure a decade before of Crédit Lyonnais, the state-owned bank nicknamed "Crazy Lyonnais" for its bizarre and reckless lending, had some of the most powerful businessmen and bankers in France felt so exposed. In addition to the class-action lawsuits, Vivendi Universal was, by early 2003, in the throes of criminal probes by the U.S. Department of Justice and French prosecutors, and formal investigations by both the chief American regulatory authority, the Securities and Exchange Commission, and the main French stock market regulator, the Commission des Opérations de Bourse (COB). Piece by piece, investigators in the United States and France started to reconstruct the last three years of Jean-Marie Messier's roller-coaster ride at the helm of a dull water and sewage company that became a French media wonder-stock and then took on the world.

"Anybody who either worked for the company or invested in the company should feel betrayed," said Edgar Bronfman Jr. One of the documents unearthed during the raids on Vivendi Universal's headquarters in December brazenly alluded to the fact that pressure was allegedly being brought to bear on the French investigators, who had started making preliminary inquiries in July 2002. One senior director of Vivendi Universal, Alain Marsaud, was discovered to have written a memo to Messier's successor, Jean-René Fourtou, on September 17, 2002, just two months into the COB investigation. "We should take care to ensure that the pressure on the investigators does not become a matter of public knowledge," Marsaud wrote. Vivendi Universal immediately denied interfering with the investigation, but the memo left many questions unanswered.

Two years earlier, Jean-Marie Messier had been feted as the "perfect Frenchman." Vivendi, the French water utility he had run since late 1994, had astonished the world. In a deal of startling audacity, Messier launched the largest ever French takeover of a U.S. company. The $46 billion acquisition of Seagram—owner of Universal Music, producer of one in every three albums sold worldwide, and of Universal Studios, an icon of Hollywood—was the boldest attempt by any foreign media group to challenge the American goliaths of the entertainment industry. A new media major— Vivendi Universal—was born.

For the first time, France could take pride in a global champion in the media and entertainment industry that could fight back against American cultural hegemony. In total, Messier would spend more than $100 billion in pursuit of his ambition to create the world's number one entertainment company. At its zenith, his empire would be second in size only to a then mighty AOL Time Warner. His deal-making addiction was fueled by the speculative hysteria that swept financial markets, driving media and telecom stocks to ludicrous valuations and media moguls to ever grander displays of machismo. Without his vision and personality—a strange blend of French technocratic arrogance, wanna-be Hollywood showmanship, and investment banker charm—Vivendi Universal would never have come into existence. Without Jean-Marie Messier's weaknesses—a love of deal making, self-promotion, obfuscation, and risk—the dream of a French champion might have survived.

The ramifications of the Vivendi Universal story are only just being felt. They extend far beyond the personal disaster overwhelming Messier, whose reputation as one of the most brilliant business personalities of the era has been indelibly tarnished by the failure of his project. Few receive a second chance after presiding over failure on such a grand scale. France's largest private-sector employer has survived its brush with insolvency, but only at the cost of being broken up and parceled off to the highest bidders.

Vivendi Universal—as conceived by Jean-Marie Messier—has ceased to exist. Mere mention of Vivendi Universal and its fallen hero now provokes severe embarrassment within French business establishment circles. The damage done to the image of French business by his Napoleonic adventurism remains incalculable.

Vivendi Universal was far more than just a media colossus. At its peak, the empire had extended beyond traditional media into the Internet and mobile telecommunications, giving France a champion in the industries of the future. The French group had led the European charge into the new economy, launching more than one hundred Internet companies in two years, including Vizzavi, whose €1.6 billion budget made it by far the most expensive and ambitious start-up of the European Internet boom. In telecommunications, it controlled the largest private mobile operator in France and had interests in others as far afield as Kenya, Egypt, Morocco, Hungary, and Poland.

Further still from the entertainment economy, the Messier empire provided the essentials of life to hundreds of millions of homes across the world. The original water business out of which the media empire had sprung pumped water into homes and factories in more than one hundred countries and to many great cities, including Paris, London, Vancouver, and New Orleans; it also built bridges in Spain; provided pest-control services in Papua New Guinea; cleaned beaches in Australia; monitored the impact of human activity on water purity in the Chilean Antarctic; treated sewage; hauled garbage; heated homes; and managed transport systems, including Connex trains in London and the southeast of England, buses in Washington, D.C., island hoppers in the Comoro Islands, trams in Nancy, and tourist trolleys in the Alps.

As the Messier empire collapsed in 2002, its three thousand subsidiaries revealed an absurd and, in some ways, wonderful collection of assets: the Citrus Technology Centre near the Three Gorges in China that aimed to produce the perfect orange; a seven-hundred-strong chain of gift stores that dominated the U.S. market for vibrators and other "wild 'n' crazy" novelty gifts; a leaky palazzo in Venice; a brand of bottled water; the Paris Saint-Germain and Servette de Genève soccer clubs; the eighteenth-century château at Méry-sur-Oise, renovated at pharaonic cost to boast an experimental garden with a miniature rain forest, hot pools for the papyrus, and a giant igloo for the Siberian irises and arctic bramble; a town house in London; the chief executive's $17.5 million Park Avenue apartment, renovated by France's leading architect, best known for his work on the Louvre; a three-thousand-item art collection, replete with Dubuffet paintings, Miró tapestries, rare photographs, and antique drinking vessels; and a private air force that included a helicopter, a Falcon, four Gulfstreams, a Global Express, and a brand-new Airbus A319.

But the story of Vivendi Universal and its charismatic leader is about more than the hubris of one man and the breathtaking creation and collapse of an industrial and postindustrial empire. It is the perfect prism through which to examine France's ambivalence toward America and to globalization. Messier had long presented himself as an exception to the "French exception," the cherished idea that France can hold back the tide of globalization and preserve the country's distinctive economic model in the face of an encroaching ultraliberal free-market capitalism. International investors welcomed the first Frenchman to master the American-inspired mantras of shareholder value.

During his rapid ascent, Messier came to symbolize a new generation of French businessmen that had become culturally more attuned to American entrepreneurialism than to the state capitalism of the Old Continent. "I am the most un-French Frenchman you will ever meet," he liked to tell American journalists. When Messier debated live on television in April 2000 with José Bové, the small farmer who orchestrated attacks on McDonald's fast-food restaurants across southern France, he did so in the name of a France ready to rise to the challenges of globalization rather than one set at all costs on defending the country's singularity and exceptionalism. In the end, ironically, it was the American investors he so dearly wanted to seduce who brought him down.

That morning in December 2002, the police faced a different Messier: beaten, angry, and bitter. "My sole revenge will be my success," he had promised on his return to Paris after a three-month holiday in Montana and the south of France. He had not kept his word. In early November he published, in French, *Mon vrai journal (My True Diary)*, a vengeful and self-serving memoir of the events that led up to Vivendi Universal's collapse and his demise as chief executive. Many advised Messier to lick his wounds in silence and await rehabilitation. They were ignored. Messier depicted himself as a prophet without honor in his own country, a crusader for a reformed, shareholder-friendly form of French capitalism who was unfairly deposed by a reactionary counterrevolution.

"The 'Vivendi Universal affair' has set back the development of French capitalism by a couple of decades," Messier claimed. His chutzpah left his peers openmouthed. The self-conscious cockiness of *j6m.com*—his first autobiography, published in 2000, the title of which played on his nickname, Jean-Marie Messier, Moi-même maître du monde—was gone, to be replaced by self-pity, petulance, and bitterness at his desertion by the French establishment, at fickle journalists, at hapless analysts, at disloyal board members, and at the "bootlegger" methods of the Bronfmans that were used to bring him down. It was not persuasive. As Richard Lambert, editor of the *Financial Times* between 1990 and 2001, wrote in a review for *The Times:* "He has rushed out his version of the story in a book which will only convince his enemies that they were right to eject him."[1]

The book shows that Messier, who frightened others for a time, had ended up frightening himself. *"Dallas . . .* Your pitiless world exists. I have encountered it," he wrote. "Surveillance; espionage of my smallest acts, of my most insignificant human interactions; tapping of my telephones; manipulation of taped recordings; photos or purported photos; rumor-mongering and the passing of documents to my board or to newsrooms: the complete amateur James Bond."[2] His paranoia expressed itself in a naive cynicism about the motivations of all who questioned him. Messier's favorite method of self-defense was to attack the credibility of others, often in the most offensive ways. To explain the mounting tensions with the Bronfmans and his credibility problem in Hollywood, he answered: "I am not a Hollywood Jew and I won't ever be one."[3]

To discredit Claude Bébéar—the chairman of the AXA insurance group, who did his utmost on behalf of the place de Paris, France's Wall Street, to save Vivendi Universal from bankruptcy—Messier claimed he was motivated by jealousy of a younger man's success in the United States and a need to be "acknowledged as *the* 'godfather' of French capitalism." To call into question the work of the analyst who undertook hard-hitting research of an opaque and aggressive company, Messier dredged up trivial stories from the banker's distant past and suggested hurtful psychological problems; board members who became angry when he did not give straight answers to simple questions were dismissed as "deranged," while those who failed to back him to the bitter end were denounced as cowards whose hands he would no longer shake.

The authors of this book are, in fact, the only two journalists to be personally attacked in his own account of his downfall. Jo Johnson of the *Financial Times* is criticized for using "methods more worthy of a tabloid rag than a business newspaper" for probing immediately into excessive spending on executive perks, while *Le Monde* has the distinction of enjoying a virulent chapter all to itself.[4] To discredit the French newspaper—whose only crime was to have been assiduous in exposing the weaknesses of his leadership and the fragility of his project—Messier alleged, unfairly, that editorial objectivity had been sacrificed to a crude personal vendetta. This, he claimed, was being masterminded by *Le Monde*'s editor, Jean-Marie Colombani, and executed by Martine Orange, its staff reporter on the Vivendi Universal story.

According to Messier, Colombani was seeking revenge for Vivendi's refusal in 1998 to sell the newspaper group *L'Express,* the French equivalent of *Time.* At one point, Messier claimed he had received a telephone call from the Corsican editor while he and his wife were being driven to a dinner with Philippe Camus, now the head of the European Aeronautic Defence and Space company, owner of Airbus. The bogus dialogue is worthy of the worst schlock writers: "'It's Jean-Marie Colombani here. If you do not sell us *L'Express,* you will see what it means to have *Le Monde* against you for twenty years!' We are into the fourth year. *Le Monde,* with Martine Orange in the lead, is running an anti-

Messier campaign. Never mind the approximations, the methods, the hunt for moles at the heart of Vivendi. Only the end counts."[5]

The evidence for this alleged campaign? Ten lead front-page articles over two years. "The harassment was permanent," Messier wrote in *My True Diary.* "Never get angry with newspapers, in particular *Le Monde.* They are so powerful. And if they decide to use this power against you unscrupulously, under the pretext of revealing the truth to the readers, you will always lose." To try to silence Martine Orange, Messier launched a €1 million lawsuit against her and *Le Monde* in May 2002 after she wrote an article that described how his wild ride at Vivendi Universal almost came to a shuddering end as early as December 2001. Soon proved to be wholly vexatious, the suit was immediately abandoned when he was fired and as the company plunged into the near-fatal liquidity crisis that *Le Monde* had foreshadowed.

Needless to say, Jean-Marie Messier chose not to cooperate with this book: "The answer is clearly no," he replied in an e-mail. Yet even if he denied us formal meetings in the context of the book, over the past two years the authors have interviewed him on numerous occasions, on the record, off the record, in his private jet, in the back of his chauffeur-driven limousine, in London, Paris, and New York. Access to Messier was never the problem. As Rupert Murdoch, with whom Messier was obsessively and self-destructively competitive, once told the *Financial Times:* "Jean-Marie's problem is that he's never met a journalist he didn't give an interview to." Messier's version of events coincides all too rarely with the eyewitness accounts given by the hundreds of people interviewed by the authors. This is still his story, as it actually happened, but almost certainly not as he might wish to see it told.

# The Man Who Tried
# to Buy the World

# Where Egos Dare

The Bronfman family regrouped in the Seagram Building in New York, the spoils of three-quarters of a century in the liquor business around them. The thirty-eight-floor skyscraper, a Manhattan landmark designed by Ludwig Mies van der Rohe at the family's behest, was a monument to the Bronfmans' power and taste. While works by Larry Rivers, Ellsworth Kelly, and Mark Rothko graced executive suites on the fourth floor, the 1920 Picasso stage curtain that they had lent the Four Seasons restaurant on the ground floor was visible to all Park Avenue. From their bootlegging origins in the Prohibition era, the family of Canadian Jews had become society regulars in Manhattan, political donors in Washington, champions of the Zionist lobby, and patrons of the arts across the country. The family empire, Seagram, had filled bars around the world with Captain Morgan rum, Martell cognac, Absolut vodka, and Chivas Regal whiskey. It also owned Universal, maker of some of the most memorable films of the twentieth century, including *Beau Geste, Billy Elliot, The Deer Hunter, Frankenstein, Notting Hill, Rear Window,* and *Spartacus*. Universal was also the world's leading record company, boasting artists such as Jimi Hendrix, Willie Nelson, Snoop Dogg, and Shania Twain, and a third share of the U.S. market. It had been a momentous morning. At the nearby offices of Goldman Sachs, the family elders—Edgar Sr., seventy-one-year-old president of the World

Jewish Congress, and his brother Charles, sixty-nine—had listened closely to Jean-Marie Messier as he outlined his vision of their shared future.

It was March 22, 2000, just two days before the decade-long bull market would hit its final peak.* That morning the Bronfmans had edged ever closer to entrusting the beguiling Frenchman with the family firm—and all the riches and influence that went with it. The forty-three-year-old chief executive of Vivendi, the French water, publishing, telecom, and pay-television group, had dazzled the assembled uncles, brothers, and cousins of the powerful Jewish family with a mesmerizing presentation. Under Edgar Bronfman Jr., the latest chief executive, Seagram had been rapidly moving into entertainment, buying the Universal movie and music businesses from Japan's Matsushita in 1995 for $5.7 billion, and then the PolyGram music empire from Philips Electronics three years later for $10.4 billion. Messier had proposed taking things several steps further. He suggested a marriage of Seagram's U.S. film and music businesses with Vivendi's next-generation distribution in Europe, the pay-television, mobile telephone, and Internet portal pipes that would take Universal's content straight to the protected European consumer. Both companies would sever ties with their pasts. Seagram would sell the family drinks empire, founded in 1928 by Samuel Bronfman, Edgar Bronfman Jr.'s grandfather, while Vivendi would disengage from its 150-year-old water business. Together they would create a transatlantic media giant. Six months earlier, the world had been dazzled by the AOL Time Warner combination of the world's largest Internet and media companies. Vivendi Universal would be their reply.

The defining act of Messier's career—the creation of a French rival to the U.S. behemoths of the entertainment industry—was fast approaching. In his presentation to the Bronfmans that morning, Jean-Marie Messier had brought all his persuasive powers to bear. Flanked by four of his French lieutenants—Eric Licoys, a col-

---

*The Standard and Poor's 500 peaked on March 24, 2000, at a value of 1527. Vivendi Universal's shares had peaked on March 10 at a value of €141. The Dow Jones Industrial Average peaked on January 14, 2000, at 11,722.

league from his Lazard Frères days; Philippe Germond, head of Cegetel, Vivendi's telecom operation; Guillaume Hannezo, his finance director; and Pierre Lescure, chairman of Canal Plus, the European pay-television company then 49 percent owned by Vivendi—Messier faced eight members of the Bronfman family. "It was a very small room given the number of people," remembers Pierre Lescure. "But it all helped create the atmosphere. This was his big act and he did it very well indeed. He was absolutely calm, clear, and utterly convincing. He explained everything about the new economy, about Vivendi's one hundred million customers in Europe and about the millions that would flock to Vizzavi, our Internet site, to look at Universal's products. I had never seen him articulate his vision so convincingly. We were all proud of him. With his strong accent, but speaking fluent English, he was at his very best, smiling, but not too much, and polite. He told the family how delighted he and his team were to be received by them in New York. It was an extremely impressive performance."

At the end of the meeting, the first between the French executives and the entire Bronfman family since informal talks between Jean-Marie Messier and Bronfman had started in Paris back in October 1999, Edgar Bronfman Sr. concluded the session by standing up and saying: "Jean-Marie, I have just one regret and that is that you don't have an American passport because if you were a U.S. citizen I would tell you to run for president." Even Charles Bronfman, Edgar Bronfman Jr.'s uncle, who had long regretted the Bronfman family's diversification into the entertainment industry, softened. "He did not comment. He did not say a word, but I had this feeling that even this little man with his narrow and suspicious eyes was more than a little impressed," Lescure would later say. "Remember that Jean-Marie had thought of every single detail. He had prepared answers to every conceivable question. It was an extremely positive meeting. Bronfman looked so satisfied, so happy. Finally, he had done something that looked like it was going to please all the different members of his family, even those that had been toughest on him over the years. He had delivered the right man and the right deal."

"We were all impressed," Edgar Bronfman Jr. would later say.

"But so was everyone at that time." He recalled Bob Wright, chief executive of NBC and vice chairman of General Electric, a man whose opinion he respected inordinately, taking him aside and telling him that Messier was going to be the future leader of the entertainment industry. As Bronfman saw it, Messier had a real record of accomplishment, in the French government, at Lazard, and at Vivendi. He was delighted to have found a solution that would finally allow Charles's side of the family to control their own destiny. As the Bronfmans controlled Seagram with 24 percent of its shares they could not sell without sending an extremely negative signal to the market and without crystallizing a huge capital-gains liability. If they succeeded in concluding the merger with Vivendi, both sides of the family would become normal shareholders, free to buy and sell as they pleased. But who would want to sell? Vivendi's share price was rocketing upward. It had doubled since October, making Vivendi France's third largest company with a stock market value on March 10, 2000, that was approaching €85 billion.

While his father and uncle returned to the Seagram building, Bronfman invited the Frenchmen back to his East Side town house for lunch. It was an all-male affair. Edgar Bronfman Jr.'s Venezuelan wife, Clarissa Alcock, was out of town celebrating her thirty-fourth birthday with their children. The Frenchmen marveled at her overhaul of the Manhattan mansion. The landmarked facade retained its neoclassical restraint, but inside, the oak-paneled walls of the entrance hall had been reclad in waxed sheets of bronze-colored steel. Where once the drawing room would have been was a sunlit atrium: the center of the house had been hollowed out to create a dazzling courtyard in the middle of which stood a larger-than-life-size Nigerian fertility statue. After they had eaten, they moved into Bronfman's library for coffee. As they sat down, their host pressed a button by his chair and a white screen descended from the ceiling: "Let's watch some trailers," he said. To Messier's embarrassment, one of the Frenchmen looked blankly back at the owner of Universal Studios. "What are 'trailers'?" he asked. Pierre Lescure offered a rapid translation. As they left his house that afternoon, after watching previews for *Meet the Parents, Erin Brockovich,* and *Gladiator,* the six-foot-three Edgar put his arm around Messier's shoulder, some distance below: "You were extremely impressive back there. You touched every member of my family. I think we have the green light."

## CHAPTER ONE

# A Perfect Frenchman

On the sweltering summer night of July 3, 2001, the limousines of the cream of the French banking, business, and political worlds drew up outside the Centre Pompidou, the modern art complex in the heart of Paris. Several members of Vivendi Universal's board, including Bernard Arnault of Moët Hennessy–Louis Vuitton (LVMH); Serge Tchuruk, chairman of Alcatel; and Marc Viénot, honorary chairman of Société Générale, were among the grandees escorted by svelte hostesses to the glass-enclosed rooftop of Chez Georges restaurant. Standing on a dais before his three hundred guests, the city spreading out behind him, Jean-Marie Messier was radiant. He could have hoped for no better going-away party than this.

A few months earlier, he had been informed that he was to be made a member of the Legion of Honor, France's foremost decoration. Most countries have an honors system, but only in egalitarian France is the status symbol, a red band worn in the lapel of the suit jacket, put on such ostentatious display. Messier had decided the award ceremony would be a fitting occasion to mark his departure from Paris to conquer the New World. In early September, he and his wife, Antoinette, along with their five children, would move to New York to start their new lives in the splendid apartment being prepared for them on Park Avenue. He could depart with the blessings of the French Republic resounding in his ears.

Protocol dictates that only someone who is already a member of the Legion of Honor, and of the same or superior rank, can confer the award. As was required, Messier was entering the order at the lowest level. At any one time, there could be a maximum of 125,000 knights, two-thirds of whom tend to be soldiers. The senior levels of the order thin out sharply, with progression based on a combination of merit and the passage of a fixed amount of time at the previous rank in the hierarchy. There are just 10,000 officers, 1,250 commanders, and a mere 75, generally former prime ministers, constitutional jurists, and the most senior ambassadors, who hold the grand cross. To lend his ceremony special prestige, Messier had asked the president of the Republic, ex officio grand master of the Legion of Honor, to decorate him. Jacques Chirac had accepted.

But when Messier specified, as if he were Napoleon dictating the terms of his coronation to the pope, that the ceremony should be held for him alone and at the headquarters of Vivendi Universal, Chirac bridled: even in this era of triumphant capitalism, the president of the Republic was not a performing clown that chief executives could hire for private parties. If Messier wanted the presidential benediction, he could attend the same mass ceremony as everyone else. Crushed by Chirac's snub, but unwilling to share the limelight on his big day, Messier decided instead to ask Bettina Rheims to preside over his ceremony. The fashionable French photographer, famous as much for her chic-porn glamour work as for the official portrait of Chirac that graced town halls across France, was a much better symbol for a modern media group than a septuagenarian politician. . . .

Messier had let it be known that he would soon become the first chairman of a big French group to direct his business in person from the United States. Too many French acquisitions in the United States had failed because the chief executive was not there to run the show, he said. "If you are not there you are not the boss," he explained. The French business world was surprised by this move and not a little put out at his decision to abandon them:

how did he anticipate being able to run a group as deeply en-meshed in French politics and society as his from New York? Through Bettina Rheims, France's leading business figures gave him some last advice before his departure.

In a subtle speech that was written with the help of her husband, the lawyer Jean-Michel Darrois, and the consultant Alain Minc, the former fashion model outlined their hopes and fears: "When a Frenchman says, 'I want to build an international company with the objective of cultural cross-fertilization,' we can only be happy. But then the chauvinist that we have in each of us tells us to hope that this immense enterprise will also remain French and that its chairman will, with all the means at his disposal, help French artists to regain the place that they once occupied in the world and that they have, today, to a certain degree, lost."

Bettina Rheims lavished praise on the forty-four-year-old star of French capitalism: "It's easy to see you in twenty years at the head of this company, which will by then have absorbed Disney, Fox, and who knows which others. Others will perhaps see you in the Elysée (Presidential palace)."

"Where will I be in a few years?" Messier responded. "Some imagine that I will be tempted by a political career; others see me as a hermit. Most probably, I will still be chairman of Vivendi Universal. . . . When we look at Vivendi Universal today, we can legitimately say . . ." Messier paused as the recorded voice of Shania Twain, Universal Music's top-selling female artist, filled the Chez Georges restaurant. Gripping the microphone, Messier then started to croon along to the country-lite barnstormer, triumphantly belting out that, like the cavalry, he had finally arrived. He topped it off by inviting the gathered grandees to look how far he'd come, yeah baby. As the cream of French society cringed, Messier turned to his five children—Anne-Laure, Claire-Marie, Jean-Baptiste, Pierre, and Nicolas—and proceeded to sing along to Stevie Wonder's "I Just Called to Say I Love You."

The various company chairmen who had followed and supported Messier in his ascension of the French *cursus honorum* over two decades were dumbfounded. Their astonishment turned to discomfort when Messier started to speak of his sadness at the death of his ten-year-old niece in an accident in the mountains and launched into Yves Duteil's sentimental "Take a Child by the Hand." In the front row, his brother, father of the young girl, dissolved in loud sobs. René Thomas, former chairman of the Banque Nationale de Paris (BNP), Jean-Louis Beffa, the financier Vincent Bolloré, and even Messier's friend Nicolas Bazire, a director of LVMH and godfather of his son Nicolas, all looked at their shoes.

Accounts of the karaoke ceremony filtered across the Atlantic. By the time Messier arrived in New York on September 2, 2001, just over a week before the terrorist attacks, *Fortune* had prepared a welcoming cover spread: "The *haut monde* of Paris is still talking about how Messier turned the Legion of Honor ceremony on its head. This reaction is, of course, exactly what he intended. Messier revels in being a *provocateur*. He's not just France's most famous businessman; he is the country's first rock-star CEO. . . . Is he the next mogul?" *BusinessWeek* was no less admiring: "Not since Napoleon has France produced an empire builder as ambitious as Jean-Marie Messier. In five years of voracious dealmaking, the 44-year-old dynamo has transformed a financially ailing French utility into Vivendi Universal, the world's number two media company behind AOL Time Warner."

Back in Paris, the business community was less gushing. "That time, he really went too far with his American boss number, or rather what he imagines American behavior to be," one of his guests later recalled. Others, in resignation, contented themselves simply by saying: "That's Jean-Marie!" Tacky and mawkish certainly, but what self-confidence and panache! Nonetheless, this sort of thing could go only so far. Someone should take him in hand because if they weren't all so fond of him . . . The reality was that many found it hard to be too cross with Messier: during the course of his astonishing career, the young chairman had seduced them all.

Jean-Marie Messier was custom-made for success in the French *cursus honorum*. From an early age he was singled out to be groomed for power in the most exclusive institutions of the French Republic. In many ways, in fact, his career coincided with the demise of this system, reflecting the shift in power away from the administrative elite toward the private sector and the market. He was at once one of the last of the great technocrats and the first of a new breed of liberal businessmen. The economic history of France is written in his résumé. As an adviser to Edouard Balladur, finance minister between 1986 and 1988, he ran the privatization program that gave birth to a French equity culture. As a managing director at Lazard Frères, then by far the leading Parisian investment bank, he helped French firms compete for international capital and seize the acquisition opportunities that globalization had suddenly made available to them.

Born on December 13, 1956, grandson of the chauffeur to the local prefect and son of a chartered accountant from Grenoble, Jean-Marie Messier was, by all accounts, a precocious child. His mother, Jeanine, says he could read by the age of five and liked to calculate the day-on-day percentage variation of the share prices displayed on the television.[1] The reality is doubtless more banal, not least because share prices rarely featured on French television before the major privatizations of the mid- to late-1980s. Still, there is no doubt that for this typical provincial middle-class family of the 1960s, education was the key to social success and personal fulfillment. The French meritocracy had served the Messiers well. "Our family climbed the social ladder in two generations," Messier liked to say. "That's why I don't believe people who say it's broken."[2]

Although the Alpine university town played a leading part in the turbulent events of May 1968, the social upheaval bypassed the Messier household. They talked about the economy, which was still at that point enjoying the prolonged postwar boom, known as the *"trente glorieuses"*—the thirty glorious years. Strongly Catholic, the family supported social causes, notably those in favor of the handicapped after the death of Jean-Marie Messier's disabled elder sister. Otherwise, the most memorable event in his childhood would seem to have been a trip at the age of ten to Rome, where he sang in a visiting choir at St. Peter's Basilica and sat on a friend's shoulders to watch the pope say Mass. Without stretching himself, Messier obtained his scientific baccalaureate at the age of sixteen from a Grenoble lycée. Perhaps through lack of anything better to do, he appeared condemned to collect diplomas: the literary baccalaureate followed the scientific one a year later.

After the normal two years of grueling preparatory classes, he was offered a place at the Ecole Centrale, a good university in Paris. He was rejected, however, by the more prestigious Ecole Polytechnique. "For the first time in my life I felt challenged," he said, describing the setback as his personal "Rosebud."[3] Against the advice of his teacher, who recommended that he settle for the certain offer rather than risk being refused again by the university of his choice, he decided to work at his mathematics for another year in the preparatory classes. His determination was rewarded: "Those were my best years. We had total freedom in all subjects," he said.

For more than two hundred years the Ecole Polytechnique had represented the acme of the French educational system and had imbued a sense of destiny in its pupils. Its statutes proclaimed its aim as being "to train men with the aptitude to become, after specialization, the top managers of the Nation." The institution was controlled by the ministry of defense, and its students wore a ceremonial uniform that included a sword and a distinctive two-cornered hat. They marched in the annual July 14 Bastille Day parade in Paris and undertook a year's compulsory military service at the start of the three-year course. An extraordinary mystique, a series of special rituals, and a private language tie those who have attended the school, known as "X."

On graduation from the Ecole Polytechnique, Messier contemplated going to business school in the United States. However, this plan collapsed after Total, the French oil group, refused to sponsor him through Harvard Business School—because, according to Messier, its analysis of his handwriting had revealed a worrying lack of ambition. In any event, Messier's final grades at the Ecole Polytechnique were good enough for him to go directly to the Ecole Nationale d'Administration without taking its competitive entrance exam. By entering ENA, Messier joined an even more exclusive cohort. Located close to government ministries in central Paris, ENA has since its creation by General Charles de Gaulle after the Liberation of France in 1944 accepted just 120 of France's brightest students each year. All university graduates, they are trained over twenty-seven months to hold the highest positions in France.

Known as *énarques,* these young men—rarely are there any women—can count themselves members of the most ruthlessly effective old boys' club in Europe. Enarques automatically use the familiar *tu* form rather than the formal *vous* when speaking to fellow graduates, irrespective of their ages. In a culture obsessed with secrecy, the closely guarded ENA alumni directory, a Who's Who of the country's leading decision makers, carries the home phone numbers of nearly all of its graduates for their exclusive use—right up to the contact details for presidents and prime ministers. They are represented in the highest offices of state: the current president, Jacques Chirac, is an énarque, as were three of the last four prime ministers: Edouard Balladur, who occupied Matignon (the prime minister's official residence) between 1993 and 1995; Alain Juppé, between 1995 and 1997; and Lionel Jospin, between 1997 and 2001. Enarques dominate the senior ranks of France's powerful civil service and public companies. They currently run about half the companies listed on the Paris stock exchange.

The Parisian school's dominance of French public life has led in recent years to growing criticism from parliamentarians eager to loosen that stranglehold. "Spain has the ETA, Ireland has the IRA, and France has the ENA," some of the school's critics like to say. When French populists need a target, ENA has long been a favorite. But during the 2002 electoral season, hostility toward énarques became more intense. Members of parliament debated ending ENA's state funding, while newspaper columnists dueled over the merits of the French system of elite formation. The college's ethos was at odds with the growing feeling that the government needed to heed *"la France d'en bas,"* the term coined by Jean-Pierre Raffarin, Lionel Jospin's emphatically non-énarque successor, to denote the overtaxed "little guy." A survey commissioned by ENA in 2002 showed that 66 percent of French people believed énarques had too much political power. It also canvassed énarques currently in business or government, who agreed that the school bred an "aristocracy" and "arrogance among the elites."

Messier's classmates recall him as smiling, likable, helpful, but not especially impressive. Short and stout, licks of brown hair lolling onto his forehead, he appeared ill at ease with sophisticated students from the smart Parisian lycées, who formed two-thirds of the intake. Unused to debating the comparative merits of Raymond Aron and Jean-Paul Sartre and irredeemably untrendy, he settled the question once and for all in his own mind. He was provincial and proud of it. From then on, he ducked the cultural questions that mattered to Parisian intellectuals. He became a highly focused, efficient machine. At ENA, Messier had a reputation for dropping people who were no longer useful to his career and for putting his considerable ability to charm to work only on those in positions of power. He had set his sights on graduating at the top of his class so that he could become an *inspecteur des finances.* This provoked him to make lengthy and often redundant interventions in the classroom, where being seen to be engaged with the material was an important step toward securing a good grade. Familiar with such tactics, Alain Minc, then teaching at ENA, called Messier to his office to calm him down. He assured the student that he had noticed him and that he would have a good mark at the end of the year: There was no need to draw attention to himself.

After leaving ENA in 1982, Messier married Antoinette Fleisch, the level-headed daughter of a French general, and secured the place in the finance inspectorate he so wanted. There he encountered an even more exclusive and tight-knit corps of politically connected public servants trained in the art of implementing ministerial orders. These were the storm troopers of the French public service. At short notice, they would find themselves parachuted to take over branches of the sprawling state, with the expectation that their brilliant minds would rapidly solve the problems facing lesser mortals. They dominated the treasury and the ministry of finance, and moved silkily in and out of the public and private commercial sectors.

Just as Messier joined their ranks, another *inspecteur des finances,* Jean-Yves Haberer, was drawing up plans for the nationalization of a large number of French financial groups. Even as

Margaret Thatcher was embarking upon a pioneering privatization program in the United Kingdom, François Mitterrand's France was heading in the other direction, with a policy of "socialism in one country." Haberer would later find himself rewarded with the chairmanship of Crédit Lyonnais, the state-owned bank. In many ways, his calamitous reign at Crédit Lyonnais, which collapsed after he bankrolled Giancarlo Parretti, a former Italian waiter, in his purchase of the Metro-Goldwyn-Mayer film studio, was a prototype for Jean-Marie Messier's at Vivendi Universal a decade later. "With Crédit Lyonnais, I was trying to build the big French and European bank that would strengthen our national identity," Haberer later explained to a parliamentary inquiry. Replace the word "bank" with "media group" and multiply the sums of money involved by ten, and the idea is the same.

It was difficult to stand out in a group that counted among its members a president of the Republic, several prime ministers, governors of the Bank of France, and all the principal bankers of the place de Paris. In the evenings, he would go to a small club, the Association pour l'etude des Expériences Etrangères, known as the A3E—the Association for the Study of Foreign Experiences—where he would encounter the future power brokers of the French business world.* Every Sunday the group would meet at the home of Charles de Croisset, future chairman of CCF bank. It would include the likes of Baudouin Prot, managing director of BNP Paribas, the French banking group, and Nicolas Bazire, who would later succeed Messier as an adviser to Edouard Balladur before becoming a director of LVMH. Against the backdrop of the left-wing government's nationalizations, the group's discussions focused on the need for a rapid liberalization of the French economy. When it came to his turn to present a paper, Messier chose a theme of Margaret Thatcher's privatization policy in the UK. The subject was topical. Messier could not fail to be noticed. Jacques Friedmann, an *inspecteur des finances* who acted as a headhunter

---

*Alphanumerics was in fashion. It was about this time that Jean-Marie Messier started to sign his name "J2M." The A3E stood for Association pour l'etude des Expériences Etrangères.

for the political center-right, was the first to spot him. A close adviser to Jacques Chirac, Friedmann had discovered Alain Juppé and persuaded him to embark upon a career in politics that would see him rise to become prime minister. Barely thirty years old, Messier, with Friedmann's imprimatur, soon found himself devising the opposition's privatization program.

When the right came back into power in 1986 on the basis of an election manifesto of privatization, the young *inspecteur des finances* was not forgotten. Friedmann recommended him warmly as an adviser to Camille Cabana, secretary of state in charge of privatization. But Messier was quickly disappointed. He soon realized that real power lay elsewhere, at the economy and finance ministry, then run by Edouard Balladur, a heavyweight figure in Chirac's government. When a ministerial reshuffle presented him with an opportunity, Messier dumped Cabana and, with the backing of Friedmann, hurried off to join Balladur at the seat of power. The right faced a problem, however. While the Chirac government approved of the free market, there were limits to its liberalism. With an underdeveloped French stock market, a lack of pension funds, and little domestic money available for investment, privatized French companies ran the risk of takeover by predatory foreigners. Messier led the handful of people at the finance ministry who set about reconciling the conflicting objectives of liberalizing the economy and preserving the French identity of the country's privatized corporations. It was his responsibility to ensure the jewels of French industry would not be plundered by foreigners once they were exposed to the stormy international capital markets.

Messier's staff revived the old idea of "core" shareholdings, or *noyaux durs*. A small group of friendly French investors would acquire large stakes in the newly privatized groups and take boardroom seats. These powerful alliances were intended to scare off hostile foreign bidders. In extreme versions, cross-shareholdings developed in which two companies would buy a stake in each other and their chairmen would sit on each other's boards. It was a system that seemed to offer protection and support, but which was riddled with conflicts of interest. The original idea was for these arrangements to last for two or three years, by which time the newly privatized groups would have become strong enough to fend for themselves. But once in place, the mechanisms stuck, and contributed to numerous failures of corporate governance. Board members often ended up fighting turf battles instead of maximizing value for all shareholders. The problem was worsened by the concentration of executive and supervisory functions in the hands of one man, the *president–directeur-générale*. While their UK counterparts tended to split responsibilities between a chief executive and a nonexecutive chairman, a single imperious PDG, addressed as "Monsieur Le Président–Directeur Générale," dominates most French boards, much like an all-powerful U.S. chairman and chief executive.

Messier would later defend the device. "The logic of the *noyaux stables* was to say, 'We are privatizing companies that are small and weak compared with their international competitors. We must give them a minimum level of protection when we throw them into the bath.' If there was an error at the time, it is not in the principle because we had to give them a way of defending themselves." He handled the privatization of some of France's best-known companies, including Saint-Gobain, Société Générale, and Paribas, the investment bank later acquired by Banque Nationale de Paris (BNP). It was a position of phenomenal influence that Messier used to its full advantage. The most powerful businessmen would arrive at the finance ministry, cap in hand, to negotiate a piece of the action. They would be greeted by a cherubic, rosy-cheeked Messier, who later admitted to fattening himself up to look older than his years. At first he watched the comings and goings of French industrialists with fascination, but he soon mastered the complex web of relationships that still characterizes the country's business life. Modest and still smiling, he listened and made himself available at all hours. Balladur displayed complete confidence in him, as did many leading industrialists. The media soon got wind of the young man in the finance ministry being credited with single-handedly reshaping the French business landscape.

When the possibility of the next step arose, all professional careers were open to him. By the time the June 1988 elections ended "cohabitation"—the term given to describe the situation in which the two branches of the French executive, the presidency and the government, are occupied by politicians from opposing political parties—Messier had received seventeen offers of employment, including one from Générale des Eaux. With the defeat of Jacques Chirac, then the incumbent prime minister and the center-right's candidate for the presidency, executive power had been reunified in the hands of the Socialists, led by François Mitterrand, who won a second seven-year term as president. The privatization program enacted by the Chirac government since 1986 was expected to grind to a sudden halt. France's returning Socialist Party had by then adopted a policy known as the *"ni-ni"* rule—neither privatization nor nationalization. For Messier, this meant that it was time to look elsewhere. His days of calling the shots from the finance ministry were over.

He had seen it all coming. In late 1987, before the defeat of the Right, he had decided to join Lazard Frères, the go-go merchant bank of the 1980s. After privatizing vast swaths of French banking and industry, he proceeded to privatize himself. Based in the chic Eighth Arrondissement, on the edge of the parc de Monceau, Lazard Frères called the shots in Parisian business. The bank existed in an atmosphere straight out of Balzac, with plush red sitting rooms from the Second Empire, ushers patrolling the corridors, warning lights flickering over the doors of occupied meeting rooms, and, above all, an atmosphere of ferocious jealousy and intrigue. Michel David-Weill, the chairman whose family controlled the bank, encouraged the internal competition: one way or another, the business would end up going to Lazard, he reasoned. Many found the atmosphere intolerable, but not Jean-Marie Messier. He passed the first few months at the New York office, where he learned about the "information superhighway" and the imminent convergence of television and telecommunications; but in 1989 he returned to France to exploit his political connections. At the tender age of thirty-three, he became a managing partner of Lazard Frères in Paris.

France is a country run by networks, and Messier's address book began to bulge. He would be seen at concerts, at the opera, in the smartest Parisian restaurants, and as the host of grand dinners and lunches in the bank's dining rooms. Aware that power in France was shifting away from the old administrative caste, Messier cultivated a more entrepreneurial set and became president of the Club of 40. This brought together forty entrepreneurs who were younger than forty years old when the club was founded. Messier argued that the club was the opposite of the old-style network: "My idea of networks is 'Let's get people talking who should logically succeed together and who don't know each other or have different specialities.' That is not the network in the sense of everybody being the same and working together because everyone is the same—that is the old-style network."[4] Its members, who would meet at the Hôtel Raphaël at least once a month, included Patricia Barbizet, who would later become the right hand of François Pinault, founder of France's most prominent retail group, Pinault Printemps Redoute; Jean-Marc Espalioux, then finance director of Générale des Eaux; Philippe Germond, at that time a manager with Hewlett-Packard; and Agnès Touraine, then working her way up the Hachette publishing group. Several of its members would later become his most loyal lieutenants at Vivendi Universal.

At the same time, he continued to cultivate his media image. Philippe Villin, a friend from ENA who had become number two at *Le Figaro*, helped by inviting him to many of the breakfasts and lunches the right-wing newspaper organized with the leading businessmen of the day. During the summers he would be found at Villin's villa at Cavalaire, near St.-Tropez, where the newspaper's socialite director entertained the rich and powerful. Within a short time of arriving at Lazard, Messier styled himself as the linchpin of French finance. More than two hundred people were invited to celebrate his tenth wedding anniversary in 1993. The networking bore fruit. After seeing Messier at the Orchestre de Paris, Didier Pineau-Valencienne, chairman of Schneider Electric, hired him to advise on the electrical components group's $2.2 billion takeover of Square D, a U.S. company. After friendly approaches failed, Pineau-Valencienne, egged on by Messier, decided to launch a hostile bid, never before attempted by a French group in the United States. Then the biggest French acquisition in the North American market, the deal sealed Messier's place as one of the leading bankers in Paris.

After Square D, many of the bank's most sensitive dossiers landed on his desk. He helped Jean-Luc Lagardère, France's media-to-missiles magnate, recover from a disastrous foray into French free-to-air broadcasting, and Bernard Arnault to develop his luxury goods group. The right's victory in the 1993 elections and Edouard Balladur's appointment as prime minister, a post he would hold until his defeat by Jacques Chirac in the race to be the right-wing candidate for the 1995 presidential election, further increased Messier's prestige and influence. The return of the right to government saw the launch of a second wave of privatizations, this time of the Elf oil group, the BNP, and the Rhône-Poulenc chemicals group, then run by Jean-René Fourtou. Lazard's success owed much to Messier. "Edouard Balladur thinks . . . Edouard Balladur says"—Messier never missed an opportunity to flaunt his ties with the prime minister. Other partners in the investment bank found themselves abandoned by their clients. "You understand," they would be told, "he's close to Balladur." His success inspired jealousy among his peers, but the rainmakers adored him. Antoine Bernheim, the veteran investment banker and chairman of Generali, the Italian insurance group, said he considered his former Lazard Frères colleague "one of the most remarkable personalities of his generation . . . I very much regret that he did not choose to pursue his career at Lazard."[5]

However, Messier knew he would never reach the top of the merchant bank. One man stood in his way: Edouard Stern. "Would I have been able to tempt him away without Edouard?" Ambroise Roux, the man who eventually lured Messier to run Générale des Eaux, would later ask. Stern was young, a talented financier and, most importantly, son-in-law of Michel David-Weill. Messier was under no illusions as to what this meant. In this type of organization, family ties always took precedence. At thirty-seven, he recoiled at the idea that his career could be blocked, and decided to leave Lazard. Didier Pineau-Valencienne, who professed to love him almost as a son, was the first to think of him as a possible successor at Schneider Electric. In his eyes Messier had the ideal qualifications: he was young, knew the group, and would accept his legacy. Messier indicated that he would accept. He met him more and more often to talk about the group and even appropriated Pineau-Valencienne's motto, a few lines from the poet René Char, as his own: "Create your luck, seize your good fortune and embrace risk: they'll get used to you."* In May 1994, when the chairman of Schneider was arrested by the Belgian authorities for fraud, Messier was there to support the executive's family and mount the defense. The business world assumed the succession was in the bag.

But Messier had plans, and they did not include Schneider. His eye was on the big prize: Générale des Eaux. The company was like a state within a state. Surprisingly, in view of the scale of state ownership in France, water management had long been considered a private-sector activity. Générale des Eaux had won its first municipal contract in 1853, under the reign of Napoleon III. From its origins in water supply and sewage, the group had gradually expanded into other local utility services. A move toward greater decentralization in 1982 encouraged local mayors to contract many other public services to private companies. Used to negotiating with local authorities, Générale des Eaux had the political contacts to ensure that it was the prime beneficiary. Its influence became tentacular. In some towns, it controlled almost everything: water, sewage, heating, transport, cable television, cinemas, school and hospital catering, hospital and clinic management, contracts to maintain public spaces and public housing, and even dry cleaning and pest control. As the owner of France's second-largest construction company, it was also one of the biggest land and property owners in the country. It owned more than a third of La Défense, the modern high-life business district to the west of Paris, and prestigious commercial centers such as the Carrousel du Louvre in the heart of Paris.

The unofficial power and influence of Générale des Eaux

---

*A lover of modern art and poetry, Didier Pineau-Valencienne had long used the lines from René Char as his personal motto: "Impose ta chance, serre ton bonheur et va vers ton risque. A te regarder, ils s'habitueront."

seemed even greater. Guy Dejouany, its long-standing chairman, was a connoisseur of France's electoral map. Its primary rival in the public utilities market was Lyonnaise des Eaux, run by Jérôme Monod, former boss of Jacques Chirac's political machine. Both groups used all the means at their disposal to win municipal contracts. Taking advantage of the deliberately opaque party funding laws, they became important sources of financing for the major political parties. Both companies had "their" mayors and "their" deputies and made the influencing of local officials their core competence. However, by the mid-1990s, Générale des Eaux was in a bad way, and beneath its solid appearance, was collapsing under its debts. The income from its various business lines was insufficient to cover losses from speculative property developments. Worse still, the justice system had just embarked on what would become an epic investigation into political party funding and corruption. Générale des Eaux and Lyonnaise des Eaux were among the judges' primary targets. The business establishment, frustrated at the stench of scandal that had hung over the place de Paris since the collapse of Crédit Lyonnais under Haberer, demanded that Dejouany take action to put his house in order.

At the age of seventy-three "and a half," as he liked to add, Dejouany was still without a successor. Several brilliant young men had been enthroned as his heir apparent in the past, but none had survived the wily old chameleon. He could dither no longer. He needed to put forward a name and do so quickly. Four years earlier he had used Messier's services for the acquisition of a small U.S. company called Air and Water Technologies, and he held a favorable impression of the young banker. "Why not Messier?" Dejouany asked Ambroise Rouxone, one of the most influential behind-the-scenes operators in France, and deputy chairman of Générale des Eaux, at the end of 1993. A friend since their days at the Ecole Polytechnique, Roux supported the idea. They agreed to put Messier to the test by asking him to find a formula that would allow Générale des Eaux to take control of Canal Plus. A large minority shareholder in the pay-television channel since its creation in 1984, Dejouany wished to increase his 20-percent stake in the company that at that time represented Générale des

Eaux's principal source of profit. Canal Plus's founding chairman, André Rousselet, a close friend and adviser of the Socialist President François Mitterrand, cultivated a tetchy independence from both his shareholders and the right-wing government.

Conveniently for Dejouany, the new right-wing government of Edouard Balladur had just relaxed the law that limited any one shareholder from owning more than 25 percent of a national broadcaster, taking the threshold up to 49 percent. Dejouany informed Messier that he wished to control 49 percent of Canal Plus without spending a single centime. The Lazard banker quickly found a solution, arranging a shareholder pact between Générale des Eaux and two other shareholders: the Havas publishing, advertising, and media conglomerate, which owned 24 percent, and Société Générale, with 5 percent. The three together would reach the magic figure. With the agreement of the others, Générale des Eaux could exercise control in the name of all three. When Rousselet heard of the pact, he resigned from the company he had founded, claiming to be the victim of a political coup. "Edouard [Balladur] has killed me," he wrote in a tirade that was published on the front page of *Le Monde*. Dejouany was doing the dirty work for the new Balladur administration, which cared little for the independent-minded television station that had long been protected by Mitterrand and the Left, he claimed. Observers commented that Rousselet had blamed the wrong man: "It wasn't Edouard that killed him; it was Jean-Marie."

The episode marked the beginning of Messier's relationship with Pierre Lescure, then Rousselet's number two at the pay-television company. For a time, there would be a sense that Lescure's role in the coup against his boss had been ambiguous, which, in some people's minds, initially diminished his legitimacy as a successor. In any event, Lescure was the prime beneficiary of the coup d'état against Rousselet, and he owed his premature promotion to Jean-Marie Messier. The success of the operation convinced Dejouany to name Messier as his successor. He gave Ambroise Roux the job of negotiating his arrival. At the time it was said that Edouard Balladur had strongly supported the nomination of his protégé to the head of Générale des Eaux. Dejouany later disputed this: "Edouard Balladur was hostile to the recruitment. When he was presented as the favorite to win the [1995] presidential election, he feared being criticized for placing his men in positions of influence. He telephoned Ambroise Roux during the summer of 1994 to try and stop the operation. 'Too late,' Roux replied. 'The patient is already on the operating table.' Afterward, Balladur continued to hold it against me and would hardly speak to me."

At the beginning of November 1994, Messier, at the age of thirty-seven, was named chief executive of Générale des Eaux and designated successor to Guy Dejouany. Only one board member, Jacques Calvet, chairman of the car manufacturer Peugeot, opposed the appointment: "How can anyone even think of entrusting a group with two hundred thousand employees to someone who has never managed more than his own secretary?" The likable young banker stood in sharp contrast to his predecessor. Messier brought a breath of fresh air into the oppressive world of Générale des Eaux, a group that deliberately refused to draw up an organization chart and lacked clear lines of responsibility. Dejouany did not even permit meetings. "Three is a demonstration," he would say when more than two people entered his office. Its headquarters on the rue d'Anjou, a small Paris backstreet, was a labyrinth whose lights would be extinguished at half past eight every evening, the moment Dejouany left the premises. Barely installed as chief executive, Messier created a committee of senior managers and started collegial discussions about the most important issues facing the company—notably the crisis in the group's property arm and the numerous legal threats. Information started to circulate. Messier also announced the end of all clandestine party financing. "Between the loss of a market and illegal financing, the choice is clear: it is better to lose the market," he decreed.

A lump in his throat, Guy Dejouany could not hide his emotion in front of the shareholder meeting at La Défense. On June 10, 1996, at the end of a long speech, Dejouany turned the page after forty-three years at Générale des Eaux. To the end, to Messier's intense annoyance, Dejouany tried to play for extra time, to obtain a year or two more as chairman. But even those closest to him said it was time to go. Everyone wanted to draw a line under an era of scandal. Barely a day passed without investigating judges launching fresh corruption probes into Générale des Eaux. Dejouany himself had been questioned about alleged corruption by a judge from Réunion in May 1995 in a case concerning the water-supply concession on the island. The affair, it seemed, was serious. A court case was in the offing that could even threaten him with prison. The pressure on him to leave with honor while there was still time was acute. In the end, the state prosecutor announced that the case against Dejouany was to be dismissed only on June 11, the day after he had handed over the chairmanship to his chief executive. "You will be the ninth chairman in 143 years," he told Jean-Marie Messier. "Try not to bring down the average."

CHAPTER TWO

# In Medias Res

If Jean-Marie Messier liked the power that came with Générale des Eaux, he had little liking for water and sewage. The trouble with brilliant minds is that they need something to occupy them. "At the beginning, he systematically visited the group's regional offices. Once he had finished his tour of France, he never returned. They no longer interested him. He only went back into the field once, for the inauguration of the bridge over the Tagus at Lisbon. After that, we never saw him again," recounted an employee. Only when the traditional business of Générale des Eaux offered an opportunity to strut the world stage did Messier's interest level rise. Such was the case at the World Economic Forum at Davos, Switzerland, in March 2001, when Shimon Peres took him aside at the prestigious gathering to tell him of his hope to carve a "peace" canal between the Red Sea and the Dead Sea. Not only would Messier be able to replenish the Dead Sea, thereby restoring the ecological balance and helping tourism, but he would personally play a vital part in alleviating the serious water shortage affecting Israel, Jordan, and Palestine that was an obstacle to peace in the Middle East. Messier was hooked. A year later, at the annual meeting of his shareholders in Paris in April 2002, Messier would still be talking of "his dream of making a gesture for world peace."

Otherwise, the gray world of local water contracts lacked the excitement of his days at Lazard Frères, or even of his time as a top civil servant reshaping the landscape of French business. The only other occasion on which people remember him becoming passionately involved was in 1999, when he set his mind on purchasing U.S. Filter, by far the largest and fastest-growing water supplier to American businesses. It would be "the biggest acquisition ever undertaken by a French group in the U.S.," he insisted. The prospect of conquering the U.S. market and of establishing the group, by then renamed Vivendi, as the world number one in water services visibly excited him. At the end of a keenly contested auction, he agreed to pay nearly $8 billion in cash for U.S. Filter.* Managers of Vivendi's water operations opposed the purchase at that price, and the acquisition subsequently proved disastrous. Vivendi Environnement, as the division was by then called, had to make a provision of €2 billion relating to U.S. Filter ahead of its stock market listing in July 2000 and a further €2.6 billion in 2002. Messier's tendency to pay way over the odds to secure what he wanted was evident early on.

The traditional businesses of Générale des Eaux were entrusted to two long-standing executives, Henri Proglio for local authority services such as water and sewage, and Antoine Zacharias for construction and civil engineering. It soon became clear that these businesses were not Messier's area of interest. Both divisions prepared to list on the stock market under the names Vivendi Environnement and Vinci. Messier, meanwhile, selected a few attractive individuals to help him transform the group's image. He called them his "Dream Team." There were his two old friends from the Club of 40: Philippe Germond, the strikingly handsome Frenchman with a taste for black shirts who had been plucked from Hewlett-Packard to run Vivendi's telecommunications group, Cegetel; and the ginger-haired Agnès Touraine, headhunted from Hachette to run Vivendi's publishing business. They were joined by Guillaume Hannezo, Vivendi's finance director, who in addition to being an *inspecteur des finances* had been a former economic adviser to François Mitterrand; and by Eric Licoys, Messier's former

---

*Vivendi paid $6.2 billion in cash for the equity of U.S. Filter and assumed $1.6 billion of net debt.

colleague from Lazard. It was with this select group of people that Messier wanted to build his own group out of the chaos inherited from Dejouany.

The devastating losses from the property arm resolved, Messier raised over €15 billion from the sale of businesses in the real estate, construction, catering, and health-care sectors and started to reinforce the group's embryonic presence in the media. The tributes rained in as he shuffled assets worth billions of dollars to transform Générale des Eaux into a new economy wonderstock ready for the new millennium. From very early on, Messier's external image became an important part of the group's transformation strategy: for a company in permanent change, the outside world needed one clear and constant point of reference.

That lodestar would be Jean-Marie Messier himself. He encouraged the idea that an investment in Vivendi—a complex hodgepodge of businesses, half of which were coming and the other half going—should be seen as an investment, or rather an act of faith, in him personally. He was no longer the representative of a group; he was the group. The French company, he would later explain, "needed the media in order to undertake a radical transformation, to bring that transformation to its conclusion as quickly as possible. It was necessary to give an image, ambition, enthusiasm. . . . It is easier to represent such a vision through a man."[1]

Employees watched with fascination as the personality cult developed: the effect on the stock price was certainly impressive during 1997 and 1998, and still positive in 1999, even if the company's shares lagged behind the French market in that year. The company's unions, up until then ignored by the haughty Dejouany management, rejoiced over the new measures they had negotiated concerning the length of the working week, profit sharing, and employee share ownership, which represented real advances when compared with the past and even with the group's competitors. "He is very different from the image he likes to give," said Guy Dejouany in late 2002. In public, Messier played the role of a modern, approachable chief executive who believed in collegial management. Inside the company, he could appear authoritarian, sometimes cutting. "He's very hard. He never goes back on what he has decided," said Eric Licoys, his closest collaborator.

Perhaps because of his youth, he worried about being able to assert his authority and showed an unhealthy concern about outward signs of status. He moved the headquarters from the rue d'Anjou to the more luxurious and prestigious quarters on avenue Friedland, overlooking the Arc de Triomphe. The ritual gatherings organized with thousands of the group's employees in large halls simply ended up wearying people once they realized they were just foils for Messier's performances. Yet he described these set-piece events as the ones that provided his "greatest frissons, a pleasure that is almost carnal." He would have a tear in his eye for every occasion and gained a reputation for insincerity: "Two words, three lies," was one often-heard description of the young chief executive's communication style. Others described him as a *"fleur bleue,"* someone who was naively sentimental, a true romantic. "People have always criticized me for faking my emotions," he would later say. "They are real. . . . I have difficulty mastering my feelings. The image of Messier-Robocop is wrong."[2]

Among the first major strategic decisions Messier made was to recognize that on its own Vivendi was in no state to be able to invest in SFR, the mobile telecom network, that it had owned since the early 1980s. Reluctantly he brought in new shareholders, including British Telecommunications and the Mannesmann, the German engineering group. Unavoidable at the time, given the financially-straitened circumstances of the company he had inherited, sharing control of France's second mobile operator was a move Messier later greatly regretted. Left with just a 44-percent stake in SFR's holding company, Cegetel, he had to share control of the rich cash flow that the operator started to generate from 2001. This semiretreat from the telecom sector soon turned into a prolonged offensive in the media.

In the summer of 1996, Pierre Lescure, by then chairman of Canal Plus, informed Messier he wanted to buy NetHold, his biggest rival in Europe after Rupert Murdoch's British Sky Broadcasting (BSkyB). NetHold had more than 1.5 million pay television subscribers in Italy, Scandinavia, and Belgium. The two men met, with their wives, to discuss the matter on the Côte d'Azur. The transaction would be costly: the owner, Richemont, a South African group that also owned the Cartier jewelery brand, Montblanc pens, and Rothmans cigarettes, was being courted by the American satellite operator DirecTV.

Buying NetHold would take Canal Plus out of its core French market. Earlier that year, Canal Plus had seen the launch of rival service TPS, which for the first time since its launch in 1984, would confront it with real competition. With Messier's backing, Lescure offered Johann Rupert, chief executive of Richemont, a 15-percent stake in an enlarged Canal Plus, valuing each of NetHold's subscribers at a record $1,600. The deal almost killed Canal Plus: its financial performance would still not have recovered seven years later. Once the most profitable pay-television operator in Europe—it made €113 million in 1996—it plunged into the red. Losses at NetHold's Italian pay-television operation, Telepiu, would prove the bane of Canal Plus and then Vivendi for years to come.

Shortly afterward, Messier put into motion his plan to take over Havas. In addition to being the largest shareholder in Canal Plus, the drifting and poorly run conglomerate owned some of the most famous names in French publishing, including Larousse, Robert, and Nathan. It also had interests in advertising, newspapers, and package holidays. After taking over the conglomerate in March 1998, Messier broke it up to get his hands on its stake in Canal Plus and its publishing business. Everything else was to be sold. At the end of the process, which also saw Messier purchase Richemont's 15-percent stake in Canal Plus, Vivendi owned 49 percent of the French pay-television operator and a handsome position in European publishing.

Yet the reshuffling of assets left several observers unconvinced. On the wave of new economy hysteria, Vivendi's share price had trebled to nearly €80 by July 1999, but remained 10 percent below its high during the winter of 1998. The *Financial Times*'s "Lex" column, ever pessimistic, wrote on July 26, 1999: "The market's ambivalence is not surprising. Vivendi has switched from restructuring mode—selling €15bn of businesses—to predator before proving it can squeeze a good return from the core business. The group remains relatively unfocused and has issued a slew of new paper. Vivendi's acquisitions have also created some confusion. Investors attracted by telecoms and media were never going to be enthusiastic about the $6.2bn purchase of a US water company. Its balance sheet does not look strong enough for aggressive expansion on all fronts."

Nonetheless, by mid-1999, Messier had unquestionably joined the ranks of Europe's leading chief executives. He had saved Générale des Eaux from the brink of failure, consummating the overhaul of its image with the adoption of the name Vivendi, chosen narrowly over such horrors as Egedia, Egery, and Eledia. His credibility allowed him to reshape his board to his liking. Opponents such as Jacques Calvet were gently pushed out, but useful representatives of old-style French capitalism—the chairmen of the major banks or their representatives, such as Marc Viénot of Société Générale and René Thomas, former chairman of BNP—were retained and flattered. He brought in friends such as Thomas Middelhoff, the chairman of Bertelsmann, a rival, but also someone who shared his vision of the business world, and Bernard Arnault, who had become one of Vivendi's leading shareholders after some property deals.

Few of them knew the group's businesses. But they all had a blind confidence in Messier's intuition and intelligence as his renown spread across Europe. He received invitations to join many of the most prestigious European boards, including that of Daimler-Benz. Jurgen Schrempp, chairman of the German engineering conglomerate that would shortly take over Chrysler, chose Messier, along with Sir John Browne of BP because they were, in the Vivendi chief executive's own words, the European bosses who "make their companies move the most."

Yet during the takeover frenzy of 1999, Messier felt Vivendi was being left behind in the two areas in which it had decided to expand: telecommunications and media. In telecommunications, Vivendi's minority stake in France's second mobile operator, SFR, looked subscale. That year had witnessed a series of multibillion-dollar cross-border deals. If Chris Gent, Vodafone's chief executive, succeeded in acquiring his German rival, Mannesmann, the Reading, England–based firm would be the first mobile operator to gain a pan-European footprint. The transaction would be the biggest takeover in European history, valued at €175 billion. Single-country operators such as Vivendi and Bouygues, another French conglomerate with a stake in a domestic mobile provider, had become the subject of bid fever.

"For several weeks, we had the impression of watching trains go by," Messier said. "The big industrial maneuvers were taking place all around us. . . . In telecom, as in most sectors, you cannot operate in just one national market. At the very least you have to be European, and, if possible, global. We were a long way from having critical mass. Cassandras were warning that Vivendi had messed up its internationalization and would soon be swallowed by its competitors."[3]

The reality was that Vivendi's investments in the media sector hung together with some difficulty and lacked coherence. In pay television, Vivendi owned 49-percent of Canal Plus, the leading European pay-television platform. By late 1999, after the acquisition of NetHold, Canal was pumping sports, movies, and soft porn to 15 million subscribers across eleven European countries. However, investors regarded Vivendi as a holding company because it only owned a 49-percent stake in Canal Plus, which in addition, started to lose ever greater sums of money as it expanded across Europe.

Vivendi was also stymied in its other main investment in European television, a 24.5-percent stake in British Sky Broadcasting. There seemed little chance of prizing control of BSkyB away from Rupert Murdoch, who had slammed the phone down on Messier in 1999 when the Frenchman informed him that he had taken the sizeable stake in one of the most valuable parts of the News Corp. empire. Although worth more than €9 billion in 2000, the stake in BSkyB had failed to deliver any tangible industrial advantage to Vivendi. As it did not even pay a dividend, it was dead money.

Since the 1998 acquisition of Havas, Vivendi also owned some of the jewels of French-language publishing. In general literature, it boasted imprints such as Plon, publisher of Charles de Gaulle; in reference publishing, it owned Larousse and Robert, guardians of the French language and powerful tools for the projection of French culture around the world; and in educational publishing its imprints included Bordas and Nathan. But these were not highly valued by the financial community because they were stuck in the low-growth French-language market.

Yet in less than two years, Vivendi had come from the obscurity of the French municipal water and sewage market to sit at the top table of European media and telecommunications companies. It ranked alongside the likes of British Sky Broadcasting and Bertelsmann in scope and ambition. This was an impressive feat of corporate metamorphosis. However, the company's shortcomings were starting to show. At the dawn of the new millennium, Vivendi still looked very much like an unfashionable holding company that, whatever the hype from the investor-relations department, consisted of four similarly sized businesses in areas that differed fundamentally from one another.

The traditional water and sewage business accounted for just 20 to 25 percent of the group's market value, the bulk of which was split equally between its three new activities: telecom, publishing, and pay TV. Vivendi could not hope to compete simultaneously in so many different capital-intensive businesses. Its lack of focus led to a situation where, like many conglomerates, it appeared to be trading at less than the sum of its parts, putting itself at risk of a takeover. When Vodafone launched its bid for Mannesmann in October 1999, Vivendi found itself blocked strategically: its traditional business had been effectively abandoned by the investment community and no longer represented more than 20 percent of the company's value; the destiny that the market had in mind for it—to become a European telecom company—was slipping out of reach.

"Everyone recognized that Vivendi had to focus on one line of business," said Guillaume Hannezo, Vivendi's finance director. "At that time, no one proposed returning to our traditional business [water and sewage] by selling or demerging the communications businesses, which, by 1999, accounted for the bulk of the value of the group. This is ironic, for it is this strategy that would have been by far the most lucrative for shareholders. The market believed that Vivendi was a kind of 'French Mannesmann' and wanted us to play the role of consolidator in the European telecom industry. Again this is ironic, as this strategy would have been even worse than the one finally chosen. We tried our hand at that strategy. We looked successively at buying Orange, E Plus, and KPN, and at bidding for UMTS licenses at auction; it failed because our cash-flow analysis always came up with valuations 50 percent lower than the prices paid; furthermore, as our share price did not enjoy a 'pure telecom' rating, we were not prepared to impose on our shareholders the dramatic dilution that would accompany an offensive acquisition strategy in the telecom sector."[4]

It seemed that with the cards he held at the end of 1999, Messier could at best only hope to preserve Vivendi's independence. Actually catching up with the competition seemed implausible. Vivendi was too small and had started too late to emerge as one of the survivors of the shakeout of the European telecommunications sector. Nevertheless, just as AOL and Time Warner were starting to negotiate their own merger across the Atlantic, Messier decided to try to find a role for himself in the Vodafone battle for Mannesmann. He would somehow make this his chance. "We needed to find a way to exploit all these great maneuvers of our competitors, that light wind that allows sailors in a regatta to steal up on their competitors. We felt it arrive when Vodafone attacked Mannesmann. A delicious little wind that makes you feel that you are in the game again."[5]

Messier decided he would try to disrupt Gent's plans. The combination of Vodafone and Mannesmann would not just be by far the largest of the recent megadeals in the telecom sector; it would create a group with strong positions in virtually every European market as well as the United States and some Asian countries. It was also a "landmark deal in the global market for corporate control," argued the *Financial Times* editorial writers, who noted that "until recently, it would have been unthinkable for a UK-based group to mount a hostile bid for a German corporate giant." To many German politicians, a hostile bid was an assault on the country's consensual traditions. Messier discussed with Klaus Esser, Mannesmann's chief executive, how they could thwart the Anglo-Saxon predator. The two agreed to explore a merger between Mannesmann and Vivendi.

They had started to discuss a potential merger in January 1999, but the talks had broken down when it became clear that Esser, whose company was larger, envisioned a takeover of the French company, rather than a merger of equals. "Whatever the shareholding structure, I wanted it to be a marriage of equals at the management level," Messier said.[6] Esser, who had successfully transformed his tubes and auto parts group into a leading European mobile operator, dismissed this suggestion out of hand.

Two months after Vodafone attacked, however, he showed himself to be considerably more understanding. Messier was now to be his white knight. "For several weeks, we thought the operation was on track," Messier said. "It would have created a magnificent business with a collection of number one positions across Europe: in mobile telephony, it would have very strong market positions in France, Germany, Great Britain, Austria, Belgium, and Italy, as well as in fixed telephony, pay-television, and Internet services."

Esser and Messier were to be co–chief executives, with the German running the telecom side from Dusseldorf and the Frenchman controlling the media and Internet business from Paris. The enlarged media and telecom business would then be strong enough to allow Mannesmann and Vivendi to shed their industrial legacies. Over the autumn, both Esser and Messier had been assailed with criticism from investors calling for them to break their companies up into their constituent parts. Critics proclaimed that Vivendi could be either a media company or a water utility, and Mannesmann a telecom giant or an engineering firm, but neither could be both at once. A merger would provide both men with the means to answer those critics. A single European telecom and media giant could emerge from the two vast industrial empires.

Accordingly, Esser asked investment banks to advise him on a sale or initial public offering of Mannesmann's engineering arm. Messier had gathered Vivendi's disparate water, waste, transport, and energy interests into a single entity called Vivendi Environnement. This would be partially floated on the stock market in July 2000, with Vivendi retaining majority control. "For Klaus Esser, this marriage would allow him to escape the clutches of Vodafone," Messier said. "But for me, the stakes were even more important. It was a question of creating the first European business able to go head to head with the American giants."[7]

Yet as the Vodafone battle for Mannesmann intensified, the agreement between the French and German companies came unstuck. The negotiations stumbled on problems of valuation as Mannesmann's share price was inflated by the bid battle. The idea of a merger of equals, according to Hannezo, was also alien to Esser's thinking. In secret, Messier started to negotiate with Gent. Messier and Esser would later disagree violently over the extent to which these talks represented a breach of trust.

"In an industrial war," Messier wrote, "as in any war, discussing with both camps is always a delicate exercise. Of course, Chris Gent and Klaus Esser knew we were talking to both of them." Reflecting on the last weeks of his negotiations with the Frenchman, Esser disagreed: "We had been discussing the merger with Vivendi since January 1999. When Vodafone launched its bid in October 1999, I knew Chris Gent would approach Vivendi. So I told Messier he was at liberty to talk to other groups, but not to Vodafone, which he agreed was a fair request." Esser said that Messier's decision to treat Vodafone as an alternative was "a highly indecent and dishonourable thing to do."[8]

The question for Gent was what to offer Messier to induce him to back out of the rival project for a Franco-German merger with Mannesmann. Gent felt able to promise three things: an agreement that for the next four years Vodafone would not launch a hostile bid for Vivendi, whose French mobile operation was the missing piece in its European coverage; a promise to sell Vivendi the 15-percent stake in Cegetel it would acquire as part of the Mannesmann deal, which would return control of the telecom business to the French company; and last but not least, an Internet alliance between the British and the French companies to create, as Messier put it, a "European Yahoo! that would be a real challenger to the Americans."

The proposed alliance with Vodafone certainly had potential, but, according to Hannezo, it was always seen internally as a second-best solution. Messier's clear preference was to achieve scale in the telecom sector through a merger with Mannesmann. But Esser's continued refusal to accept a merger of equals with the smaller French company meant that this now looked impossible. "By default we decided to ally ourselves with Vodafone and to accept, like Judas, our thirty pieces of silver," Hannezo would later say.[9]

News of the impending AOL Time Warner merger on January 10, 2000, undoubtedly eased the decision to abandon all hope of concluding the telecom merger with Mannesmann. Messier first learned of the deal in a phone call from Thomas Middelhoff of Bertelsmann, a board member of both Vivendi and America Online. Like Messier, Middelhoff seemed to personify a new generation of young, dynamic, and America-loving European executives. Their two families skied together and their children had become close friends.

"Jean-Marie, perhaps you know already, AOL and Time Warner are going to merge. Not a joint venture. Merge." Middelhoff explained that America Online was, in fact, poised to pay $165 billion to buy Time Warner, the blue-chip New York media empire. It was to be the largest takeover in history, putting together companies whose market values prior to the deal exceeded $350 billion, the equivalent of the GDP of Australia. The new company would be the fourth largest in the United States, behind Microsoft, General Electric, and Cisco by market capitalization. The news was almost too much to bear.

Suddenly, the nebulous Internet project with Vodafone gained allure. If Vivendi failed to consummate its merger with Mannesmann, it could try to sell itself as the European AOL Time Warner. The alliance with Vodafone would be a clear statement that

Vivendi's future lay not with telecommunications, but with the Internet. "The 10th of January was a wake-up call," says Alex Berger, a former senior executive at Canal Plus. "It was a very violent, very powerful day—an accelerator for everything that happened subsequently."[10]

Messier admitted to being stunned. AOL had done something few would ever have predicted possible just eighteen months before: it had acquired Time Warner, the world's largest media company, cashing in its shares for Time Warner's fabled brands. In the seven years since the AOL initial public offering in March 1992, the company's market value had soared to more than $120 billion, 20 percent higher than that of Time Warner. One hundred dollars invested in AOL at its first public offering was worth $28,000 by the end of 1999. All the trends appeared in AOL's favor. In 1992, users spent only five minutes a day on AOL; by 1999 that figure had multiplied by ten. The logic of the deal was rooted in the voguish concept of "convergence." At their merger presentation on January 10, 2000, AOL founder Steve Case and Time Warner chief executive Gerald Levin promised to create "the world's first Internet-age media and communications company, delivering branded information, entertainment, and communications across rapidly converging media platforms."

Messier immediately interpreted the announcement as a call to arms. "Nothing will be the same again. AOL and Time Warner are the first to understand that the new and the old economy must merge."[11] The merger reinforced Messier's belief that the Internet was the media distribution platform of the future. Every communications device—from mobile handsets, personal organizers, and laptop computers to hotel toilet seats and exercise-bicycle handlebars—would allow consumers to download music, films, and games from the Web. He felt the omnipresence of the Internet would enhance the value of such content because owners of distribution platforms—the mobile telephone giants, pay-television operators, cable companies, and Internet access providers—would need branded content to win and keep customers.

Content would be the equivalent of "location, location, location" in the new economy. Why else would AOL pay a 70-percent premium for Time Warner? It was clear that AOL feared its main business as Internet-access provider to middle America risked being commoditized by the falling cost of communications and growing familiarity with the Internet. AOL argued that by acquiring Time Warner—owner of such brands as CNN, *Time,* Warner Bros., Warner Music, *Sports Illustrated, People,* HBO, *Fortune, Entertainment Weekly,* and Looney Tunes—it could offer its 20 million subscribers a privileged taste of the world's best media content. It would also be able to market its broadband Internet-access services to Time Warner's 13 million cable households.

For Time Warner, the lure was a guaranteed, controllable showcase for its brands in the vibrant cyberspace community behind AOL's "walled garden." The marriage of the old economy and the new was finally happening: convergence had arrived. Levin shaved off his mustache and removed his tie; Case put on a suit. The message was that the distinctions between the two worlds—the "old" traditional media represented by Time Warner and the new economy represented by AOL—would soon disappear. Nothing could have been further from the truth.

Vivendi's negotiations with Mannesmann soon ran into terminal problems. Messier was easily diverted from the stodgy world of German engineering by the powerful aphrodisiac of Hollywood. The Bronfman family had been tentatively sounding out buyers for their Universal Pictures film studio for some time. John Weinberg, a Goldman Sachs partner and a board member of Seagram, had approached possible buyers, including Canal Plus, Yahoo!, News Corp., Disney, Sony, and Bertelsmann. One by one they had ruled themselves out of the running. Canal Plus was too small on its own to afford it. Rupert Murdoch balked at the price. Thomas Middelhoff was constrained by Bertelsmann's family foundation. Sony had its hands full. Others either could not afford Seagram or would confront insuperable cultural or competition issues.

Edgar Bronfman Jr. decided in the autumn of 1999 to broaden the search. A call was placed to Jean-Marie Messier at Vivendi even though at first glance, the water company looked like an improbable buyer. Bronfman would be "vacationing" in Paris in

October; would Mr. Messier be interested in meeting him? They set up a forty-five-minute breakfast at Vivendi's offices at 42 avenue Friedland; it lasted two hours longer than planned as the two men discussed their visions of the new economy. Later, Messier said, "We had identified Seagram as a very interesting partner. But there was no reason for me to think Edgar was looking for partners. For me, the main objective of this meeting was to understand who Edgar was."[12] They did not touch on the idea of a merger. Nonetheless, the subtext was evident. At the end of the breakfast, Messier recalls, Bronfman said: "Your strengths and our strengths just naturally seem to go together."

On January 20, ten days after the AOL Time Warner merger and just over a week before the Vivendi board was to decide whether the company should merge with Mannesmann or ally itself with Vodafone, Pierre Lescure and Jean-Marie Messier flew to New York to once again discuss with Bronfman his vision of a potential combination of the two companies. At the end of the meeting, it seemed to Messier that a transatlantic merger with Seagram had every chance of meeting his criteria for Vivendi: it would be a bold step into the unknown that would leave him in charge of a world leader in an industry of the future.

The ideas remained fluid at this early stage, but nonetheless undoubtedly influenced him as he weighed the final proposal from Klaus Esser in Dusseldorf. The Messiers spent the weekend of Saturday, January 22, at their country house near Rambouillet, about thirty kilometers to the southwest of the capital. Messier felt that he had done his best to secure the future for his shareholders. He was in a position to offer his board a choice between a traditional industrial merger with Mannesmann that would create considerable value, above all through economies of scale on the one hand, and an alliance with Vodafone, which would have a much more entrepreneurial logic and rely on the development of new revenue streams on the other. With the first, Vivendi would base its strategy on telecommunications, whereas with the second it would become more of a media and Internet company, like AOL Time Warner. The talks with Bronfman had left Messier certain that if an agreement with Mannesmann failed, he would not be starved of future opportunities to show his daring.

That weekend, hopes of an agreement with Klaus Esser died. On Saturday morning, the fax machine at Rambouillet disgorged an unsettling missive. Esser was demanding that they revise their agreement over the division of management positions in the new company. Instead of having five representatives from each company on the executive committee, Esser suggested, it would be appropriate for Mannesmann, the bigger company, to have six, providing it with a symbolic majority. A few hours later, Messier sent a terse fax back. The negotiations were over. The Vivendi board would not consider the merger with Mannesmann when it met the following week. "It was all over between us," Messier later wrote. "This was not a rush of blood to the head, but a perfectly considered decision: operations such as this, which involve hundreds of thousands of shareholders and as many employees, can only be undertaken in complete trust. Klaus Esser had broken the pact of trust."[13]

Esser called back on Sunday to explain that he was merely trying to obtain a board seat for Hans Snook, the charismatic Dutchman who had founded Orange, the mobile operator Mannesmann had bought in the UK. Vivendi and Mannesmann had agreed to adopt the brilliant brand Snook had invented as the new name for their Franco-German company. Even though Esser agreed to revert to the original five-a-side agreement, leaving Snook off the board, the squabble hardened Messier's resolve to abandon the merger project. Their personal relations had worsened to the point of mutual incomprehension: "I no longer understood Klaus Esser," Messier said. "There was something Shakespearean about him as he became more and more hesitant, anxious and isolated. Extremely introverted, solitary and torn between his desire to stay independent and his wish to act in the interests of his shareholders, he was no longer able to conduct himself as a chief executive."[14]

By Thursday, January 27, 2000, Messier had decided that there would be no merger with Mannesmann. He went downstairs to the Vivendi dining room, where his team was still working on the last details, and thanked them as warmly as he could for all their work.

Esser would later say that he still believed Messier intended to recommend the merger to his board at its forthcoming meeting on Saturday, January 29: "By January 29, I certainly did not feel that the deal had collapsed."[15] His media consultants from the Maitland Consultancy had the merger announcement ready to be released on Monday morning. Media speculation about Messier's intentions peaked in the hours leading up to the meeting. Although Messier admitted to suffering "force 10 stress," Messier relished his influence, having positioned himself as kingmaker in the Anglo-German contest. He had sold his support for Vodafone as dearly as possible. In reality, he knew Chris Gent would probably win regardless of his decision. Gent could again raise his offer for Mannesmann, wreck any agreed merger between the German company and Vivendi, and leave Messier with nothing. The Frenchman would recommend to his board that Vivendi abandon Mannesmann and enter into an alliance with Gent.

"Messier played his hand perfectly," said Hans Snook of Orange.[16] For several of the grandees of French capitalism around the Vivendi boardroom table, eschewing a Vivendi-Mannesmann combination, one that fell squarely in the politically approved tradition of other recent Franco-German mergers, was not an easy decision. Rhône-Poulenc and Hoechst had just joined forces to create the highly successful pharmaceutical group Aventis. Aerospatiale and Deutsche Aerospace had combined forces to create the European Aeronautic Defence and Space Company, owner of Airbus, the archrival of Boeing. To dump Mannesmann, consigning it to almost certain defeat at the hands of Vodafone, would go against the grain of Franco-German cooperation. In the end, though, Messier's wishes were clear. Vivendi's board members backed the alliance with Vodafone that would lead directly to the creation of Vizzavi and then Vivendi Universal.

Messier immediately telephoned Gent to inform him of the board's approval. To the Frenchman's astonishment, Gent did not have a fax machine at home. Unable to exchange a signed agreement, they would have to take each other's word as a guarantee. They scheduled a press conference the next day in Paris. Messier waited until Sunday morning to tell Esser and was forced to leave four messages on his voice mail, so brief was the space for messages on the German executive's answering service. Messier's rambling messages, which lasted twenty minutes according to Esser, reached the German as he was en route to Paris for a final meeting with Gent.

"You are going to lose this thing," Esser was told by the Englishman on his arrival at Le Bourget airport. According to Messier, Esser "immediately indicated to Chris Gent that he would accept Vodafone's offer, but on one condition: that Vodafone renounce its alliance with Vivendi! In short, he asked Gent to betray us. Some would have done it. But not Gent. We were right to trust him."

On the afternoon of Sunday, January 30, less than three weeks after the announcement of the AOL Time Warner merger, Messier and Gent launched their Internet alliance at a packed press conference at Vivendi's headquarters in Paris. Vizzavi, as the alliance would be baptized later that year, was Chris Gent's reward to Messier for winning him Mannesmann: it was to be the Taj Mahal of Internet start-ups. With a budget of €1.6 billion, it was the most extravagantly funded start-up in the history of the European Internet and a handsome consolation prize for Messier, whose hopes of catching up with the new giants of the telecommunications industry could now never be fulfilled. No cost was to be spared in its development. At a time when media companies who failed to spray cash at their Internet investments were attacked for not "getting" the new economy, Vizzavi was reassuringly expensive.*

The buzz around Vizzavi in the financial community was deafening. Shares in Vivendi and Vodafone both rose sharply when stock markets resumed trading on Monday. Anxious to distract attention from his failure to consummate a merger with Mannes-

---

*The cost would be split between the two 50-percent shareholders, Vodafone and VivendiNet, a joint venture between Vivendi and its 49-percent-owned pay-TV arm Canal Plus.

mann, Messier stoked the frenzy, promising an initial public offering of Vizzavi shares within twenty-four months and confidently asserting that Vizzavi would be raking in the profits within three years.

If the idea was to create a European version of Yahoo!, the leading U.S. portal, the difference was that from day one Vizzavi would be the default home page for Vodafone and Vivendi's combined subscriber base of 75 million mobile-telephone and pay-television customers. Just as AOL's subscribers would pay for privileged access to Time Warner films and music, so Vodafone's 55 million mobile subscribers, Canal Plus's 14 million pay-TV subscribers, and SFR's 6 million mobile subscribers, as well as anyone else who wanted, would use Vizzavi as the platform from which to download Vivendi's media products via Internet-linked mobile phones, personal organizers, and computers. Vivendi would sell computer games, sports highlights, and movie clips from Canal Plus's huge rights library over this new mobile platform. Vizzavi had a convincing claim to be the most desirable European shopping mall on the World Wide Web. Everyone wanted in, from Rupert Murdoch and British Telecom to the smallest start-up. Only Hans Snook, the visionary marketeer behind Orange, expressed his doubts: "It looks like a Yahoo! me-too. You can't win with a me-too product."[17]

Messier and Gent agreed to rotate their chairmanship of Vizzavi, with the Frenchman taking the helm for the first two years. It was Vodafone's prerogative to appoint the chief executive, and Gent chose Evan Newmark, a thirty-five-year-old American with a Harvard Business School and Goldman Sachs pedigree that made him the paragon of a new economy executive. Vizzavi, Newmark said, had "twelve to eighteen months, not much more" to seize a top-three position in the European portal market. Late to the race, it would have to elbow aside existing Web brands such as Yahoo!, AOL, Microsoft's MSN, and local players such as France Telecom's Wanadoo and Deutsche Telekom's T-Online. With market leadership secured, Vizzavi would then go public within two years. As easy as that.

Anxious to find a unifying force for Vivendi's disparate publishing, television, and telecom interests, Messier hyped Vizzavi with either naive optimism or frightening cynicism. Vizzavi, he promised, "delivers on technology's promise to make life better. It helps you deal with the inevitable, and focus on the enjoyable. It helps put you in control of how and where you spend your time. It inspires and empowers you to get more out of living. Vizzavi is life unlimited."[18]

With Gent and Messier, perhaps Europe's most powerful businessmen, giving Vizzavi the hard sell in a bubble market, investors soon held unrealistic expectations of what the start-up could achieve. Vizzavi rapidly transformed perceptions of Vivendi. Analysts now virtually ignored Vivendi's traditional water and waste businesses when valuing the stock. Almost all of the group's value resided in its telecom, media, and Internet arm.

"By surfing on the Internet wave, Vivendi let the market make its strategic choice for it," said Guillaume Hannezo. "By the spring of 2000, Vivendi was a media and telecom company. In addition to the stake in Cegetel, which was then valued at around €20 billion, Vivendi consisted of €20 billion of Internet promises in Vizzavi and about €25 billion in stakes in European pay TV (€10 billion for BSkyB and €15 billion for Canal Plus). The traditional businesses with solid cash flows such as Vivendi Environnement and Havas publishing accounted for just €10 billion each."[19]

"The market reacted to the agreement beyond all expectation," said Hannezo. Vizzavi had the electrifying effect on Vivendi's share price that Messier had hoped. Within two months of the Vizzavi announcement, Vivendi's shares had soared 130 percent from their mid-November 1999 lows to reach €142, six times their value at the moment of Messier's arrival. In just under four months, Vivendi's market value had increased by €50 billion to €84 billion, making it the third most valuable French company, after France Telecom and TotalFinaElf, the privatized telephone and oil giants.

The rise in Vivendi's value was in large part attributable to the Vizzavi business plan. High on the Kool-Aid of the new economy, analysts argued the portal was worth €40 billion or, to put it in context, more than the value of the global airline industry. And this despite the fact that the start-up had yet to achieve a single sale. The Vivendi share price rose in double-digit leaps in the days following the agreement as analysts produced studies that attached ever higher values to the Orwellian Vizzavi, then just a sketch on a spiral notepad.

## CHAPTER THREE

# Hurry Up Please, It's Time

After his first meeting with the Bronfman family in New York, on March 22, 2000, Messier became Concorde's best customer. Every week he would fly to New York to woo Edgar Bronfman Jr. It seemed he was making all the moves: Bronfman had come to Paris just once in order to cast an eye over the blueprints for Vizzavi. The negotiations had not progressed entirely smoothly. At a meeting in New York on April 24, Messier had proposed a firm all-paper offer to buy Seagram that valued the company's shares at around $72. However, Bronfman, backed up by his finance director Brian Mulligan and investment bankers from Goldman Sachs and Morgan Stanley, dismissed the offer out of hand. Seagram's shares had been worth $64.50 at their peak in March 2000. On that basis, Messier was offering little more than a 12 percent premium. "It was purely a question of price. What he was initially offering was far too low," Bronfman remembers. "So I said, 'Ciao,' and he went back off to the airport."

The talks were off. Less than an hour later, however, Bronfman's telephone rang. It was Jean-Marie Messier on the line, calling from his car: "I want you to know that I have great personal admiration and respect for you and for the Bronfman family," he said. For the Seagram chief executive, the courtesy call was yet another giveaway sign. "I knew he'd be back." The investment bankers, paid primarily on a success-related basis, worked the phones frenetically in order to keep the two sides talking. Lazard had profited handsomely from its close ties to Messier. It had earned €40 million in fees from Vivendi in the two years leading up to the merger and would be paid a similar amount again—based on 0.11 percent of the value of Seagram—if Messier succeeded in acquiring the U.S. company.* In total, the four main banks (including Merrill Lynch, which was advising Canal Plus) stood to gain $110 million if the deal was completed. By the end of May, after a telephone conversation between Guillaume Hannezo and Brian Mulligan had smoothed the waters, it was time to try again.

On June 8, Messier once again flew to New York on the Concorde from Paris, accompanied by his two trusty bankers from Lazard Frères, Georges Ralli and Erik Maris, as well as Jean-Francois Prat, one of Paris's leading corporate lawyers. As ever, the supersonic jet—which would be grounded the following month after a New York–bound aircraft crashed into the northern Paris suburbs, killing 113 people—had been full of familiar faces. By coincidence, three of Vivendi Universal's board members—Bernard Arnault, chairman of the LVMH luxury goods group; Jean-Louis Beffa, chairman of Saint-Gobain, the world's leading glass manufacturer; and Henri Lachmann, chairman of the Schneider electrical components company—were all on the flight. Messier discreetly informed them that, once again, he was off to see Edgar Bronfman Jr. with a refined proposal for a merger between Vivendi and Seagram. On his arrival in Manhattan that Thursday afternoon, the two sides immediately sat down to negotiate. By 7 P.M. Messier

*Lazard acted as adviser to Vivendi in connection with the acquisition of the United States Filter Corporation in 1999, the acquisition of Superior Services in 1999, and Vivendi's joint venture with Vodafone to create the Multi Access Portal in January 2000; adviser to Vivendi Environnement in connection with the joint venture of Dalkia and Electricité de France in July 2000; adviser to Vivendi Environnement in connection with the disposal of Kinetics Group in August 2000; adviser to Vivendi in connection with the initial public offering of Vivendi Environnement in July 2000; and adviser to Vivendi in connection with the acquisition of Loot by Scoot.com Plc in June 2000. Georges Ralli, a partner of Lazard, is a member of the supervisory board of Vivendi Environnement.

thought they had a deal, but thirty minutes later, all seemed up in the air once more. Messier felt the Bronfman lawyers were starting to go back on points already settled to their mutual satisfaction.

Moreover, he was late for dinner. In a few minutes, he was expected at a function hosted by Felix Rohatyn, the U.S. ambassador to France, in the presence of Madeleine Albright, U.S. secretary of state under President Bill Clinton. Rohatyn, the former Lazard star who became famous after he oversaw the rescue of New York City from the brink of bankruptcy in the early 1970s, had set up the French-American Business Council to help erode French fears of economic liberalization and U.S.-led globalization. Messier was billed as one of the main attractions of the evening. Explaining that he felt personally insulted by the lawyers' behavior, Messier told Bronfman that he was prepared to return to the negotiating table after dinner, but only on condition that the pointless quibbling stop. "We either reach an agreement or we go our separate ways," he said. Three hours later, after slipping out of the dinner before coffee, Messier returned to find the tension gone. By three o'clock in the morning, after three further hours of discussion, both sides appeared satisfied. Yet as he climbed into the car waiting to drive him back to his Upper East Side town house, Bronfman hesitated, "Give me some more time. This is a once-in-a-lifetime decision. I'll never make it again. I want to sleep on it."

Did Bronfman think hard enough as chief executive of Seagram? Rarely has any man been given an opportunity to press home his advantage in such a prestigious array of businesses. The strategic choices he made would affect not just his family's wealth and influence, but the shape of the entertainment and drinks industries. During his time at the helm of Seagram, Bronfman could have pursued greatness in many different fields. He could have concentrated all his energies on developing the Seagram drinks and fruit juice empire. The Canadian company could have played the role of consolidator of the liquor industry, stealing the thunder of the now-dominant British and French groups, Diageo, Allied Domecq, and Pernod Ricard. He could have nursed the family's 24-percent stake in Du Pont, harvesting the chemical company's rich dividend stream on behalf of his numerous relations. He could have pushed harder to take over Time Warner in the mid-1990s, possibly averting the group's calamitous merger with AOL, which created the role model for Vivendi Universal. If he had turned down Jean-Marie Messier's advances and retained Universal Studios and Universal Music, he would now be praised, along with Sumner Redstone of Viacom, for being one of the few moguls to have focused on lucrative traditional media and avoided the convergence bust.

In its heyday in the mid-1950s, Seagram accounted for one in three alcoholic drinks sold in the United States. Yet its origins at the end of the First World War could not have been more modest. After fleeing Bolshevik Russia, Samuel Bronfman—father of Edgar Bronfman Sr. and Charles—and his brothers opened a small bar with a pool table and a couple of rooms for rent in Winnipeg, Manitoba. When Canadian Prohibition barred alcohol retailing, the Bronfman family began shipping by mail order from Montreal. After Quebec too gave way to prohibitionist pressure in 1924, the brothers went into distilling. In cooperation with distillers in Great Britain, they opened a distillery in Ville LaSalle, outside Montreal, and bought a second distillery from the Seagram family. Under the name Distillers Corporation–Seagram, the Bronfman brothers established a lucrative business selling whiskey, much of which was bootlegged to the dry United States. Anticipating the end of U.S. Prohibition, they began stockpiling, and by 1933 they had the world's largest supply of aged rye and sour mash whiskey.

Cleansing the family name of its association with bootlegging was of primary importance to Samuel Bronfman. The U.S. government was bringing lawsuits against Canadian companies that had dealt with smugglers. Moreover, clandestine hooch had given whiskey a harsh image, which Bronfman softened by introducing the smoother, blended Seagram's 7 Crown in 1934 and then Crown Royal, in honor of the June 1939 visit to Canada of King George VI, the first by Britain's reigning monarch.

A driven, insecure person, Samuel Bronfman had a lifelong ambition to "be somebody," a status that in his own mind he never quite attained, according to his eldest son, Edgar Bronfman Sr.[1] Mr. Sam, as he was known, tried at one point to make the family change its name to Seagram-Bronfman and claimed to have been born in Canada. Only after his death did Edgar Bronfman Sr. find a passport that proved his Russian origins. Mindful of the anti-Soviet feeling that prevailed for so long in the West, he hid the truth about his birth, and was never betrayed by his siblings.

The Bronfmans were Montreal's most prominent Jewish family and enjoyed a lifestyle consistent with that status. Their home in the suburb of Westmount boasted a butler, a cook, a kitchen maid, a parlor maid, a lady's maid, a laundress, a gardener, a chauffeur, a "mademoiselle" for the girls, and a nanny for the boys. "Conspicuous by its absence was love," remembered Edgar Bronfman Sr., who once said he was closer to the family chauffeur than to his parents and described his father as a man who would have "made Queen Victoria look like a swinger." Edgar Bronfman Sr. believed his brother, Charles, to be their father's favorite and retained few fond memories of Montreal. Edgar Bronfman Sr.'s family moved to New York in 1955, six months after the birth of Edgar Bronfman Jr., returning to Canada only for meetings of the Seagram board. Charles Bronfman played a much greater part in the Canadian community as owner of the Montreal Expos baseball team and as a major benefactor to philanthropic causes.

"Father believed in the old British foreign policy of divide and conquer. While Charles was in Canada and I was in the U.S., he told each of us uncomplimentary things about the other and deliberately kept us apart," Edgar Bronfman Sr. said. "His insecurity was such that he had a fear that we might combine and throw him out. Our friendship survived, thank the lord."[2] Bronfman so thoroughly dominated his brother during their long, exasperating apprenticeship to Mr. Sam that he assumed Charles never aspired to running Seagram. While Charles remained close to the family seat in Montreal, Edgar became an American citizen and married into Wall Street's "Our Crowd" Jewish aristocracy. He and his wife, Ann Loeb, the daughter of John Loeb Sr., the philanthropist and politically active scion of the banking dynasty that eventually formed part of Shearson/American Express, had three children: Samuel II, Edgar Jr., and Holly.

Edgar Bronfman Sr. succeeded Samuel Bronfman as president

in 1959. Recognizing that the U.S. spirits industry was likely to suffer from slower growth as consumers grew more health conscious, Edgar Bronfman Sr. executed a scattershot diversification. He bought Texas gas fields, Israeli supermarkets, and a 5-percent stake in the Hollywood studio MGM, and even ended up with a 24-percent stake in Du Pont after the U.S. chemical giant acquired shares Seagram had bought in the Conoco oil company. In 1988 Seagram bought Tropicana, at that time a fading orange juice brand, and then, in the early 1990s, as Edgar Bronfman Jr.'s influence started to be felt more and more strongly, a 15-percent stake in Time Warner.

The radical repositioning of Seagram in the mid-1990s was the work of Edgar Bronfman Jr. Born in May 1955, one and a half years after Samuel II, Edgar Bronfman Jr. was from an early age earmarked to lead the third generation of Bronfmans. He was forced to grow up quickly when his parents went through a messy divorce. Tall, straight-backed, and soft-spoken, Bronfman now shows little trace of his years of rebellion against an overwhelming father. Instead he has the conscious tranquility of someone who feels comfortable admitting to never having flown on a commercial airline. One story has it that at the age of twelve, he made a trip alone across New England in the Seagram corporate jet to look at prep schools. "Are you here with your father?" one headmaster asked. "No," the young Bronfman reportedly replied. "I'm here with my pilot."

On another occasion, the following year, Bronfman watched his father on the telephone at home. "I don't remember what he was talking about but I remember I must have been very impressed because I said to him: 'Dad, you're very powerful, aren't you?' He looked at me and said: 'Always remember, son, you never have any power if you have to use it.' That means if you walk into a room and you have to tell people who you are, you are not powerful." Bronfman was seventeen when his parents separated. He took it hard, and his unhappiness probably accentuated a certain wilfulness in him. "I don't ever remember consciously trying to rebel," he says now. "It's not like I went off somewhere in India to chant. I just never liked school."[3]

Edgar Bronfman Jr. picked up his interest in film from his father. In the late 1960s, Edgar Bronfman Sr., while chairman of Seagram, began investing in films and plays on the side and set up a small movie production company called Sagittarius Productions. The son would sift through the piles of scripts left around the family's Park Avenue apartment, and when he was fifteen he persuaded his father to put up $450,000 to produce a film comedy called *Melody.* Edgar Bronfman Sr. hired first-time producer David Puttnam, who would go on to produce such classics as *Midnight Express* and *Chariots of Fire* and then run Columbia Pictures for Coca-Cola. That summer, Edgar Bronfman Jr. moved to London, where he stayed with Joan Collins and her husband Ron Kass and ran errands for the British film producer.

During his junior year of prep school, he took time off to complete *The Blockhouse,* a grim World War II film. Puttnam found it bleak, but the young Bronfman considered it an important work. "It was everything Puttnam said," he told Ken Auletta of the *New Yorker.* "It was dark and it was depressing and absolutely no one wanted to see a movie that took place underground with seven men slowly starving to death."

Nonetheless, the experience encouraged him to skip college to become a movie producer. At the same time, he began to write Simon and Garfunkel–derived ballads, often under the pseudonym Sam Roman, with titles such as "The Quiet Sound of You and I" and "In Your Arms." In 1979, aged twenty-four, Edgar Bronfman Jr. seemed to be living out one of his lyrics when he eloped to New Orleans with Sherry Brewer, a beautiful black actress he had met through the singer Dionne Warwick. Edgar Bronfman Sr., president of the World Jewish Congress, regretted his son's marriage, even though it gave him three grandchildren. "I very much wanted for him to end the relationship because all marriages are difficult enough without the added stress of totally different backgrounds. His children would have problems being accepted by either black or white society."[4] The two did not speak for a year. "Mom closed ranks immediately. It took Dad a little longer. He threw a cocktail party for us, but I could see he was not happy. We remained estranged."[5]

After divorcing Sherry Brewer in 1991, Edgar Bronfman Jr. re-married three years later. On a trip to Caracas, he said to the wife of a local Seagram partner, "If there's anyone as pretty as you, I'd love to meet her." That night, he was introduced to Clarissa Al-cock, daughter of a senior executive of the Venezuelan national oil company. Again, her background clashed with Edgar Bronfman Sr.'s sensibilities, but less dramatically than Sherry Brewer's had in 1979. Father and son had been reconciled since 1982, when Edgar Bronfman Sr. asked his son to join the family firm. After his sec-ond film, *The Border,* starring Jack Nicholson and Harvey Keitel, also bombed on its release in January 1982, the younger Bronf-man, whom the family nicknamed Efer, accepted a job as executive assistant to the chief executive.

Samuel Bronfman II, victim of a kidnapping in 1975, had also been encouraged to join the family firm in expectation of one day taking over from his father. With both his sons competing to suc-ceed him, Edgar Bronfman Sr. sensed the same destructive ten-sions that his father had encouraged between him and Charles. In a non-family-owned business, competition is good, he reasoned. The winner takes over and the loser gets another job elsewhere. The adherents of the loser swear fealty to the winner, and some of them manage to keep their jobs. "Having my two sons line up supporters as if it were an election was not good for them, for the corporation, for the family or for me. I already knew that Sam would not be the next chief executive. It was clear even when they were teenagers that the brilliant, tough-minded businessman in our family would be Efer."[6]

Upset at the looming battle, Edgar Bronfman Sr. let slip in an interview with *Fortune* that Edgar Bronfman Jr. was to succeed him. "What I should have done, of course, was discuss the issue with my brother Charles, then with Efer and Sam. It took Sam a long time to get over the hurt I inflicted." Charles told reporters that he objected to the way the appointment had been handled. This was the first public rupture within the Bronfman family. It would not be the last.

Edgar Bronfman Jr. joined the board in 1988 and was made responsible for the firm's U.S. operations; eleven months later he became president and chief operating officer. By June 1994, Bronfman, then thirty-eight, had risen to become chief executive, a position in the gift of the Bronfman family, which held at that time 35 percent of the shares. His intelligence and thoughtfulness impressed those who worked with him. But he often failed to help himself, making light of concerns about his aptitude to lead a public company at such a tender age. On one occasion, he explained his qualifications to a heavily pin-striped crowd in New York by saying: "You just have to be real smart and choose the right father." Unencumbered by high expectations, Bronfman nonetheless stamped his mark on Seagram. In March 1995, he argued for the sale of Seagram's stake in Du Pont. This would have a fundamental impact on the group: Du Pont accounted for more than 40 percent of the drinks group's earnings and paid a handsome dividend. Edgar Bronfman Jr., however, doubted whether Du Pont could be expected to do much better than track the S&P 500. "Both Efer and I felt that Du Pont was a boring investment," remembered his father. "Du Pont is still a great company, just not an exciting one."[7] Charles Bronfman looked at it differently. He reasoned that Du Pont, the archetypal blue-chip investment, would be there forever. As long as the family had good managers at Seagram, it would be protected generation after generation. Not for the last time, his nephew and brother ignored his words of caution. The sale of the Du Pont stake the following month netted Seagram around $7.7 billion after taxes.*

Edgar Bronfman Jr. had a clear idea of how to put the cash to use. After briefly considering the luxury-goods industry, father and son agreed that leisure offered the best opportunities for the next century. As technology reduced the need for manual labor, a shorter working week would leave more time for recreation. By combining a strong presence in entertainment with Seagram's position in beverages, the family would be ideally positioned for

---

*Seagram had acquired its shares in Du Pont for $3.28 billion in 1981.

decades to come. The question was what to buy. For the best part of fifty years, the entertainment industry had been dominated by a handful of major studios: Warner Bros., Walt Disney, Paramount, Twentieth Century–Fox, Metro-Goldwyn-Mayer/United Artists, Columbia Pictures, and MCA, the parent of Universal Pictures and MCA Records. In the decade that followed Rupert Murdoch's acquisition of Twentieth Century–Fox in 1985, six of the seven studios would change hands. Time bid $14 billion for Warner Communications in June 1989. Sony's purchase of Columbia for $3.4 billion later that same year prompted its domestic rival Matsushita to buy MCA for $6.1 billion in 1990. Giancarlo Parretti and Crédit Lyonnais joined the action in 1991, paying Kirk Kerkorian $1.3 billion for MGM/UA, and Viacom bought Paramount for $10 billion in 1994. By then, the Japanese were looking to sell. Sony started to seek a buyer for 25 percent of Columbia Pictures, and Matsushita decided in January 1995 that it too had had enough.

Sony and Matsushita had between them spent almost $10 billion acquiring Hollywood studios in the hope that gaining control of large libraries of film and music would promote sales of electronics equipment. Not long after Matsushita's acquisition of MCA, Japan's bubble economy burst. During 1993 and 1994, Matsushita's sales and profits dropped substantially, forcing it to veto MCA's acquisition of Virgin Records and plans to join with ITT to bid for CBS. Cultural clashes hardly helped. Matsushita executives spoke little English, rarely visited the United States, and had little contact with MCA managers other than to turn down requests for funds. America was experiencing "the Japan that can say no,"* and did not like it. These clashes boiled over in October 1994. MCA chairman Lew Wasserman, then eighty-one and the

---

*The title of a controversial book by Akio Morita, chairman of Sony, and Shintaro Ishihara, a right-of-center member of Japan's ruling Liberal Democratic Party. Published at the same time as Sony acquired Columbia, its cover depicted a For Sale sign stuck into a map of the United States against the backdrop of the rising sun. The book bashed U.S. business and called for more assertive Japanese economic and foreign policy-making.

industry's most revered elder statesman, and his number two, Sidney Sheinberg, indicated that they and many other top executives would leave unless MCA was granted sufficient capital to compete with the other movie studios. Steven Spielberg said that he too would stop working for MCA if Sheinberg, his close friend and mentor, left the studio. In short, MCA had turned into a nightmare.

By this time, Edgar Bronfman Jr. had already built up a 15-percent stake in Time Warner, but found himself frustrated by poison pills put in place by Gerald Levin that would frustrate any attempt at a takeover. When Bronfman heard in March 1995 from Michael Ovitz, the Hollywood superagent, that MCA was for sale, he flew to Osaka in his Gulfstream IV to meet Matsushita president Yoichi Morishita. As negotiations unfolded, the Edgar side of the family confronted determined opposition from Charles. Edgar Bronfman Sr. attempted to counter his brother's arguments by pointing out that even staid Coca-Cola had bought a movie business—Columbia Pictures—and made a fortune when it sold the film company to Sony. Charles was not convinced, nor would he become more so after the decision to buy MCA had been made. Edgar Bronfman Sr. put their difference of opinion down to Charles's essentially "conservative" character as opposed to his own more "adventurous" personality, although he admitted that the Hollywood egos, stars, and hype could make him uncomfortable too. He argued that buying MCA represented an enormous opportunity for his son. Edgar Bronfman Jr. would have full control of MCA, a company in an exciting and fast-growing field, as opposed to having to play the role of a boring fund manager, which would have been his destiny if Seagram had retained the Du Pont investment.

"You can't ask a 40-year-old to come as the new C.E.O. and tell him that 2/3rds of the business is sacrosanct," said Bronfman's father. "If you do, you know what kind of a businessman you are getting. As the third generation C.E.O., Efer wanted to build stockholder value far beyond the S&P 500 and to do that we would have to look elsewhere."[8] In April 1995, Edgar Bronfman Jr. agreed that Seagram would pay $5.7 billion for 80 percent of

MCA, valuing the entire business at $7.1 billion. Gratifyingly, this was exactly the same price Matsushita had paid in 1990.* Yet Seagram stock fell 20 percent in a week as the press and the investment community crucified Edgar Bronfman Jr. If Coca-Cola had failed to apply its marketing power to the entertainment business when it owned Columbia in the 1980s, what hope had Seagram? "Dumb and Dumber" proclaimed one *Wall Street Journal* headline. Others were barely kinder. From almost any angle, analysts argued, it was a bizarre cocktail. On the one hand, orange juice, ginger ale, and whiskey; on the other, rock bands, film stars, and the glamour of Tinsel Town. If the Bronfmans had always seemed solid if uninspiring managers, they suddenly seemed to be allowing Edgar Bronfman Jr. to indulge his passion for the movies.

Bronfman was unrepentant. "People are more skeptical of a person's ability if he's born with money," he told *Vanity Fair* shortly after the acquisition. He found a refrain to justify the purchase: "There are only six major seats at the production table. Not one major has been created in the last fifty years. And we had a chance to buy MCA, one of the best baskets of assets in the entertainment industry, which is the fifth-fastest-growing sector of the U.S. economy." Universal Pictures, he noted, had just made *Jurassic Park,* the highest-grossing film of all time, and it produced television programs such as the whodunit series *Murder She Wrote;* MCA music had the rights to more than 150,000 songs; through Putnam it published bestselling authors such as Tom Clancy; and Universal's theme parks were set to be the boom businesses of tomorrow's leisure economy. In the space of seventy-two hours, he said, Seagram had been transformed. This was how long it had taken to clinch the sale by Seagram of its stake in Du Pont and sign the purchase of 80 percent of MCA from Matsushita. The net effect, he enthused, was to give Seagram control of its own destiny. The acquisition of MCA was to Edgar Bronfman Jr. what the investment in Du Pont in the early 1980s had been to his father: a large, controversial deal that transformed and expanded Seagram. But, as Edgar Bronfman Sr. noted, it was also different. The Bronf-

---

*Matsushita paid $6.1 billion for MCA and took on about $1 billion of net debt.

mans had control of MCA, which had never been true of Du Pont, and were able to appoint their own managers and set their own strategy.

Perhaps because the Bronfmans themselves were now in charge of a business they did not yet fully understand, the tensions within the family worsened. At the same time, the end of the Wasserman and Sheinberg era—a partnership that had spanned twenty-two years—introduced managerial upheaval at MCA that Bronfman never resolved. The Bronfman years in Hollywood started off on a poor footing when he embarked upon a long and public mating dance with Mike Ovitz, the all-powerful talent agent at the head of Creative Artists Associates, who was demanding $250 million and a large slug of Seagram equity as payment for becoming the Bronfmans' hired help at MCA. An exasperated Charles finally flew to New York to kill the negotiations. He remained unhappy about the direction in which Seagram was heading. Edgar Bronfman Sr. tells how one day Charles came into his office, sat down, and said: " 'I thought as we got older we were supposed to get closer and be better friends.' 'Well that's what's happening.' 'No it isn't,' said Charles. 'What are you talking about?' 'MCA.' 'All right, Charles,' I said. 'Now the rules are that if you say "no," we don't do it. Did you ever say no?' 'Well no, but . . .' 'Charles, did you ever say no?' 'No. I didn't want to start a family feud.' 'There probably would have been one, but if you had said no, we wouldn't have made the deal. Now stop it. We've already made the deal; let's get on with it.' "[9] Thus began the Bronfmans' five unhappy years in Hollywood.

Within two years of turning Seagram upside down to acquire MCA, it appeared that Bronfman had lost all enthusiasm for Hollywood. Instead, he suddenly seemed intent on refocusing the entertainment arm of Seagram on the music industry, where MCA had a small, successful record division with about 6 percent of the market. This shift was confirmed in October 1997 when he announced the sale of Universal's cable channels—USA Networks and Sci-Fi—and television programming assets to Barry Diller for $4.1 billion. In other words, more than half of the MCA assets by value that Seagram had bought from Matsushita were suddenly being sold again. It was a strange transaction that went against the trend in the industry to integrate TV and film production and distribution, and it confused investors. Yet there was a contorted logic to it. Bronfman felt that only Barry Diller, then fifty-five years old, had the raw talent necessary to develop MCA's television business on Seagram's behalf. Because Diller refused to work for anyone else, he would take actual ownership of the business, while leaving Seagram the right to buy it back later. Bronfman described the complex arrangement as a means of "hiring Barry without hiring Barry" because he had a "clear path to control" the moment Diller stopped running the business. As partial payment for the business, Seagram received a 43-percent stake in Diller's enlarged company, USA Networks, enabling it to share in all the anticipated increase in the value of the business under the control of the Hollywood legend. Bronfman retained the right to veto large transactions at USA Networks, but otherwise ceded total management control of the business the Bronfmans had just bought from Matsushita to "Killer" Diller, one of the most powerful men in the history of Hollywood.

Later described by Tina Brown, former editor of *Vanity Fair* and the *New Yorker*, as "the reigning daddy cool of American business,"[10] even in 1997 Diller had a near-mythical status in the entertainment industry. He had skipped college to join the William Morris Agency, starting out in the mailroom, where he learned the intricacies of the industry by reading the contracts of the stars on the talent agency's books. Within a few years, Diller became head of programming at ABC, then in a distant third position behind CBS and NBC. With the help of Michael Eisner, later to become head of Walt Disney, Diller transformed the network with innovations such as the *ABC Movie of the Week*. In 1974, aged thirty-two, he was headhunted from ABC to rescue Paramount. With Eisner at his side, he revived the ailing studio with a flurry of hits including *Raiders of the Lost Ark* and the TV show *Cheers*.

The two men made Paramount the top Hollywood studio during the late 1970s. But the crowning achievement of Diller's career would follow his move to Twentieth Century–Fox in 1984, shortly before the studio's sale to Rupert Murdoch. At the height of the power of the Big Three TV networks, he and Murdoch started to build Fox into a fourth television network. Its success was based on low-cost "reality" programming, with shows such as *Cops* and *America's Most Wanted*, as well as youth-oriented hits such as *Married . . . with Children* and *The Simpsons*. Diller was the only person whose demands to be made an equal partner Murdoch ever seriously considered. In the end, the naturalized American reportedly told Diller, "There is only one principal in News Corporation." A mogul in search of an empire, Diller quit Fox in 1992, promising that henceforth he would work only for himself.

Barry Diller's acquisition of Universal's cable channels compounded a sense of drift in the early years of the Bronfmans' ownership of MCA. Bronfman was fast becoming the joke of Hollywood, a dangerous development in a town that cannot abide the taint of failure. The studio had been churning out a gut-wrenching sequence of box-office failures and had slipped to ninth in the box-office rankings during the Bronfmans' ownership. Dog after dog trotted off the Universal lot: *Blues Brothers 2000, Dante's Peak, Mercury Rising,* and *Primary Colors* were just some of the studio's unmemorable productions from this period. To make the challenge tougher, Bronfman was splitting his time between Seagram's beverage operations and Universal Studios, commuting between a rented home in Malibu and a town house in New York. It seemed an additional disadvantage he could ill-afford when competing against seasoned pros like Rupert Murdoch of News Corp., Michael Eisner of Walt Disney Company, Gerald Levin of Time Warner, and Sumner Redstone of Viacom. Nor was it as if the drinks world was a sea of tranquility and ever-rising profits. The Asia crisis was starting to hurt Seagram's drinks business. Moreover, in May 1997, Guinness and Grand Metropolitan announced their plan to merge to form Diageo, the world's largest drinks company. Bronfman seemed unable to articulate a clear vision for either of the family company's divisions.

In April 1998, Peter Bart, editor in chief of *Variety,* wrote a cutting spoof memo to Bronfman:

Have you noticed a whirring sound lately, Edgar? It may be unfamiliar to you, but those of us who have worked in Hollywood for a time know it all too well. That whirr is the sound of Hollywood collectively turning on someone, Edgar. In this case, turning on you. Magazines and newspapers are lining up to blast you. The revisionist thinking on your deal with Barry Diller is that Barry got the best of you. Your various spokesmen may keep emphasizing that you have deftly positioned yourself ultimately to take over Diller's empire several years down the road, should you opt to do so, but the fact remains that Hollywood is persuaded that you have let the fox into the henhouse—that Diller is positioned to take you over.

The public memo from one of the most respected pundits in the industry, which urged Bronfman to communicate a clear strategy, electrified the young chief executive. The following month, Bronfman decided to double up on Seagram's exposure to the entertainment industry, but also to shift its focus away from Hollywood, which he had taken to describing openly as a "dumb town." At a recent media conference, he had been ridiculed for suggesting that the movie industry consider changing its ticket-pricing structure so that moviegoers paid more for big-budget movies than they did for less expensive ones. He felt it was time to react.

At the end of a lightning negotiation with Cor Boonstra, chairman of Philips, the Dutch electronics group, Bronfman announced the purchase of PolyGram, the world's leading music company and Europe's leading film producer, for $10.4 billion.* While Uncle Charles shuddered, many pundits applauded. MCA's music division, by far the smallest of the big six music majors and once mocked as the "Music Cemetery of America," had become the surprise success story of the original MCA acquisition from Mat-

---

*The acquisition was completed on December 10, 1998. Seagram paid $8.6 billion in cash and 47.9 million Seagram shares for PolyGram, which was 75 percent owned by Philips. With 10.8 percent of the equity, the Dutch electronics group became Seagram's second largest shareholder after the Bronfmans.

sushita. Under Doug Morris, the former head of Warner Music, MCA Records had released a string of hits from acts such as Beck, the Wallflowers, and Bush, and was one of the few growth stories at a time of sluggish sales across the industry. Nonetheless, MCA was still by far the smallest of the big six music groups worldwide and was in fact regarded as more of a "mini major." With the PolyGram acquisition, it would leap from the number six position to the number one spot overnight, its market share soaring to 24 percent from 6 percent. The move reverberated through the $38 billion music industry. Bronfman and MCA's Doug Morris found themselves in charge of the world's biggest music business. Morris, another former songwriter, who could claim the credit for "Sweet Talkin' Guy," said the merger would yield annual savings of around $300 million. Seagram's old music operation within MCA had been strong in the United States, but weak overseas. Poly-Gram, which was strongest in Europe and Asia, would transform its position and radically reshape Seagram's focus within the entertainment industry.

Bronfman was gambling that the deal would restore his personal credibility in the financial community, which continued to regard him as a pampered charmer who had inherited, rather than earned, his power at Seagram. He reassured Seagram's investors that the acquisition of PolyGram was the final step of Seagram's transformation. "It's been a large and, I think, pretty dramatic series of asset transformations. Those are behind us now." Seagram, he claimed, was no longer a holding company, but a leader in the field of entertainment on the one hand, and spirits and wine on the other. He promised that the strong cash flow from a bigger music business would provide ballast for the volatile finances of Seagram's Universal film subsidiary. A few years earlier, when the music industry had enjoyed double-digit growth, a similar strategy based on cost cutting would doubtless have succeeded; but Bronfman was plowing his family fortune into music at a time when the industry was entering a far less favorable cycle. After a heady decade when consumers not only bought new releases but replaced old vinyl albums with compact discs, global record sales had stalled in 1996. Growth was expected to remain sluggish until the economic situation stabilized in the once-buoyant Asian market. By 1998, some observers suspected the music industry's difficulties reflected long-term structural changes. They feared that Internet piracy would spiral out of control with the advent of on-line file-sharing services, such as Napster, which were enabling Web surfers to build huge personal libraries of music for free from the comfort of their personal computers.

By mid-1999, just a few months after the completion of the PolyGram acquisition in December 1998, the Bronfmans decided it was time to sell Seagram, whose value was by then overwhelmingly tied up in its media assets. Media-content companies such as Universal were attracting record valuations. In the first six months of 1999, Seagram's shares had risen by more than 35 percent, making the family's stake worth around $7.5 billion. AOL's purchase of Time Warner the following January confirmed the family's decision to seek a buyer. "Even before the Time Warner/AOL deal was announced," Bronfman said, "it was becoming quite obvious to me that, in order to create value for our shareholders in the future, we would have to look at new business opportunities— a partner, a joint venture, an alliance, a merger. Why? Because it was clear that the communications and media industries were being reshaped significantly by the convergence of entertainment, telecommunications, computers, and mobile devices." The acquisition of PolyGram had already left Seagram's balance sheet seriously stretched. Uncle Charles was in favor of cashing in his chips while the bull market in media stocks still raged. However, selling his family's stake in Seagram would require them to accept a large discount to the market value of their shares and would also expose them to a substantial capital gains tax liability. The only way they would be able to realize the full value of their stake would be to sell the whole company—at a premium—to a trade buyer offering to pay in shares.

The meetings with Pierre Lescure and Jean-Marie Messier acquired greater urgency after the AOL Time Warner announcement on January 10, 2000, and the collapse of Vivendi's planned merger with Mannesmann at the end of the same month. Messier wanted to move fast to exploit the high rating attached to Vivendi's shares in the aftermath of the launch of Vizzavi on January 30. In mid-February 2000, he and Lescure again asked Bronfman to meet in New York. On Friday, February 25, and Saturday, February 26, Messier, accompanied by Lescure and Guillaume Hannezo, gave a detailed presentation to Bronfman and Brian Mulligan, Seagram's finance director. That Vivendi owned just 49 percent of Canal Plus complicated the negotiation. Without full ownership of the pay-television business, it was impossible for Messier to promise that Canal Plus could be seamlessly integrated into any new transatlantic entertainment company.

For Bronfman, controlling Canal Plus, a vital European distribution platform for Universal's film output, was a fundamental part of the deal's logic. Direct access to the heavily protected European consumer was a long-standing Hollywood dream. Without Canal Plus, they would be taking shares in a mishmash of a company that controlled a water business and a publishing business, but that had only large minority interests in its pay-television media distribution platforms. Without full ownership of Canal Plus, Messier would find it hard to convince anyone that real synergies would ever be possible. There was no choice: to live the Hollywood dream, Messier would have to buy not just Seagram, but Canal Plus too. Moreover, it was what Pierre Lescure wanted: Canal Plus was in poor financial shape after the acquisition of NetHold in 1996 and needed the security of being part of a large group. It would have to be a two-pronged attack, on Hollywood and on the leading European pay-TV operator. The scale of the endeavor was daunting. Not only would Vivendi have to pay perhaps as much as $43 billion to secure Seagram, but acquiring the half of Canal Plus that it did not already own would cost a further $15 billion, taking the total cost to nearly $60 billion. Such an ambitious and complex three-way transatlantic merger had never before been attempted.

Immediately, Messier ran into difficulties with Pierre Lescure. One of the Canal Plus chairman's demands as part of his agreement to join the three-way merger was that he was to be put in charge of all film and television activities, from Canal Plus to Universal Studios. This would require the veteran Hollywood executives who ran Universal to report to a French television executive in Paris. Edgar Bronfman Jr. thought this was lunacy. Already, 2000 was set to be a second year of strong recovery for Universal Pictures at the box office. In 1999, the studio had suddenly started to produce knockout hits. It had surpassed its all-time domestic gross with $934.5 million in revenues and 13 percent of the domestic market, and had climbed to third place among the major studios. Domestic box-office revenues would surpass $1 billion for the first time in 2000, giving Universal a year-end market share of around 15 percent, which would leave it second only to Disney. Ron Meyer and Stacey Snider, president of Universal Studios and chairwoman of Universal Pictures, would soon to be named Man and Woman of 2001 in *Variety*. They had nothing to learn from Lescure about how to run a Hollywood studio.

It helped that Vivendi's share price continued to rocket upward. Since the announcement of the Internet alliance with Vodafone six weeks earlier, Vivendi's shares had risen by more than 40 percent. The vertical hike in share price in the first three months of 2000 lifted Messier's purchasing power. In an all-stock transaction, this meant that he would have to give away fewer Vivendi shares in order to buy Seagram. This was of vital significance in Messier's thinking as he negotiated the terms of the transaction with Bronfman. As one banker said: "If you double the value of my currency, I don't mind overpaying. You have to remember that Messier was offering to pay with shares that were fundamentally overvalued because of the hype surrounding Vizzavi. He had at least €20 billion of Vizzavi in his share price." Messier understood that he had a limited opportunity to exploit the Internet hysteria surrounding Vizzavi to launch himself into the big leagues of the global media industry. He would seize the chance with impeccable timing, striking a deal with the Bronfmans when Vivendi shares were only just past the all-time highs they had reached in March 2000. "Why did we sell to Messier? Because he was the most ardent," Bronfman would later say

At the formal meeting with the whole Bronfman family in New York on March 22, 2000, Messier had clearly understood that Vivendi was the favorite to buy Seagram. The discussions he had since been having with Bronfman revolved around the purchase not just of the entertainment arm, but of the entire company, including the drinks business. For tax reasons, it was unattractive for the Bronfmans to try to sell Universal Studios and the music business separately. It was also unappealing for the family to sell the whole company to a cash buyer, as that would have triggered a huge capital-gains liability on their shares in Seagram. The reality was that no one else was interested in paying the amount Bronfman was asking. Messier would later say he believed the Bronfmans found other partners "less sexy." Other suitors had their different drawbacks. Bertelsmann was controlled by a private German foundation, which made share deals impossible. Thomas Middelhoff, who was interested in the Seagram opportunity, told Messier he had little hope of engaging Edgar in a serious discussion. A few days before Messier's trip to New York, he told the Frenchman: "Go for it. You can succeed where I today have no chance."[11] Disney and News Corp. were uninterested in buying Seagram at such a high price, especially when it was clear that the music industry was facing serious structural problems due to piracy and new forms of music retailing over the Internet. Yahoo! did not want to contaminate its stock market rating as a pure Internet play with old media assets.

Messier appeared to offer the Bronfmans the best of both worlds: an exceptionally high price for their company, and more freedom for Uncle Charles's side of the family to sell their shares than had been possible when they were part of a controlling block of shares at Seagram. Moreover, Bronfman had negotiated a tight corporate-governance agreement that would give the family a powerful voice in how the new company would be run. The Bronfmans demanded important safeguards to protect their power. Remembering how they had failed to influence Du Pont and Time Warner, they insisted on a substantial boardroom presence. Messier agreed that five Seagram directors, including three members of the Bronfman family, should sit on the eighteen-person Vivendi board for at least the first four years of the merger. The family would be entitled to three board seats for as long as it retained 75 percent of their 7.7-percent stake in the new company. In return, the Bronfmans agreed not to attempt a takeover of the company, or even to acquire more than 10 percent of its shares. They promised not to seek to oust Messier as chief executive of Vivendi Universal—as it would be called—or to put forward any resolution calling for a change of the management at a shareholder meeting.

On the morning of June 9, 2000, Bronfman, after a night of hesitation, sought the approval of his father and uncle for the deal Jean-Marie Messier had proposed on his return from dinner with Madeleine Albright and Felix Rohatyn. In the end, Messier had offered $77.35 per share, based on a ratio of 0.7 Vivendi shares for each Seagram share. That would represent a handsome premium of 54 percent to Seagram's closing share price of $50.31 on June 9. It was 20 percent more than the all-time high of $64.50 that Seagram shares had reached on March 6, 2000. In absolute terms, this was not substantially more than he had offered on April 24, but in the intervening period stock markets had started to fall from their peaks. In view of the fact that all media valuations were starting to slide, Bronfman did not risk pushing for more. If they did not reach a deal now, it would be harder later on if the relative values of their companies started shifting. He had already secured a handsome premium for his family. Furthermore, over the weekend of June 17–18—several days after reports of the talks leaked into the press and started to depress the Vivendi share price—Bronfman won an agreement that Messier would tilt the ratio in Seagram's favor if the French company's shares fell more than 12.5 percent.

"We sold Seagram for an awful lot of money," Bronfman said. On top of the $35 billion for Seagram's shares, Messier would also assume around $8 billion of its debt. In addition, it would pay $15 billion for the outstanding half of Canal Plus that Vivendi did not already own. The total cost of the three-way deal was nearly $60 billion.* The new company would be headquartered in France,

---

*Vivendi would issue Canal Plus shareholders two new shares for each of their existing shares. In total, it would issue 130.6 million shares to Canal Plus shareholders, which, on the basis of Vivendi's share price of €115 ($110.5) at the time of the negotiations, valued the transaction at around €15 billion.

with Jean-Marie Messier as its chairman and chief executive. Bronfman agreed to report to Messier, a significant diminution of responsibility for a man who had been chief executive of a major U.S. corporation for more than five years. He would become vice chairman of Vivendi Universal, with overall responsibility for Universal Music and the Internet. With all this agreed to, on June 19, they signed the merger agreement. Edgar Jr. was convinced he had done the right thing for his family. "You know what they say in the U.S. about entrepreneurial families?" Bronfman said. "The first generation creates a business, the second makes the fortune, and the third destroys it. I represent that third generation. But with this merger, I'm assuring the future of the generations to follow."[12]

## CHAPTER FOUR

# Bonjour Hollywood!

The $42 billion price tag on Vivendi's acquisition of Seagram stunned Wall Street and the City of London.* News of "Operation Secret" had leaked into the market six days before the terms of the "collar" had been agreed. A few pundits called on Messier to abandon the transaction. The "Breakingviews" comment column that appears in the *Wall Street Journal Europe* berated Messier for being an old-fashioned empire builder: "The industrial logic for combining Vivendi and Seagram is pretty spurious." By Tuesday, June 20, the day the deal was formally announced, Vivendi's share price had fallen nearly 20 percent to €96. The Canal Plus transaction would not be affected, but the drop made it highly likely that the Seagram leg of the deal would now take place on terms that were less favorable to Vivendi shareholders. Because of the collar, Vivendi would now have to offer 0.8 Vivendi shares per Seagram share, not 0.7. The deal was rapidly becoming less attractive for

---

*Vivendi would issue Seagram shareholders 319.5 million new shares. The agreement was reached when Vivendi's shares were trading at $110.5, giving an implied equity value for Seagram of $35 billion at the time the deal was negotiated. Seagram also had $7 billion to $8 billion of net debt, taking its enterprise value to $42 billion to $43 billion. The value of the deal would fall as Vivendi's shares lost their value following the merger announcement. The transaction is often described as having been worth $34 billion.

Vivendi's own shareholders, who recoiled at paying top dollar for two indebted companies facing structural problems in their respective industries. In another economic climate, the share price fall would have killed the transaction.

But not in the heady days of the first six months of 2000. For Messier and Edgar Bronfman Jr., there was no turning back. Messier dismissed the share price fall as "classical arbitrage." The plunging share price, he said, in no way reflected the intrinsic merits of the deal: "The market is right, but not every day." He blamed "flowback"—the tendency of U.S. investors to sell the shares of European bidders—and parasitic Anglo-Saxon hedge funds for depressing the shares for speculative gain. "Between the arbs and flowback, we had a tough day yesterday," Messier said on Wednesday, June 21. "It will remain tough today. But we expect it to get less tough day by day." In New York, he predicted the flood of U.S. selling would reverse. Over time, he said, the percentage of U.S. shareholders in Vivendi Universal would rise to 50 percent, compared with just 20 percent before the Seagram deal. Vivendi would soon start to trade on the New York Stock Exchange with a coveted single-letter ticker, V, which Messier had reserved two years earlier. In Churchillian fashion, he started to wave with the first two fingers of his right hand. Messier drew on his large reserves of credibility to help him through the difficult weeks that followed the announcement of the merger.

A large part of the cost, he argued, would be offset by the sale of the drinks business, which he expected to fetch $8 billion to $11 billion in an auction, or more than enough, after tax, to pay off the existing Seagram debt. But that still left an implied enterprise value of over $30 billion for the media businesses being acquired. The implied valuation made analysts gulp: after all, Edgar Bronfman Jr. had paid just over $16 billion to acquire Universal Studios and PolyGram (renamed Universal Music), which represented the bulk of the assets Vivendi was proposing to buy. Messier attempted to soothe investors' nerves by walking them through a breakup valuation for Seagram. The 43-percent stake in USA Networks was worth $6 billion at a share price of $20. He pointed to the fact that many analysts in fact had a share-price target for USA Networks stock of nearer $30, which would have valued the Seagram stake in Barry Diller's company at $9 billion. Universal Pictures, by then well into its second year of recovery, with hits such as *Erin Brockovich* and *Nutty Professor II*, was valued at around $4 billion, and the theme parks were worth another $2 billion to $3 billion. The difference of nearly $20 billion was the residual value Messier appeared to be placing on Universal Music, the heart of the transformed Seagram business. This looked like more than a full price, even for a world-leading business such as Universal Music. Messier was surely overpaying. Vivendi's shares continued to fall.

Messier said Vivendi and Seagram shared a common vision: that the world of communications was set to undergo a revolution with the appearance of the high-speed Internet. All forms of content, including music and film, would soon be streaming onto the various devices consumers carried with them daily. People would be able to order films and games over their televisions, listen to live debates or concerts on their personal computers, or scroll through video clips or trailers for the week's new films on their mobile phones before clicking to reserve a seat in the movie theater nearest their home or wherever they happened to be, which their mobile phone would have identified all by itself. It was an exhilarating vision of the future, which few analysts doubted would one day become a reality. The question was when.

Vivendi Universal and AOL Time Warner, Messier claimed, were the only big media groups that understood that the future lay with convergence. "Which groups are building direct relationships with customers and which are not?" he would ask rhetorically. "I think you have clearly in one camp AOL Time Warner and Vivendi Universal, building these direct customer relationships. And on the other side you have another group which is not doing it, where you find Disney, where you find Viacom. And you have someone in the middle, which is News Corp." What Messier and Bronfman were describing was in reality just a rehashed version of the old idea of vertical integration. AOL Time Warner had been the first to give it a new economy spin. But Vivendi Universal extended the logic. AOL Time Warner's pipes to the subscriber were rusty old things stuck in the back of defunct personal computers. Vivendi Universal's wireless ones were the real deal. Vivendi Universal, moreover, was genuinely global. Messier liked to stress the A in AOL to underline how parochial its business was.

Messier would steer investor attention away from the glamorous but risky world of Hollywood toward the supposedly stable cash flows of Universal Music. The world's leading record company, producer of one in three albums sold worldwide, was the prize Vivendi was really seeking, he would confide. On a sum-of-the-parts basis, Vivendi was acquiring Universal Music at around eighteen times its forecast cash flows of €1.1 billion, he said. This compared favorably to the multiple Bronfman had paid for Poly-Gram less than two years earlier and to Warner Music's planned purchase of EMI.* "We are at the bottom of that range and we are comfortable," he said. Why was the price so much higher? Because profits had almost doubled under Edgar Bronfman Jr. and would continue to grow at more than 12 percent a year between 2000 and 2002, he promised. Was the music sector not plunging into a crisis brought on by falling sales, a lack of fresh acts, and rampant piracy? On the contrary, he replied, music would be the segment of the entertainment industry that would benefit most from the development of the wireless Internet. Why had he not bought Poly-Gram in 1998, when it was on the market at a significantly lower price? It was too early, Messier said. Vivendi had arrived late in the consolidation of the global entertainment industry and now had to run fast and jump high to catch up.

Many wondered how Messier could justify paying such a large premium without being able to point to any cost savings within the music operation. Seagram had managed to extract $300 million of cost savings by combining PolyGram with Universal's existing music business. Vivendi, by contrast, would have to run Universal Music as a stand-alone operation. But Messier pointed to the "huge" synergies on offer through Vivendi's European dis-

---

*Seagram paid $10.4 billion for PolyGram, which had earnings before interest, tax, depreciation, and amortization of €540 million on a pro forma basis in the year to June 30, 1998. (Seagram SEC filing, November 25, 1998.)

tribution in the form of its stake in French mobile phone operator SFR and its 50-percent share in Vizzavi. Downloading Shania Twain or Eminem onto your SFR cell phone via the Vizzavi portal would be as easy as calling your mother, he said. The broadband wireless era was just months away. Bronfman predicted that the music business would grow from $40 billion to $100 billion over the next ten years as on-line and wireless sales accelerated. "At the moment, you have fifty thousand to sixty thousand music retail outlets around the world," he said. "More people than that join Yahoo! every day." How would convergence work between U.S. content and European distribution? Messier happily explained: "By offering our customers an exclusive opportunity to listen to the new song by Celine Dion, on the one hand we can boost Universal Music, but also the usage and loyalty of customers to Vizzavi." Bronfman interrupted: "Er, Celine Dion is not one of our artists." "Well, you will have to go and attract her," Messier muttered through gritted teeth.

For the third time in ten years, the French were laying siege to Tinsel Town. Even tub-thumping French nationalists suspected the triumph of hope over experience. There were many who asked how any Frenchman dared to risk buying a Hollywood film studio. Six years earlier, Crédit Lyonnais, the mighty state-owned French bank, had been brought to its knees by a reckless Hollywood venture that ended up costing French taxpayers more than €10 billion and enmeshing the bank in years of lawsuits and scandal. Its mistake had been to back Pathé, a French film group then in the hands of a former Italian waiter by the name of Giancarlo Parretti, in a $1.3 billion bid for MGM in 1990. After appointing an industry insider, Alan Ladd Jr., to run the studio, Parretti memorably informed the press of the division of responsibilities: "Ladd, 'e make-a the deals while I fuck-a the girls," he promised. He was true to his word, keeping a lion in his office and driving around Beverly Hills in a gold-colored Rolls-Royce. After Parretti turned out to be an accomplished fraudster, the state-owned bank in 1991 became the unhappy owner of a loss-making Hollywood studio and started a decade-long battle with the U.S. Department of Justice, which had decided to pursue the bank's senior officials for fraud too. Even though it managed to sell MGM back to Kirk Kerkorian in 1996, Crédit Lyonnais was still being prosecuted in the United States by the time Messier bought Seagram. The wheel of experience had not had time to turn full circle.

Canal Plus, which was now at the center of Messier's plans for Universal, had also suffered the worst of Hollywood. It lost hundreds of millions of dollars in the early 1990s by backing Carolco, a megabudget producer of so-called event films that hoped to blast its way into the big league of Hollywood studios by doling out double-digit salaries to A-list writers and directors. Carolco is still blamed for almost single-handedly ruining the economics of filmmaking in Hollywood. It produced the town's biggest-budget pictures, some of which still rank among the top grossers ever: *Terminator 2* took in $490 million worldwide to become the highest-grossing movie of 1991; the following year, the Michael Douglas–Sharon Stone vehicle *Basic Instinct* achieved the same distinction, with a $353 million worldwide gross. Its chief executive, Mario Kassar, set new standards for corporate extravagance, boasting the biggest yacht at the Cannes Film Festival. Despite numerous cash calls on its obliging foreign partners, led by Pioneer Electronics, Canal Plus, and Crédit Lyonnais, Carolco filed for Chapter 11 bankruptcy protection in 1995.

To allay these primal fears, Messier would wheel in Stacey Snider, chairman of Universal Pictures. One of the most powerful women in the U.S. film industry, Snider had made the studio the hottest in Hollywood. She would address head-on all the investors' preconceptions about Hollywood. "You may have in mind historical losses. You may assume we still have old-style Hollywood management. That is no longer accurate and it no longer applies. Today, process is everything. We're confident that a consistent and profitable slate is achievable and that we can plan multimillion-dollar projects in a sane and responsible manner." Universal Pictures, she explained, now planned its film releases over a twenty-four-month period, with the aim of releasing about fifteen films a year. Two to three a year would be so-called tentpole films, such as *The Grinch* and *The Mummy Returns:* special-effects-driven movies that offered cross-promotional opportunities in merchandising. Four to six would be event films, such as *Meet the Parents,* starring Robert De Niro and Ben Stiller, that were star driven and story led. And the last four to six would be smaller, niche-oriented portfolio films, such as *American Pie* and *Bring It On.* The continuing strength of the Universal slate was undeniable: in March 2000, *Erin Brockovich* grossed $255 million worldwide, and *Gladiator* grossed $420 million in May. Snider said she had high hopes for *Billy Elliot* in November 2000 and for *A Beautiful Mind* and *Hannibal* the following year.

Messier also encouraged investors to dwell on the prospect of closer cooperation with Barry Diller. Vivendi Universal would inherit the 43-percent stake in his company, USA Networks, that Seagram had acquired in partial payment for its cable television channels in 1998. "Barry alone is 50 percent of the asset," Messier crowed. "He creates value in whatever he does." Messier intended to revive relations with Diller. These had soured since Bronfman, who had the right to veto any deal worth more than 10 percent of USA Networks' market value, had thwarted Diller's attempt to buy NBC, the General Electric–owned TV network. Messier promised to be more supportive of Diller's ambitions. "With Vivendi, that deal can get done," said PaineWebber analyst Christopher Dixon. The reality was that Messier instinctively felt uncomfortable having no voting control over such a large asset—the stake in USA Networks was worth $6 billion to $7 billion—and was looking for ways to take back control. The agreement with Diller left Vivendi Universal unable to claim any direct presence in the U.S. television market. "Basically, our domestic television strategy is our piece of USA Networks and our ability to ultimately control that company," Bronfman said. Boxed out of the U.S. television market, Messier was forced to emphasize new, unproven forms of distribution over the Internet. These synergies, which left analysts scratching their heads, were supposed to lead to a 10-percent jump in sales. The combination with Vivendi, it was claimed, would allow Universal to reinvent itself for the digital age.

The French company's purchase of the Hollywood studio raised few protectionist hackles in the United States. Even so, there was a degree of nervousness at Universal Studios. "There were people who thought we'd have to put Gérard Depardieu in every movie," recalled Ron Meyer, chairman of Universal Studios. Universal employees quickly discovered that what had been billed as a merger was no marriage of equals. "At my first integration meeting, there were ten French guys and me," says one U.S. executive at Universal. "In America, that's not what we call integration. Integration was something my mother told me I shouldn't be afraid of. . . . It was then that I realized this was not a merger. This was a takeover." Yet for all the anxiety about conflict and crossed wires between Paris and New York, the French and the Americans seemed to be getting on well. At a breakfast in Paris in March 2001, for example, Ron Meyer would greet Pierre Lescure and Denis Olivennes, the number one and number two at Canal Plus, with hugs and kisses on both cheeks. It may have been ostentatious, but it did not seem forced. The Americans seemed to be enjoying the cachet of a relationship with the French.

In the early days, Bronfman maintained that fears of an impending French-American culture clash were being much exaggerated. "There were huge cultural issues when Time and Warner merged, but no one focused on them because they are American companies. It is two company cultures being merged, not two country cultures," he said. By March 2001, the Vivendi takeover certainly looked as though it were treating the Bronfman heir well. He was tanned, and his beard was meticulously cropped. Dressed in a cream cashmere polo shirt and gray slacks, rather than his trademark Armani suits, he looked so relaxed some started to wonder whether he would not soon be spending most of his time at home. His name was rarely heard in discussions with senior Vivendi Universal executives. The only person who talked of him as a boss was Doug Morris, head of Universal Music. Yet Bronfman insisted that he was playing a crucial role that spring. "There are two decision makers at the company—that is, Jean-Marie and myself." He said this shared power had been crucial to the smooth integration of the two businesses. "The fish always stinks from the head. To the extent that people see a strong relationship between Jean-Marie and myself, that always helps things."

Messier did his utmost to reassure his U.S. executives that he was on the same cultural wavelength: "I feel like an American and I like the culture here," he said in New York. "I lived in New York for a year and have come to the U.S. at least once a month for fifteen years." Few were surprised that Hollywood had rushed to extend a warm welcome to the new owners of Universal. As Rupert Murdoch pointed out after buying Twentieth Century–Fox in 1984, Hollywood was "founded by émigrés" and is a town where money has no nationality. Cash is simply the raw material of moviemaking, and lots of it is needed when a single blockbuster can cost up to $150 million and the competition is fierce for scripts, directors, stars, and glitzy mansions in the better parts of Beverly Hills and Malibu. As Peter Bart of *Variety* noted, to a certain extent Hollywood had only survived thanks to its ability to attract wave after wave of foreign money. Competition for funds in Tinsel Town had never been fiercer, not least because it had virtually become an investment truism that the film industry suffered structurally lousy economics. Foreign investors might have wised up a little since the days of Crédit Lyonnais, Giancarlo Parretti, and Carolco, but word that a big French conglomerate planned to take over Universal Studios could be nothing but good news. "Instead of 'Bonjour Hollywood,' the *Financial Times'* headline should have read 'Au Revoir Profits,'" commented Terry Smith, chief executive of the independent broker Collins Stewart in London and bestselling author of *Creative Accounting*.

The expectation was that Vivendi would follow what had become Hollywood's most predictable script. An outsider spends billions of dollars to acquire an entertainment empire, harbors dreams of meshing technology or marketing prowess with the "content" Hollywood churns out in the form of films, TV shows, and music, enriches several hundred already fabulously wealthy Tinsel Town insiders, and eventually impoverishes itself. The only variable in the tale would be the time frame. Matsushita bailed out after five years, as did Seagram. Coke lasted seven. Sony was still gritting its teeth after eleven years of pain. A month after the deal was announced, the *Los Angles Times* gleefully described Messier as "an easy target since he's virtually an alien in Hollywood and since Vivendi-controlled French pay-TV giant Canal Plus, headed by Pierre Lescure, has a long history of spending pots of dumb money in Hollywood." Here they were again, this time backed by a big water utility. As Ron Meyer would later say: "Did people take Jean-Marie seriously? No. But this is a cynical town. A lot of people come and go; they come and go. Parretti, Matsushita, Seagram. It takes a long time to establish credibility in Hollywood."

Vivendi suffered from remarkably little of the xenophobia that had scarred Matsushita's and Sony's arrivals in Beverly Hills a decade earlier. The insecurity behind the Japan-bashing of those recession-hit years was long forgotten in the optimistic economic climate that prevailed in the middle of 2000. As the U.S. economy cruised through another year of record growth, American politicians were more confident than ever in their country's prosperity and cultural appeal. Moreover, many were well aware that Universal had not been in U.S. ownership for a decade, but had shuttled from a Japanese consumer electronics group to a Canadian drinks company. If a French water-and-waste conglomerate now wanted to own the studio, so be it. That Vivendi would suddenly think it worthwhile to start trying to make Universal produce auteurist French movies appeared as unrealistic as it would have been for Matsushita to have "orientalized" the studio or for Parretti to have insisted MGM make more Italian movies. Few expected Lescure, who was infatuated with American popular culture, to see any commercial merit in asking Universal to produce low-budget European art films. Nor did Messier look as if he would interfere too much. "If I read a script, it will be for pleasure, not for decision," he promised.

Messier delighted everyone with his thick accent and by repeating at every opportunity that Universal would be run by Americans in Hollywood. His praise for Stacey Snider and for her boss, Ron Meyer, smoothed over the fact that Pierre Lescure would henceforth be their boss. Lescure, who never made any effort to move to Los Angeles, was hardly a threatening presence. In this respect, the acquisition of Universal succeeded. No irreplaceable executives left Universal following the deal, in marked contrast to the management turmoil that had marred the first three years of Bronfman ownership. However, the cost of this management stability was unwitting largesse on the part of Vivendi's share-holders. Edgar Bronfman Jr. had already created a special $40 million bonus pool to retain key staff after the 1998 acquisition of PolyGram. Two years later, Messier bought the peace by creating another jackpot—this time worth a minimum of $50 million—to keep the talent from walking out the door. How this $90 million was carved up among the players is unknown, but it would appear to have helped buy the alien a lot of loyalty in a fickle town.

The newly formed Vivendi Universal would certainly be big: it would have sales of €54 billion ($52 billion) in 2000. Half of that, of course, would come from Vivendi Environnement, which was starting life as a semi-independent company following its stock market debut in July 2000. But even so, with 2000 sales of €24.3 billion ($23.3 billion) in its music, publishing, film and television, telecom, and Internet arm, Vivendi Universal would join the superleague of global media powerhouses, and Messier could claim to be the undisputed king of the European media sector. It would be just smaller than Walt Disney, which had turnover of $25.4 billion in 2000, but would overtake Viacom. It would be 50 percent bigger than its nearest European rival, Bertelsmann, and almost twice the size of News Corporation, the fiefdom of Vivendi's arch-rival, Rupert Murdoch. Gerald Levin and Steve Case of AOL Time Warner might be number one for the moment, with 2000 sales of $36 billion, but it was Messier's clear intention to overtake them as soon as he possibly could.* The trouble was that no one seemed to be giving him credit for the size of his empire. On the contrary, the breadth of Vivendi Universal's interests counted against it in the eyes of the financial community. Its complexity was a barrier to understanding and to valuation.

"When I do VU, I could do at least five other stocks," grumbled one U.S. investor. French investors had been evaluating

---

*The merger between AOL and Time Warner was held up for months by antitrust authorities, but was finally consummated on January 11, 2001, a year and a day after it was announced. Vivendi Universal came into existence on December 8, 2000, less than six months after it was announced.

Générale des Eaux for decades and were familiar with the business models of the conglomerate's constituent parts. Havas and Canal Plus had both been listed companies in France since 1986. But for U.S. investors Vivendi Universal seemed an extraordinary and exotic company. Seagram itself was already a conglomerate. Merging one conglomerate with another multiplied the analytical effort required to estimate a fair value for the group. Vivendi Universal presented its financial results according to French accounting standards. These were considered deeply suspect—if not completely worthless—by U.S. investors, and had the additional drawback of making Vivendi Universal's financial ratios hard to compare with those of conventional U.S. media groups. It was easier to leave the exotic French media group out of the analytical cohort altogether than to wrestle with the innumerable differences between U.S. and French accounting standards.

To complicate matters further, U.S. media investors were relatively unfamiliar with the satellite pay-television model. DirecTV did not have its own stock market listing, but was a subsidiary of Hughes, which in turn was part of General Motors. Echostar had only started to attract investor attention as its share price took off in the late 1990s. This left Canal Plus, a large proportion of Vivendi Universal's value, something of a mystery to many of the biggest U.S. funds. In the face of such complexity, many preferred to steer well clear of the new French media group. The retention of Vivendi Environnement within an aspiring media group had also laid Messier open to the charge of being an empire builder. The attacks sharpened when it was revealed that RWE, a powerful German utility, had offered Messier €30 billion to buy Vivendi Environnement prior to its flotation in July 2000.

Media analysts said that accepting the offer would immediately have clarified Vivendi Universal's identity as an entertainment, telecom, and publishing stock that was more comparable to the big U.S. media groups. It would also have provided Vivendi with a colossal war chest for acquisitions. Instead, the conglomerate seemed destined to remain an equity analyst's nightmare. Lehman Brothers, for example, in its first thorough investment appraisal after the merger announcement, had to call upon the services of no fewer than ten analysts from four different teams of sector specialists—media, telecom, drinks, and utilities—to come up with an overall valuation for Vivendi Universal's shares. Not surprisingly, Lehman concluded that Vivendi Universal needed to radically simplify its asset base if it wanted to be treated on a par with the pure plays of the media sector.

Yet doubts surrounded each step in this direction. First, there was uncertainty over the price Vivendi would be able to get for Seagram's spirits, which few believed would fetch the top end of the $8 billion to $11 billion range that Messier was targeting. The right was to distribute Absolut vodka was called into question by the Swedish state-owned liquor monopoly. Second, even after the partial flotation of Vivendi Environnement in July 2000, there was a lack of clarity over whether Messier intended to retain majority control of the utility in the long term. He had promised not to offload any more Vivendi Environnement shares until the end of 2003, which, in Internet time, was a century away. Third, analysts saw little sense in Vivendi Universal's owning a disparate portfolio of stakes in public companies, including British Sky Broadcasting, Havas Advertising, Saint-Gobain, Alcatel, and Du Pont. Investors did not want Messier to tie up their capital on low-returning investments. And fourth, while analysts recognized that the Universal assets gave Vivendi critical mass on the media front, these assets did not change the group's problems in telecommunications. In an industry that was consolidating in waves of mergers, Vivendi owned less than half of Cegetel, which lacked the scale of the giants of the industry. Most analysts wanted Messier to sell the small telecom business to Vodafone.

In public, Messier would rapidly pass over the question of Vivendi Universal's profitability, pausing only to celebrate the group's limited exposure to the advertising cycle, "so often the Achilles' heel of media companies." Less than 5 percent of Vivendi Universal's revenues would come from the cyclical advertising market. In terms of its profits, though, Vivendi Universal ranked far behind the remaining old economy media giants. Its €989 million of operating profit in 2000—a margin of just 4 percent—was a feeble performance set against Disney's $4 billion on only slightly higher sales.* To mask this weakness, Messier had long since become a master at presenting his group's results in their most flattering light. By the summer of 2000, the dot-com bubble had started to deflate, but it was still standard practice to spoon-feed the markets only those voguish measures of profitability—such as earnings before interest, tax, depreciation, and amortization, abbreviated to *ebitda*—that disguised the true cost of rapid growth. The ebitda measure was particularly flattering to Vivendi Universal. The French group, controversially, consolidated 100 percent of Cegetel's financial results, even though it owned only 44 percent of its shares. Once analysts stripped out the 56 percent that Vivendi Universal did not own, the group's ratios of enterprise value to profits, a key measurement tool for stock pickers, started to look far more demanding. Needless to say, this did not stop Messier from complaining that Vivendi Universal deserved to be rerated in line with the multiples of other media groups.

For Messier, the real measure of success for the media conglomerate of the new millennium was "synergy." And this was something that Vivendi Universal claimed in spades. The Seagram acquisition, he said, was "a marketing-driven merger, not a cost-savings merger." Although he believed he could achieve €400 million in straightforward cost savings, that was not where the value of the merger lay. "The merger will offer us the possibility of numerous revenue synergies—the creation of new businesses, products, and services. Thanks to the great progress made by our teams, we can already estimate that these will represent additional ebitda of €220 million in 2002, and more than €400 million in 2003. That means we are talking big, and we are talking rapid growth," Messier said. "The figures are reliable and concrete." To achieve additional ebitda of €220 million, Vivendi Universal would need to achieve €1 billion of extra sales. If these synergies were concrete in Messier's mind, they were almost comically neb-

---

*Operating profits were $1.63 billion for News Corp. for the year to June 30, 2000; $1.3 billion for Viacom; and $1.2 billion for Bertelsmann. AOL Time Warner recorded a pro forma operating loss of $383 million in 2000.

ulous to investors. Internally, senior Vivendi Universal executives such as Ron Meyer and Denis Olivennes, chief operating officer of Canal Plus, were deeply skeptical about these synergies.

The €1 billion of additional sales seemed hard to correlate with the vague projects Messier managed to articulate. He claimed the group had thirty-five specific new revenue-generating projects. Yet the handful that he would frequently cite sounded severely underpowered. For example, the education division within Vivendi Universal publishing and Universal Pictures would soon launch an English-learning program using scenes from Hollywood movies. In May 2001, he promised, the company would launch Universal Mobiles in France, giving Vivendi's mobile-phone customers access to Universal Music. The biggest source of synergies, and the one that most symbolized Vivendi Universal's claim to be the company at the forefront of converging content and connectivity, would, of course, be Vizzavi. But by March 2001, after more than a year in development, the multi-access portal being created in alliance with Vodafone had yet to live up to its grandiose billing as the key to "life unlimited." The €1.6 billion start-up that aimed to compete with the likes of Yahoo! and Microsoft's MSN on every technological front remained little more than a business plan.

The unit's growing staff in London, Paris, and elsewhere promised a full range of interactive services—games, information, and entertainment—but problems with mobile technology meant that downloading a Web page would often take half a minute or more. This was a "prohibitive" amount of time, according to Messier. Even within the company, Vizzavi was viewed as either a huge potential business or a huge potential embarrassment. Indeed, Ron Meyer inadvertently gave a sense of the doubt and bewilderment that surrounded the project: "Everyone has had so much focus on Vizzavi because Vizzavi is clearly the future of this business, whether it works or not." It was clear that influential figures inside the company felt the future was some way off yet. Some executives described Vivendi Universal in distinctly old economy terms. "You need to look at it [Vivendi Universal] as the General Electric of entertainment—then it is a beautiful company," said Denis Olivennes, referring to the famous counterexample of the conglomerate that works. "If, on top of that, you create the convergence, then it is even more beautiful. But even if we fail, you still have the GE."

Terry Smith was one of the few analysts who dared to say right from the start not only that these synergies were bogus, but that the deal would actually destroy value for shareholders. On June 18, 2000, before the deal had been formally announced, Smith sent out a research note to his clients: "Seagram is no media empire. While numerous newspapers echoed the *FT*'s claim that this deal 'would redraw the map of international media,' in reality the most far-reaching impact is likely to be on the global drinks industry. Acquiring a music company that was in European hands until a few years ago anyway and a loss-making film business doesn't do that much map redrawing for me." Smith criticized Bronfman for his "almost comical" focus on ebitda, as if the interest bill he had acquired while building Seagram from a drinks company into a media business were somehow unfair.

Smith noted that Seagram had highlighted a $285 million profit at the ebitda level for its results for the quarter to March 31, 2000, burying the fact that its operating profit was negative to the tune of $1 million and that it still faced $278 million of interest and tax charges. The great Seagram empire was leaking money. Only two of Seagram's four divisions were actually profitable. And one of those, the drinks business, which accounted for 29 percent of sales, was to be sold. The only profitable division set to remain within Vivendi Universal was the group of theme parks, which accounted for just 5 percent of total sales. The music division, which accounted for 40 percent of sales, had contrived to lose $23 million on sales of $1.36 billion. The film division lost $32 million on sales of $877 million.

The "Lex" column of the *Financial Times* was equally scathing about the merger, describing it as without doubt "the most heroic act of value destruction so far this year." On July 13, just as Messier and Bronfman were winding up their first wave of investor road shows, "Lex" waded in again. It said that Messier's "vision of Johnny Hallyday music and Universal films piped down mobile phones cost shareholders about €10bn at a stroke." Indeed, it was the unbridled optimism about the music industry that most worried independent thinkers. No one seemed to buy the idea that Vizzavi would be the great tool to hold the disparate wings of the empire together, allowing millions of teenagers to listen to Universal music over their SFR handsets.

Bronfman's claim that music-industry revenues would double to $100 billion over the next decade, with digital downloading accounting for a large part of the growth, also met skepticism. Terry Smith commented: "It is very hard to believe the Internet is going to be a one-way street for PolyGram when it comes to revenues. All these players' vision of more people listening to more music is surely right, but what they will pay for it is another matter. What we may well have here is a potential situation which is so awful to contemplate they have no alternative but to live in a world of complete denial."

As shareholders in Seagram, Canal Plus, and Vivendi gathered in Montreal and Paris to approve the merger at the start of December 2000, many were furious. In Montreal, the end of an era was gloomily noted as the Bronfmans presided over the most perfunctory of shareholder meetings. The 35-percent fall in the value of Vivendi's shares, from around €115 at the time of the merger discussions to €75 at the end of 2000, meant that each Seagram shareholder now stood to receive only $57 worth of Vivendi stock, much less than the $77.35 that had been trumpeted in June.

There was no chance of pulling out of the transaction. Both the Bronfman family and the Philips consumer electronic group, Seagram's largest shareholder since the acquisition of PolyGram, had already committed their stock. A yes vote was guaranteed. Bronfman reached for some corny lines to mark the passing of the company founded by his grandfather: "The heart is more stubborn than the mind. It's not easy letting go of so much of our past, and none of us—myself; my father, Edgar; my uncle, Charles; my brother, Sam—have taken this decision lightly. It's been particularly difficult to make dispassionate decisions about a company that has been so integral to my family's life."

In a spectacular set piece before his shareholders gathered at the Carrousel du Louvre in central Paris, Messier enjoyed his moment of triumph: "In the space of four years, our share price has quadrupled, our market capitalization has increased sevenfold, and our operating income tenfold." He acknowledged the drop in Vivendi's share price—"from excessive highs we have now gone to excessive lows"—but pointed out that Vivendi had performed better than either the telecom or the media sector. The merger had actually had a positive effect on Vivendi's share price, he said, hinting that it would have fallen more if the group had not acquired Seagram. In fact, he suggested that if they looked at it another way, the fall in the Vivendi share price meant they were now paying far less for Seagram. So Vivendi shareholders were getting an even better deal!

Looking back at that event almost two years later, Guillaume Hannezo said that the moment Vivendi Universal closed the Seagram and Canal Plus deals, the group's senior managers believed they had resolved the strategic dilemma that had bedeviled them since the late 1990s. Vivendi was no longer confused about its identity: it was essentially a Franco-American media group with a strong position in the important segments of the entertainment industry, notably music, films, television, and games. "Even if hopes of convergence have now been pushed back ever further into the future, the rationale that led Vivendi to acquire Seagram remains exactly right," Hannezo said. "If one considers what Vivendi was at the beginning of 2000—essentially a company whose market value was embedded in its pay-television, telecom, and Internet assets—one could legitimately ask what would have happened to it in the absence of a merger, if it had stayed on its own."[1]

Like Messier, Hannezo argued that Vivendi on its own, without a merger with Seagram, would have been in worse shape in terms of its share-price performance. All the Internet value in the stock related to Vizzavi would have disappeared; pay-television valuations had fallen 80 percent, and so had those of telecom stocks. In other words, he argued, Vivendi had done well to capitalize on its high share price by buying Seagram because its old economy media businesses had held on to more of their value. Universal Music's value had fallen by "only 50–60 percent" and that of Universal Studios by 20–30 percent. "The merger with Seagram therefore created value for the Vivendi shareholder," Hannezo argued.

Not everyone would agree with his logic: shareholders would surely have preferred Messier to use his shares, overvalued or not, to buy businesses that at least maintained and preferably increased their value. Furthermore, no one could deny that the purchase of Canal Plus had been anything but catastrophic for Vivendi's shareholders. Vivendi bought the 51 percent of Canal Plus it did not already own practically at the peak of the bubble, putting over €17 billion on the table—in shares, of course—for a company that was losing around €700 million a year and whose value had been puffed up by the hopes embedded in its 25-percent stake in Vizzavi.* The deal actually turned out to be far worse because Vivendi belatedly discovered numerous off-balance-sheet commitments to U.S. film studios, to the organizers of Formula One auto racing, and to French soccer clubs that would eat further into the operating cash flows of the business. None of this, of course, would be fully appreciated until the ink on the deal had long been dry.

Vivendi Universal came into existence on December 8, 2000, with a market value of €79.9 billion. Some noted that all three companies—Vivendi, Canal Plus, and Seagram—were worth less together than Vivendi had been on its own. The majority of investors, however, accepted that Vivendi had fared no worse than other media and telecom companies since the merger announcement. Messier had a strong record. It was now up to him to justify their trust.

"So far, Messier has demonstrated that he's a fantastic financier," said André Lévy-Lang, the former chief executive of Paribas. "The test now is going to be management. I think he can do it, but that's what the challenge is—and that's why the market has been so skeptical."[2] Erik Israelewicz, commentator on *Les Echos,* the

---

*Prior to the merger, Canal Plus and Vivendi had each owned 50 percent of VivendiNet, which in turn owned 50 percent of Vizzavi. Canal Plus therefore had an economic interest in Vizzavi of 25 percent.

leading French business newspaper, asked whether it sufficed for a chief executive to be nothing more than a deal maker: "The first reel of the film has been exciting. But will he be for Générale des Eaux what Jean-Yves Haberer was for Crédit Lyonnais, who, [in the early 1990s] through a series of ever more spectacular gambles, led the public bank to its famous catastrophe? It is too soon to say."

## CHAPTER FIVE

# Maître du Monde

In Paris, the Vivendi Universal project assumed an overtly nation-
alistic tone. Speaking to his shareholders at the closing of the deal
at the Louvre, Messier rallied them around the Tricolore: "There
are seven thousand of you here this evening, which is a record in
Vivendi's history, over twice as many as in April. . . . This unprecedented level of shareholder participation shows that you all
have a very strong feeling of belonging, that you have sensed the
full importance of the stakes that have brought us here today, to
witness the birth of a project the likes of which is rarely seen. A
French group is about to become the world's number two in communications, an industry where, for decades, no European group
has managed to come anywhere close to troubling American domination. Who would have thought it possible? Who could ever
have dreamed that, in communications, from the first foundation
stones laid by Guy Dejouany, we would reach the event that has
brought us here today: the creation, through the friendly merger
between Vivendi, Seagram, and Canal Plus, of Vivendi Universal,
which will weigh in ahead of such communications giants as Disney, CBS-Viacom, and the Murdoch group, News Corp."

With the AOL Time Warner deal ensnared in competition
probes, Messier reveled in the idea that Vivendi Universal could,
for a time at least, describe itself as the world's largest media and
communications group. "Before the AOL and Time Warner

merger takes place, which will be in a few weeks' time at best, Vivendi Universal will enter the new century and millennium as the world leader in communications.* What a symbol for our future ambitions. And what a response to the skeptics, the naysayers, and those who want to stay in their own backyard. To all of them, Vivendi Universal will demonstrate that it is possible to be both French and global, and that defending French culture sometimes means stepping out for a breath of fresh air." The irony that it was a French company storming the bastions of U.S. popular entertainment was not lost on Hollywood pundits. "Vivendi's intended takeover of Seagram underscores the following paradox," Peter Bart wrote in *Variety* the day Messier and Bronfman signed the deal. "The French have been most vocal in protesting Hollywood's domination of the world marketplace. Yet the Vivendi deal, along with several other Euro initiatives, underscores the fact that it is Euro money that increasingly is financing Hollywood's domination. What in God's name, therefore, are the Euros complaining about? . . . Europeans would do equally well to recognize that it is they who are emerging as the cultural imperialists."[1]

Messier had long been at the forefront of the French business community. With the Seagram merger, he transcended the place de Paris. In the days following the merger, his cherubic features graced the cover pages of all the international weeklies—*Time, Newsweek, Fortune,* and *Business Week* were just a few of the U.S. magazines that attempted to interpret the significance of the forty-three-year-old Frenchman. Many depicted him as a symbol of the changing face of French capitalism and of a new, self-confident country liberated from a wearisome complex over its own relative decline. Messier incarnated *"la France qui gagne,"* the France that wins. Nor was it just the international media that puffed the new-economy-miracle boss du jour. Messier was an unbeatable advertisement for an economically vibrant France, one that was ready to lead Europe in the race to dominate the industries of the new millennium. Both the Gaullist president, Jacques Chirac, and his So-

---

*This would not prove true: Walt Disney's 2000 sales would be more than $25 billion, versus $23 billion for Vivendi Universal's media and communications arm.

cialist prime minister, Lionel Jospin, raced to bask in his reflected glory. In the year that followed the announcement of the merger, Messier experienced the kind of flattery that would have turned the head of an Easter Island statue.

At a ceremony to anoint Messier the Franco-American Chamber of Commerce's Person of the Year, the French ambassador to the United States, François Bujon de l'Estang, set the tone. "Jean-Marie Messier, you have shown truly exceptional leadership and vision in taking the helm of the prestigious but somewhat stodgy company, Générale des Eaux, a major actor in water services and construction activities, and changing it almost overnight—well, five years—into the service group of the twenty-first century. You have shown along the way a clear will to become a major actor of globalization and seize the opportunities that it offers, instead of concentrating on the threats that it can bring. On a more personal note," the ambassador continued, "you are the prototype of a new breed of French executives that dispels the traditional clichés about France. You have championed a new type of corporate governance, more in line with international, and, yes, American standards, and more attuned to the expectations of investors worldwide. In you and with you, Jean-Marie Messier, the chamber recognizes today the new French economy that has enjoyed a tremendously good coverage in the American press these past few months, an economy of entrepreneurs (reminding us all that this is a French word), of business creation, of Internet start-ups that are the avant-garde of 'la France qui gagne.'"

" 'We are the champions! We are the champions.' Once again this refrain is on everyone's lips," observed Erik Israelewicz in Les Echos. "Messier's landing in Hollywood is a symbol of a new-found French aggression." France, it seemed, was winning everything: less than a fortnight after Messier bought up a chunk of Hollywood, Zinedine Zidane led the French football team to a brilliant victory in the European Championship, repeating the national side's triumph at the 1998 World Cup. Even the cautious governor of the Banque de France, Jean-Claude Trichet, let himself get carried away on French radio the following morning, saying the historic French victories would be "fantastic for consumer confidence." Israelewicz contrasted the euphoria with the somber mood that had overshadowed France three years earlier: "The country was worrying about 'the end of work' and 'austerity without end.' Today, it sees only *'la vie en rose'* and *'la France qui gagne.'* After a decade of depression, French consumers and businesses are euphoric. Confidence indicators are off the charts. Sales of cars and mobile telephones are soaring. On almost every front, the France that considered itself lost, crushed by American imperialism, or by the German steamroller, has suddenly become 'champion of the universe.'"[2] The country, according to the World Health Organization, had the best health system in the world. Unemployment was falling. Trade balances were improving. Airbus had overtaken Boeing. France was the world's number one tourist destination. And, of course, in José Bové, France could even claim the world leader in antiglobalization. A winner in every category.

Even philosophers such as Bernard Henri-Lévy, author of *Barbarism with a Human Face* and probably France's most famous living intellectual, felt sufficiently roused by Messier's spunkiness to attack the skeptics: "I don't know much about economics, still less the mergers and takeovers that we have been hearing so much about lately. But when French business leaders like Jean-Marie Messier and Pierre Lescure take to the high seas because they are fed up with seeing French culture and cinema live in permanent surrender to large American corporations, when they force destiny, reverse the prescribed order of things and start to hunt down one of these businesses, when they contribute, in other words, to shaking the dust off parochial national capitalism in order to give it a global destiny and when the market punishes them so brutally, who is right? Them or the market? The incredible bravery of some or the Franco-French faintheartedness of others? Those who bet on a France open to the world or on a France that is perennially small-minded and provincial in its outlook?"

The acquisition of Seagram was of far greater significance in France than comparable transatlantic deals—notably Daimler-Benz's takeover of Chrysler, one of Detroit's Big Three, or British Petroleum's acquisition of Amoco, one of the Seven Sisters—had ever been in Germany and the UK. It confounded French "declinists" who argued that the cards were stacked against France in the new global economy. This camp of naysayers included Gaullist president Jacques Chirac, Socialist prime minister Lionel Jospin, and a cross-party swath of politicians, who would all regularly inveigh against the excesses of the market economy and champion government intervention to "tame" globalization. As Hubert Védrine, France's Socialist foreign minister, put it, "Let's admit it, globalization does not *automatically* benefit France. Globalization develops according to principles that correspond neither to French tradition nor to French culture: the ultraliberal market economy, mistrust of the state, individualism removed from the republican tradition, the inevitable reinforcement of the universal and 'indispensable' role of the United States, common law, the English language, Anglo-Saxon norms, and Protestant—more than Catholic—concepts."

The declinist case rested less on the relative performance of French business—which had, after all, continued to produce world leaders in numerous fields (Michelin in tires, Moët Hennessy–Louis Vuitton in luxury goods, EADS in aerospace, TotalFinaElf in oil, for example)—than on the sense that France's capacity to project its own values, its *rayonnement*, had suffered irreparable damage from globalization. How much longer, the declinists asked, might France hope to export its culture when fewer and fewer foreigners studied French, or sustain a welfare state that demanded burdensome levels of taxation in an age of flighty capital and ever-fiercer fiscal competition between governments? With government expenditures still over 50 percent of GDP and nearly 25 percent of French workers employed by the state, many in France still looked to the government rather than the market to ensure their wellbeing. That globalization appeared to deal all the cards to the infinitely adaptable Americans, with whom France still competed for worldwide influence, added further weight to the declinist camp. Philip H. Gordon, director of the Brookings Institution's Center for the U.S. and France in Washington, argued that many French people feared not just the disappearance of *dirigisme*—the idea that the state takes an active role in all aspects of life—but the end of France itself. "Uncontrolled globalization, many French worry, will oblige France to abandon some of its most distinctive and best-loved aspects of its entertainment, art, culinary traditions and language—in short those things that most make it France."[3]

Védrine characterized France as being colonized by the United States: "America today is much more than the British Empire and closer to what the Roman Empire was compared to the rest of the world in that era. American globalism . . . dominates everything everywhere. Not in a harsh, repressive, military form, but in people's heads. Americans have mental power to inspire the dreams and desires of others, thanks to their mastery of global images through film and television." The foreign minister argued that the desire to preserve cultural diversity in the world was not a sign of anti-Americanism, but of antihegemony, a "rejection of impoverishment." The French were only keen on watching American movies, he claimed, because these films, initially made profitable in a vast internal market, were backed by huge resources to help them flood markets abroad.

Many left-wing French nationalists believed that the Internet risked accentuating the United States' "soft power." The new American invention would be a "diversity killer" operated by the U.S. corporations that designed and dominated it. The monopolistic "Wintel" duopoly (composed of Microsoft's Windows operating system and Intel's chips) was American. Economies of scale in electronic commerce and content were high and therefore favored the large and early entrants from the United States. The most successful Internet companies, such as Amazon, AOL, and Yahoo!, were all American. At the start of 2000, nearly 90 percent of all Web pages were in English; more than 40 percent of all Internet users resided in the United States; and nearly half of all electronic commerce was expected to still be generated in the United States in 2004.

The creation of Vivendi Universal raised hopes that France would now have the ability to organize its own resistance to American cultural hegemony. "We will beat all the Yahoo!s of the world," Messier promised. Mobile technology had long been a rare area where Europe led the United States. Through Vizzavi, Messier would enable the Old Continent to overcome the U.S.

dominance of the first-generation PC-based Internet. The wireless Internet of the future would be led by Europeans. He even pronounced the Internet to be "left-wing," to the delight of the former Trotskyites in the Jospin government. He promised that Vivendi Universal would become a powerful force for diversity: "Vivendi Universal is French by nationality, global in ambition. One often hears that 'globalization is going to kill culture, that it harmonizes everything, Americanizes everything.' I don't believe that for a second. I believe that tomorrow's world will be one of cultural diversity and the renewal of local and national cultural identities. Globalization does not erode cultures, it wakes them up and makes them communicate with each other. In my mind Vivendi Universal will only be judged to be a real success, aside from its financial results, if, in years to come, the group is recognized as being the one that best represents this cultural diversity to which we are all so attached." France's commentariat applauded: the *"petit village gaullois"* of the Astérix comics was still resisting the yoke of the Roman Empire.

It is this spirit of Gallic resistance that in part explains the fierce cross-party political support for the phenomenon known as the "French cultural exception." This is the term given to the welter of quotas and subsidies that allows France to protect its domestic film, television, and music industries from the ravages of U.S. competition. Literally it means that French audiovisual products are exempted from the free-trade rules monitored by the World Trade Organization that prohibit states from implementing protectionist measures. The exemption means that France can specify minimum national content requirements on radio and television and, through levies on movie ticket sales and television broadcasters, can funnel half a billion euros each year toward the national film industry. The policy undeniably sustains a depth of creative activity in France that no longer exists in any other European country. A record 172 feature films were made in France in 2001, easily the most in any European country.[4] Spain made 107, and Italy 103, while Germany and the UK each made 83. Thanks mainly to the box-office success of *Amélie*, 2001 was a bumper year for the share of French films in the theaters. French films accounted for 41.5 percent of total admissions in France in 2001, up from 28.5 percent in 2000. It would fall back to the low thirties in 2002, but the French still appear to enjoy their own culture far more than other European Union nations. British films account for just 20 percent of UK admissions, and German films for less than 10 percent of sales in Germany. The ministry of culture crows that the 46.4-percent market share of U.S. films in France in 2001 was the smallest since 1998.

Yet there remained plenty of room for doubting the efficacy of the cultural exception, particularly as an instrument for the projection of French culture and language around the world. Low-budget movies made in France bomb overseas. Only 9 of the 172 films had budgets of €15 million, and just 1 (Roman Polanksi's English-language *The Pianist*) had a budget of more than €30 million. Nearly 25 percent of films had budgets of less than €1 million, which is often simply not enough to make the slick productions cinema audiences have come to expect. Exports of French films generated revenues of just €71.5 million in 2001. More embarrassing still from the viewpoint of *la francophonie,* of the ten highest-grossing "French" films, five were actually made in English. French films make no dent at all on Hollywood's monopoly of its huge domestic market, where it accounts for more than 92 percent of all admissions. If France is simply trying to keep its filmmakers alive and to provide for a degree of cultural diversity, it is certainly succeeding, albeit at a cost. But if it is hoping to rival Hollywood on the global stage, it fails on almost every tangible measure. While subsidies for French cinema ensure that more films are made, they do not make them widely watched or exported.

Many French filmmakers worried about Messier's commitment to the cultural exception as actually practiced in France. Fine talk about diversity was all very well. Messier could continue saying "I like Hollywood movies, but I adore French cinema" to his heart's content, but for the powerful creative community in Paris what was most important was for Messier to promise never to call into question the nuts and bolts of the cultural exception itself. For the *gauche caviar,* the snobby left-leaning commentariat, Canal Plus had over the years become a symbol of the nation's cultural vitality because of its status as the indispensable crutch of French cinema. Enshrined in Canal Plus's charter was an obligation to give 12 percent of its revenues to European film production, including 9 percent for French cinema alone. Every Canal Plus subscriber in France therefore contributed around €2.50 a month to cinema production. This was no small financial obligation for the loss-making pay-television operator. In 2001, Canal Plus spent €153 million honoring its commitments toward the French film industry. Its funds helped finance 122 French films—71 percent of the total number of films made in France and 21 percent of all investment in the French film industry that year.

Messier was not alone in believing that Canal Plus had created an unhealthy culture of dependence in the French film industry. Many films financed by Canal Plus or the French state were unwatchable exercises in narcissism. "Their survival is due not to support by moviegoers, who desert these movies in droves, or to high cultural aspirations, which are generally wanting, but to the industry's perceived right to support from Canal Plus and the taxpayer," argued Guillaume Parmentier, head of the French Center on the United States at the French Institute of International Relations in Paris. "The result is cronyism and, too frequently, mediocrity. . . . The French value their contribution to the art form, but increasingly resent having to subsidize mediocre productions and lazy artists." Messier firmly believed that while it was important for France to maintain a home-grown industry capable of producing original and high-quality pictures, making Canal Plus carry the burden like this was no longer the right way for the system to operate. Vivendi Universal is not the ministry of culture, he would patiently explain. Nonetheless, as a condition for being allowed to proceed with the merger, Messier committed to stick to the terms of Canal Plus's funding obligations until 2004. However, he made it clear that after that grace period, he would negotiate hard to loosen the terms of its broadcasting license.

Fears over Canal Plus's medium-term commitment to French cinema were compounded by worries about what would happen to its maverick style if it was swallowed up by a large conglomerate. Pierre Lescure had been virtually alone in supporting the pay-

TV operator's absorption into a conglomerate run by French technocrats. He found his position and authority endlessly challenged by his free-spirited colleagues and also by André Rousselet, Canal Plus's founder and his trusted mentor. Rousselet, who had resigned from Canal in 1994 after Générale des Eaux became its controlling shareholder, lashed out bitterly at the merger in a page-long article in *Le Monde*. The former adviser to President François Mitterrand argued passionately that Canal Plus would find itself a provincial outpost of Messier's new U.S. empire and would suffer, along with French cinema, if Vivendi were to find itself taken over by new owners: "Are Canal Plus employees not entitled to demand that France's leading media company not be sacrificed to the uncertain fortunes of businesses, however prestigious, that are 9,107 kilometers away from the Quai André-Citroen? Don't be pushed into this merger. Before accepting this fate, remember these words: a group without culture has no future."

His polemic stunned Lescure, who turned to the company's chief operating officer, Denis Olivennes, to draft a reply for the following day's paper. "Canal Plus has changed," replied Lescure, who knew that its weakened finances left him no choice but to find a large media conglomerate as a parent. Satellite television, he said, was now at the heart of the globalization that was erasing borders, sharpening competition, and creating a race for size and strength. "That's the real danger. It's that, unless Canal can compete with the biggest, it will progressively lose its subscribers, even in France. They will go directly to other, more powerful foreign operators, who will be wholly indifferent to our preoccupations about defending our cultural diversity. We cannot defend our cultural exception from behind the Maginot line. The merger will bind Canal within the world's second largest media group, worth more than €100 billion and led by Jean-Marie Messier. In other words, a group with an international footprint, but with a European, indeed French, center of gravity, one that is proud of its roots, but happy to compete on the global stage, a modern group, free from complexes about its competitors or the financial markets and unafraid of the open seas."

The wrangles with Canal Plus employees and pampered French

filmmakers, who demanded a special charter guaranteeing that Vivendi Universal would renew the pay-TV operator's cinema-funding commitments for a further four years, had a profound impact on Messier. "He stopped listening after Seagram," said one of his closest bankers. Suddenly, everything French seemed to appear small-minded and parochial. "We will neither be apostles of U.S. cultural domination, nor of *l'exception française*," he began to say. He was not creating a French national champion in the media industry just to preserve the masturbatory output of a small clique of Parisian filmmakers. He wanted to build a strong group that could compete on a level playing field with the giants of the sector. His frustration soon became evident. He began to squabble publicly with other French chief executives—and when talking to U.S. journalists, he started to refer to France as an "exotic little country." Above all, he refused to be appropriated as the champion of domestic protectionist lobbies. While he waited for the European Union competition authorities in Brussels to approve the three-way merger—which they did in October 2000, on the condition that Vivendi sell its 24-percent stake in Rupert Murdoch's British Sky Broadcasting—Messier sat down to express his frustrations.

Aided by Christine Mital, a friendly journalist from *Le Nouvel Observateur*, Messier produced his personal manifesto: *j6m.com*. The ironic alphanumeric title displayed a self-conscious cockiness that elicited horror, but also a certain admiration. How he captured the daringness of the time, that Messier! He had adopted the nickname given to him by *Les Guignols*, Canal Plus's satirical puppet show, which lampooned Vivendi Universal in its sketches about grotesque "World Company." The perennial target of the show's jibes at modern capitalism, Messier's J6M was made to personify the bumptiousness and arrogance of the new economy's chief executives. If Messier signed his name "J2M"—so far removed from the formality of the typical French chairman—the show's creators would poke fun at him by adding an epithet: on their nightly shows, he was satirized as Jean-Marie Messier, *Moi-même, Maître du Monde*. When it appeared in September, just three months after the Seagram announcement, *j6m.com* (subtitled, just as embarrassingly, *Why Fear the New Economy?*) provided a readable response to the flood of antiglobalization tracts that had been hitting the bookstands in railways and airports throughout France in the late 1990s.[5]

From the success of this burgeoning literary genre, it appeared that a significant section of French opinion was firmly in thrall to "Forresterism," the idea put forward in Viviane Forrester's best-selling 1996 book, *L'horreur économique,* that the U.S. liberal economy was imposing horrific social costs on France. In the summer of 2000, José Bové, the charismatic leader of a militant confederation of small farmers' unions, had just published his rabble-rousing antiglobalization tract, *The World Is Not for Sale.* The small town of Millau in southern France had just been the scene of an extraordinary protest: responding to America's hike of import duties on the locally produced Roquefort cheese, an angry group of local farmers, led by Bové, marched to the site of a McDonald's fast-food restaurant, then under construction, and dismantled it. They piled the building on the back of their tractors and drove it through the town in front of cheering supporters. The protest made front-page news around the world as the latest indication of burgeoning public concern about the impact of untrammeled free trade and the spread of American fast-food culture on local communities.

"This is the first time that a leading chief executive has undressed in public," noted Erik Israelewicz, who reviewed *j6m.com* for *Les Echos.* "His candor surprises and sometimes shocks this side of the Atlantic, as some of his peers have already let him know." Messier applauded the advent of stock options, long frowned upon in France, and defended high levels of executive pay. "Senior executives are the first 'victims' of globalization. It is appropriate that they should be in the first rank of those to benefit from it. Our executives are expected to be supermen and superwomen. They endlessly need to retrain, work in all languages, change countries and culture, decide quickly and act even faster, constantly produce better results." He lamented the traditional French hostility to the nouveaux riches that stifled entrepreneurial drive. "We applaud the wealth of an Anelka or a Depardieu, but not that of a future Bill Gates." There should be an outcry, he said, over the hundreds of young French people leaving France to set up businesses overseas. "I once heard one French politician even welcome the phenomenon, saying 'at least, it will help the spread of the French language.'" France had to wake up to the reality that there would never be a French Silicon Valley if the country did not profoundly alter its attitudes toward money.

Messier revealed his pay—a salary of €1.06 million in 1999 and a 200-percent bonus—to the irritation of the numerous French chairmen who had refused to let light in on such "private" matters. He was certainly not the first to do so, but he was the first to make a song and dance about it. Outside France, what was shocking was less Messier's €3 million remuneration in 1999, but the fact that a chief executive of his apparent caliber running a company of Vivendi's size could end up with just €1 million after taxes. Few carped at his revelation that in his five years at Vivendi he had received 2 million stock options, roughly a third of 1 percent of Vivendi's share capital. At the time, although not yet exercisable, those options were in the money to the tune of €22 million. "Am I worth that amount?" he asked. Messier justified the package in relation to Vivendi's increase in market value from €9 billion to €55 billion between 1997 and 2000. "My share represents half of one-thousandth of the €46 billion increase in value. . . . There is the saying, 'If you pay peanuts you get monkeys.' Brutal, but true."[6]

*j6m.com* confirmed Messier's status as France's first celebrity chief executive. His willingness to offer an opinion on any subject—from the thirty-five-hour work week and pension reform to antiglobalization, the role of NGOs, and the clash of civilizations—made him the darling of the media. He was funny, quick-witted, frank, and, above all, accessible, in contrast to the sobriety of other French chief executives. Their cautious relationships with the media through press conferences, respectful interviews with "reliable" journalists, and staged photo-ops looked old-fashioned and unspontaneous. Messier, by contrast, took on all comers. He debated live on television with José Bové. He posed for *Paris Match*, lying on his bed like a starlet and clutching the latest antiglobalization tome, *La Bourse ou la vie.* His fast responses, delivered in language devoid of the pomposity of the énarque, encouraged the talk shows to invite him onto France's most popular programs. Messier was the first boss, for example, ever to appear on *Can't Wait for Sunday,* the most watched show on the France 2 network, and he bounded into the television studio in an open-collared shirt. For two hours and before a live audience, he chatted with a parade of guests, from the actress Sophie Marceau to a young French ski champion to whom Messier gushed: "For me, skiing is a physical necessity. I have a need for risk." Periodically, the cameras would cut away to interviews with Messier's relatives and video clips of him cooking dinner or visiting his old high school in Grenoble.

Many began to wonder if Messier might consider running for public office. One unexpected and probably unwanted endorsement came from Silvio Berlusconi. The Italian prime minister, who had long been arguing that France, like Italy, needed to be run by a businessman, announced that Messier would make an ideal leader. The young Frenchman would brush aside such speculation. "My main driver is not money. If it were I would have stayed with Lazard and had a nice quiet life. Nor is it power. Otherwise I would have stayed around politics with Balladur. I like to be responsible and rewarded for what I do. In politics, life is too short: politicians make decisions they are not responsible for. They are also too national. I am international." Interviewed by the *Financial Times* in his private jet as he flew to London to give the keynote speech at a media conference, he said his one ambition was to run Vivendi Universal for another fifteen to twenty years. It was too much fun to contemplate giving it all up for politics. Others could see why. "He is at least as powerful as the president or prime minister of France," said Pierre Lellouche, a leading member of the ruling Gaullist Party.

Not everyone was in thrall to "Jean-Magic Messier," as *Le Monde* described him in a full-page profile after the Seagram merger. His harshest critics were within Canal Plus, which never accepted the Vivendi Universal yoke. Bruno Gaccio, the comic genius behind *Les Guignols,* never disguised his loathing. In a column in *Time,* he lamented the impact that the adulation of Messier was having on French values:

> Many of you ill-informed Anglophones naively think that Jean-Marie Messier is French. Wrong. He's not American either. Or Swiss, Argentine, Canadian or anything else. Jean-Marie Messier is, in fact, part of a unique community that extends its empire across the entire planet: the Go-Getters. These marvelous man-machines are the ones who make the consumer goods, who strut their certitude across the world stage, corseted in their dark gray suits, admired by those given to admiration. I don't admire Monsieur Messier. I don't hate him either. I don't give a damn about him. I come from a small, exotic country, France, which represents a little less than one percent of the world's population and which has a great number of citizens with no ambition other than to have a beautiful life. I'm like that myself. The Go-Getters bore me. Competition cheeses me off, and professional success leaves me cold. . . . Don't force us to succeed. Don't impose your life on us. Don't be an example. Remain a mystery. An anomaly. A Jean-Marie.

## CHAPTER SIX

# Vivendi Frères

Barely had shareholders approved the acquisition of Seagram and Canal Plus than Messier started to put the Vivendi Universal deal machine through its paces. In its actual form, the company was still just a skeleton of what he had in mind. His image of the company he wanted to create was grand: "the world's preferred creator and provider of personalized information, entertainment, and services to consumers anywhere, at any time, and across all distribution platforms and devices." With this sweeping objective, the list of potential acquisitions was endless. Messier believed he had the resources to achieve his goal. "We have zero debt. We are rich," he crowed. That was, of course, far from true: Vivendi Universal's net debt actually stood at €25.5 billion at the end of 2000.* He could only make the claim at all because he had parked €15 billion of its debt with Vivendi Environnement, which since July 2000 had become a semi-independent but still majority-controlled company, with its own stock market listing. He had also reached an agreement in December 2000 to sell Seagram's drinks business to Diageo and Pernod Ricard for approximately €8.5 billion.† Ignoring the debt of Vivendi Environnement and as-

---

*Vivendi's net debt was €22.8 billion in 1999 and just €6.5 billion in 1998.
†The purchase price was $8.15 billion, which was expected to result in after-tax proceeds of $7.7 billion.

suming that the cash from the sale of the drinks division was already in the bank, Messier could claim this half-truth with conviction. Within two weeks of the completion of the $60 billion acquisitions of Seagram and Canal Plus, the next multibillion-dollar deal was ready to roll.

"He went and bought a telco in Africa!" laughed Bronfman. "I was not disappointed with the Maroc Telecom deal. I was furious. It was done without my knowledge. In terms of the message we were trying to send to investors it was disastrous. I'd just spent six months on the road selling the story. In that context, the Maroc Telecom deal made no sense. Why did he do it? I have no idea. But then why did he do so many things?" Unbeknownst to his new American partners, Messier had secretly negotiated with the Moroccan government to take a 35-percent stake in the state telecom monopoly for €2.4 billion.* The transaction immediately confused investors, who had been given the impression over the previous six months that Vivendi Universal wished to become a media and entertainment player. There seemed no rationale whatsoever to acquiring a minority stake in a North African telecom operator. Furthermore, Messier was paying a high price, at almost ten times the operator's forecast 2001 earnings before interest, tax, depreciation, and amortization. He described the deal as the first time a foreign company had ever taken a large stake in a major Moroccan enterprise and as the start of a "strategic global partnership" with the North African kingdom. The Moroccan market, he promised, would open up for Vivendi Universal.

To general disbelief, Messier insisted that the purchase of the Moroccan telephone operator would yield bountiful synergies: Vivendi Universal Publishing would enter into discussions with the Moroccan ministry of education to provide on-line teaching materials and, apparently, reinforce a partnership with the Al

---

*Vivendi Universal later disclosed that it had contracted a reciprocal put and call option related to a 16-percent interest in Maroc Telecom, owned by the kingdom of Morocco. The options can be exercised between September 1, 2003, and June 1, 2005. (See Vivendi Universal 2001 20F, pp. 67, F-42.)

Akhawayn University in Ifrane; Universal Music would open an office in Casablanca; and Vivendi Environnement would benefit in its bids for local authority contracts. A few weeks later, on March 1, 2001, Vivendi Environnement did indeed win two twenty-five-year concessions to supply water, waste, and electricity services to the 1.2 million inhabitants of Tangier and Tétouan. But this was not the type of synergy U.S. media investors had expected or wanted. Few believed that it would make good business sense for commercial agreements to be cross-subsidized by the expensive acquisition of a strategically redundant stake in Maroc Telecom. Similar telecom transactions in Poland and Kenya appeared equally scattershot. The more Messier attempted to explain the potential synergies that could be created through the investment in Maroc Telecom, the less the market believed in his entire vision of convergence and in his ability to weld a cohesive group out of such disparate assets.

During 2001, it seemed that Messier was the last big spender in cyberspace. Long after dot-com dreams had vaporized across Europe and at the same time as other media companies were frantically trying to curb their Internet losses, Messier still had his foot to the floor as if it were 1999. Guillaume Hannezo despaired of these Internet investments, which he said destroyed nearly €2 billion of capital invested in 2000 and 2001. "Vivendi Universal was much slower than the other media groups (Disney, Viacom, and even News Corp. or AOL) in reducing and then stopping investment in the Internet once it had become clear that the new technologies (cable broadband, ADSL, UMTS) would take longer to develop than anticipated and that Internet companies were failing to find profitable business models. These investments in businesses without any sustainable economic model might appear naive, and one can wonder why simple common sense did not prevent them. But at the time, anyone who questioned the rationale for an Internet investment was seen as an obscurantist."[1]

As Vizzavi burned its way through €1.6 billion of seed capital, Messier made almost weekly announcements of new dot-com ventures. On January 31, 2001, he launched Viventures 2, a €630 million Internet venture capital fund.* Five days later, he paid $140 million to buy Uproar, the owner of U.S. on-line game-show and lottery portals. On February 12 he launched Education.com, an on-line learning network with a $25 million budget and aspirations to break even in 2002. On February 23, Vivendi Universal and Sony launched Duet, an on-line rival to Napster that offered teenagers the chance to pay for music they were downloading for free. In April, he bought Emusic.com and said he was considering purchasing Scoot.com, the UK portal in which he had invested €443 million for a 22-percent stake the previous summer.† Finally, in May, he splashed out $400 million on MP3.com, the San Diego–based on-line music platform.

According to Hannezo, Messier came close to bidding for Yahoo!, the pioneering American Internet portal, and Europ@web, a motley assortment of doomed dot-coms. Messier was on the point of paying Bernard Arnault €700 million for the incubator's various holdings when the cohead of Goldman Sachs in Paris, Philippe Altuzarra, dissuaded him on the grounds that it "did not fit the Vivendi Universal equity story." Nonetheless, these loss-making businesses would hit Vivendi Universal's results hard in 2001: the Internet division lost €290 million at the operating profit level in 2001, 50 percent more than in 2000. To celebrate the six-month anniversary of Vivendi Universal, Messier indulged himself with dreams of a much bigger deal. He thought hard about buying Club Med, the French package-holiday operator. The logic behind such a move in Messier's mind was that Club Med's one hundred villages, which were dotted across holiday spots in Europe, Asia, and the United States, were similar to Universal Studios' theme parks

---

*Vivendi Universal would put up a third of the fund. Other partners included the Belgian financier Albert Frère, Société Générale Asset Management, Goldman Sachs, and Azeo, an investment fund linked to Lazard.
†Vivendi Universal paid $24 million for Emusic.com. It wrote off virtually the entire investment in Scoot.com in June 2001. (See Vivendi Universal 2001 20F, p. F-20.)

in California, Florida, and Osaka, Japan.* According to Henri Giscard d'Estaing, then Club Med's general manager, the project died only once Vivendi Universal's financial position weakened after September 11. It is just as well, for the investment reaction to that deal would have been one of utter bemusement.

Messier's attention had in the meantime turned elsewhere. It settled on Houghton Mifflin, the last of the great Boston publishers. Over the years, as the rest of the trade publishing industry migrated to New York, Houghton Mifflin's trade arm—which boasted authors such as Philip Roth and J.R.R. Tolkien—had shrunk in relation to its vast textbook-publishing business, which by 2001 accounted for approximately 90 percent of its sales. This increased its appeal to Messier, who believed education would be one of the five types of content—along with music, film, sports, and games—that would be most valued in the digital era. The ongoing auction of the Boston company soon had his full attention. Private equity firms were in the lead as the large educational publishers, such as Pearson and McGraw-Hill, were ruled out of the running for antitrust reasons. But on June 1, Messier waded into the bidding with a winning offer of $2.2 billion, including $500 million of debt.† "We now have world-leading positions in music, films, games, and education," Messier announced. "The acquisition of Houghton Mifflin propels Vivendi Universal Publishing to the number two position worldwide in education publishing. We have the tools to become number one." In fact, the number two position seemed to belong, by a nose, to McGraw-Hill.‡ Either way,

---

*Universal Studios owned Universal Studios Hollywood in Los Angeles, Universal Studios Florida, and Universal's Islands of Adventure in Orlando, Florida. It also owned Universal Studios Japan in Osaka and Universal Mediterranea near Barcelona, Spain.

†The $2.2 billion enterprise value represented 10.7 times ebitda after book plate amortization.

‡Vivendi Universal's educational publishing turnover would rise to around $2.2 billion in 2001, compared to $3.8 billion for Pearson and $2.3 billion for McGraw-Hill.

Messier had signaled his determination to compete for leadership of yet another segment of the media marketplace.*

The deal left Bronfman cold: it effectively reversed his 1996 decision to quit the publishing business with the sale of MCA's general fiction arm, Putnam Berkley, to Pearson. Messier continued to promote a vision of a world unified by the wireless Internet. "When I see a great book, I think movie rights, interactive games, and so on," Messier said. "The digital broadband revolution is going to make all content accessible across all platforms and devices." But to many investors, education appeared marginal to the new core entertainment business. They wondered how Universal Studios would make blockbuster movies or video games out of Houghton Mifflin's dry textbooks. How realistic was it to imagine English-language material selling to Moroccan teenagers via Maroc Telecom mobiles in the souks of Marrakech? Investors admitted that Houghton Mifflin was a fine and venerable stand-alone business. The problem, as ever, was that Messier's belief in the value of his new economy synergies had led him to pay far, far over the odds.

The long bull market in mergers and acquisitions, which had been struggling for over a year, finally died in the autumn of 2001. On October 22, an era of naive innocence suddenly ended when Enron, the U.S. energy giant, disclosed that the Securities and Exchange Commission had opened an informal probe into certain "related part transactions." The announcement followed a rapid sell-off in the stock in reaction to Enron's surprising revelation the previous week of a $1.2 billion charge related to one of its controversial financing vehicles. Over the following weeks America was shocked to discover that the third largest company in the United States had been systematically defrauding investors and that Arthur Andersen, its auditor, had knowingly approved misleading accounts.

---

*Vivendi Universal estimated the global educational-publishing market to be worth €50 billion, half of which was in the United States. However, in September 2002, Merrill Lynch estimated spending on instructional materials to be just $27 billion (€28 billion), with the United States accounting for 30 percent of the total.

Steven Spielberg and Seagram President and CEO Edgar Bronfman Jr. *(Gamma)*

Jean-Marie Messier at his office overlooking the Arc de Triomphe, at 42 Avenue Friedland, Paris. *(Alain Bull)*

Jean-Marie Messier and his wife Antoinette were among seven hundred guests who came to honor Edgar Bronfman Sr. and Jr. at the 92nd Street Y's Premier Corporate Gala on January 30, 2001.
*(Patrick Andrade)*

Two best friends: Edgar Bronfman Jr. gets a pat of encouragement from Jean-Marie Messier at the 92nd Street Y's Premier Corporate Gala, just under two months after the closing of the Vivendi/Seagram merger.
*(Patrick Andrade)*

Marc Viénot, honorary chairman of Société Générale and one of Jean-Marie Messier's most determined supporters on the Vivendi Universal board. *(Alain Bull)*

Jean-Marie Messier with Lionel Jospin at the hotel Matignon, the French Prime Minister's official residence, in the summer of 2001. *(Daniel Simon)*

Jean-Marie Messier at Universal Studios, where the set is ready for the shooting of *The Scorpion King*. He takes the director's chair. *(Fanthomme Hubert/Paris Match)*

Jean-Marie Messier sits next to Jodie Foster at the 54th Cannes Film Festival closing dinner in May 2001. *(Benainous-Duclos)*

Jean-Marie Messier poses at the Olympia, the famous Parisian concert hall bought by Vivendi Universal in August 2001. *(Esch Thierry/Paris Match)*

Barry Diller and his companion, designer Diane Von Furstenberg, at the premiere of *The Others* at the Paris Theater in Manhattan on August 2, 2001, a few weeks before he started to negotiate the sale of USA Networks to Vivendi Universal. *(Nick Elgar)*

*(right)* Jean-Marie Messier at a press conference announcing Vivendi Universal's first half results for 2001 just before the start of his season in hell. *(Alexis Duclos)*

*(left)* Jean-Marie Messier faces Rupert Murdoch, chairman of News Corporation and with whom he was obsessively and self-destructively competitive, at a media conference in Scottsdale, Arizona. *(Fanthomme Hubert/Paris Match)*

In his office at the Seagram Building at 375 Park Avenue, Jean-Marie Messier is proud to announce that the painting hanging behind him, Mark Rothko's *Brown and Black in Red*, will soon be donated to a French foundation established by François Pinault, owner of Christie's auction house. *(Fanthomme Hubert/Paris Match)*

At 7:00 A.M. on Wednesday, January 9, 2002, Jean-Marie Messier poses for *Paris Match* ice skating in Central Park, two days after a disastrous sale of Vivendi Universal shares soured sentiment toward him and the company.
*(Fanthomme Hubert/Paris Match)*

Pierre Lescure waves to Canal Plus employees demonstrating outside Vivendi Universal's headquarters following his dismissal on April 17, 2002.
*(Bassiguac-Lehnof)*

November 2002: Jean-Marie Messier strikes a Napoleonic pose in his first public appearance following his exit in July 2002. *(Fred Kiehn)*

Jean-Marie Messier opening one eye to reality as he launches his version of his downfall, a book titled *Mon Vrai Journal* (*My True Diary*). *(Fred Kiehn)*

Enron's 144 most senior managers were revealed to have received $744 million from the company in the year before its collapse, ten times the likely severance payments for the 4,500 Enron employees who lost their jobs in the energy trader's bankruptcy. The crisis of capitalism had begun.

The deal-making era in which Messier had thrived ended in the aftermath of Enron's collapse. Complex, acquisitive, and highly indebted companies dropped out of favor. Rapid corporate transformations, such as were being attempted by Enron, Marconi, and Vivendi Universal, were suddenly as unfashionable as they had been admired eighteen months earlier. Those companies that displayed a concentration of power in a single, almighty chairman and chief executive were particularly suspect. Although few U.S. companies showed signs of being tempted to shift to the British structure with a nonexecutive chairman, investors expected board members to apply tighter restrictions on the chairman's and chief executive's freedom of action. Virtually every chief executive in the United States and Europe had been advised to keep his head down. Media interviews were axed, press conferences canceled. Messier, however, behaved as though the lessons from Enron and all the other corporate scandals that had collectively created a sense of mistrust and panic on Wall Street simply did not apply to him. "He had no idea how to make the mental transition from 2000 to 2002," said one person close to Bernard Arnault. For Jean-Marie Messier, the crescendo of self-delusion had not yet reached its climax.


Jean-Marc Espalioux, chairman of the Accor hotel group, was more familiar with Vivendi Universal than almost anyone else on the board. He had been finance director of Générale des Eaux for ten years, before leaving shortly after Messier's arrival. On this occasion, he, like a number of other members of the board, was genuinely perplexed. That Friday, December 14, 2001, Messier had summoned them at short notice. Such short notice, in fact, that he found them scattered across the globe. Pierre Lescure was in Los Angeles, the American members were in New York, and the majority were in Paris. Unable to meet in the flesh, the board members had agreed to a video conference. After the purchase of Houghton Mifflin in May 2001, Messier had vowed once again that the shopping spree had ended. He had repeated his pledge to focus on integration of the various businesses. Yet to their surprise, Vivendi Universal's board members suddenly found themselves being asked to approve not one but two more huge transactions.

Vivendi Universal was poised to take a 10-percent stake in Echostar, the U.S. pay-television operator. The operation would cost $1.5 billion. Messier said owning a small stake would help Universal Pictures secure commercial agreements with the U.S. pay-TV operator, which was then in the process of trying to buy its rival DirecTV—a move that would make it the largest satellite player in the country. No one understood why Vivendi Universal needed to own 10 percent of Echostar in order to sell it programming. Many suspected Messier had done the deal just to spite Murdoch, who had repeatedly failed to break into the U.S. satellite television market. The board scarcely had time to dwell on the details, for Messier was simultaneously proposing a second, much larger acquisition. Vivendi Universal would repurchase from Barry Diller the very same television businesses Bronfman had sold him in 1998. This time, however, they would pay three times as much as the $4.1 billion Bronfman had received for them. Messier had celebrated his forty-fifth birthday the previous evening. He felt at the peak of his energies and power. No one was going to be allowed to obstruct his plan to take over USA Networks. Since June 2000, he had been planning this transaction. With Universal, he owned the Hollywood studios and the second largest film library in the world. If he bought back USA Networks—maker of programs such as *Law and Order* and *Murder, She Wrote*—the integrity and logic of Universal Studios would be restored. The studio would at last be reunited with its television arm.

Several directors said the documentation was too sketchy to enable them to evaluate the proposals properly. Tracking problems incessantly interrupted the videoconference. "That meeting was all part of a pattern of the board not being kept properly informed," says Bronfman. "There's a record there for all to see." Messier could sense their reticence. For the first time, there was real hesitation. So soon after the collapse of Enron, the board members were suddenly more attuned to their responsibilities. One or two directors even started to pose serious questions about the group's financial situation, a departure from the normal somnolence of board meetings. But Messier was master of his board. The older members—seventy-three-year-old Marc Viénot, honorary chairman of Société Générale, and sixty-nine-year-old Jacques Friedmann, the retired chairman of the supervisory board of AXA-UAP*—would eat out of his hand, fascinated by the confident and ambitious young man who knew how to build eye-catchingly complex financial structures and understood the jargon of the new economy: the Internet, third-generation mobile telephony, and so on. That Messier sat on so many of his directors' own boards also stifled debate. He sat on the boards of LVMH, Alcatel, and Saint-Gobain; and their chairmen, Bernard Arnault, Serge Tchuruk, and Jean-Louis Beffa, in turn sat on his. He was also a director of BNP Paribas, represented at the media group by its honorary chairman, René Thomas, and one of its directors, Jacques Friedmann.

Barry Diller fascinated Messier, just as he had Bronfman. Diller had left Fox in 1992, promising that he would work only for himself. He had spent twenty-five years shaping American popular culture but had never achieved his dream of owning a Hollywood studio or television network. The 1990s had been years of frustrated ambition on a grand scale but, paradoxically, had boosted his reputation. The more deals he turned down, failed to pull off, or withdrew from at the last minute, the more people loved Barry. In 1994, he had bid for Paramount Communications, but was outgunned by Sumner Redstone at Viacom. "They won. We lost. Next," Diller said. Next was CBS. Fox's surging popularity had hurt the rival network, as the newcomer had won over several CBS

---

*Marc Viénot, the author of two reports on French corporate governance, was also chairman of the supervisory board of Aventis, the Franco-German pharmaceutical group, of which Jean-René Fourtou was vice chairman. Jacques Friedmann was replaced as supervisory board chairman of AXA by Claude Bébéar, previously chief executive of the French insurance group.

affiliates and outbid CBS for the rights to televise the National Football League. Diller was days away from success when his backers withdrew support for the deal. He started again in 1995, and with the backing of John Malone, the king of U.S. cable, bought the Home Shopping Network, which he had used in 1998 as the vehicle for the purchase of Universal Studio's cable channels—USA Networks and Sci-Fi—and television production business from Seagram. Diller paid Seagram $4.1 billion, in the form of a 43-percent stake in HSN, which was renamed USA Networks, and $1.2 billion in cash. This did not stop Diller's insatiable pursuit of the bigger prize: a studio or a network. The following year, he almost succeeded in buying NBC from General Electric, but was thwarted by Bronfman's decision to veto the operation. The stream of failures continued: Diller tried furiously to buy Lycos, the Internet portal, in 1999, but failed after wisely refusing to increase the value of his offer to Lycos shareholders.

The contrast with Messier's own impulsive acquisitiveness was obvious to everyone. "Diller did the thing really smart businesspeople are supposed to do—that is, bide their time and wait for it to come to them—as opposed to what media moguls invariably do, which is, at vast cost and assuming great risk, go out and get what they want when they want it," argued media pundit Michael Wolff. "You just have to be cold enough, or disconnected enough, to walk away from any deal . . . which almost no other media person has been able to do. Then there is the toughness thing, which in terms of the Diller legend should not be underestimated—Barry, evidently lacking the need to be liked, is a very scary guy. It is surely this very lack of sentiment that makes a good deal-maker." Diller's apparent maturity in accepting seeing his dreams repeatedly frustrated had impressed the U.S. business community. "This has made Diller, in an age of excess, seem like the last prudent man—and a not unheroic one. . . . While he has still not achieved his obvious goal, he's achieved this other thing, this mythicness, this invincibility, this all-knowingness—and he's achieved this, his legendariness (which has, not incidentally, allowed him to make billions), precisely because he failed to achieve the other thing. Barry is one of the luckiest losers in history."[2]

Messier envied Diller's credentials as a media visionary and flattered him at every opportunity. But by the end of 2001, he had received little in return. How could he leverage the relationship? Messier regarded Vivendi Universal's stake in USA Networks as the key to unlocking numerous opportunities in the U.S. media market. "He represents a good half of the assets on his own," Messier had said at the time of the Seagram merger. With Barry Diller as his partner, he believed, the entertainment industry would fall at his feet. As the months passed, however, the relationship appeared to be delivering little except bruising clashes with Diller's ego. The interactive television and e-commerce veteran had turned down Messier's invitation to help out Vizzavi. Cooperation between Universal Studios and USA Networks had been frustrating. Valuable synergies were unexploited: there were savings to be made between USA Networks' television production on the one hand and Universal's film production and film catalog on the other. Both companies were developing businesses where the other was already strong. Universal was losing money building on television production, and USA Networks in producing films at its small studio. Diller's obsessive desire to control everything was poisoning the partnership. As part of his deal with Bronfman in 1998, Diller had the right to vote the 43-percent stake in USA Networks owned by Seagram for as long as he ran the company. The only power Seagram, and subsequently Vivendi Universal, retained was the right to veto large transactions.

"I want to make sure that we don't leave money on the table," a frustrated Messier said in the autumn of 2001. It was absurd, he felt, that Diller's TV operation had not been making shows based on Universal's movie library or even working to identify ways of "leveraging Universal's success." Diller, for his part, was cutting. "He can say what he wants. We own it, all talk aside. If there were anything to talk about, we'd talk about it. Otherwise, it's just noise." As for any loopholes in the original Seagram agreement that Messier might use to force Diller to change the way he operated the TV unit? "Zero, nothing," Diller said. Yet on no account did Messier want to lose access to the Diller name and touch. As 2001 drew to a close, the Frenchman felt the need of a new mentor to steer him through the treacherous waters of Hollywood. Pierre Lescure had served a useful role at the start of the Hollywood adventure, introducing Messier to his contacts from Canal Plus and letting Messier tag along at his side at Herb Allen's annual media industry get-together in Sun Valley. But Lescure had reached his limits as a power broker. The Canal Plus chairman seemed happier reminiscing with Lew Wasserman, then in his eighties, over lunch in the Universal black tower than theorizing about the deals that would shape the future of the media industry. "Pierre is a wonderful guy, but he didn't know his ass from his elbow when it came to the U.S.," Bronfman would later say.

More worryingly, relations with the Bronfmans continued to deteriorate. At meetings of the executive committee, where Edgar Bronfman Jr. was responsible for Vivendi Universal's music operations, Messier barely acknowledged the former chief executive of Seagram and squeezed his opportunities to express his views. Tensions grew between the two men as they adjusted to unfamiliar roles. In March 2001, Bronfman planned to attend the opening of Vivendi Universal's theme park in Osaka, Japan. The theme park had originally been conceived by Matsushita during the Japanese company's ownership of MCA, but it had been financed and executed by Bronfman. However, when he examined the opening day schedule, he realized Messier had left him no role in the ceremonies and so decided not to attend. Other incidents also betrayed personal tensions. After his move to New York in September 2001, Messier tried to transfer a Rothko canvas, *Brown and Black in Red,* from the fourth floor of the Seagram Building into his new apartment on Park Avenue. The idea that the collection put together by Phyllis Lambert, sister of Edgar Bronfman Sr., might piece by piece vanish into Messier's private quarters irritated the Bronfmans. A message was sent to the Frenchman requesting that paintings stay in their original positions. In the end, the two sides reached a compromise when Messier agreed to move it into his office. He would appear to have enjoyed the last word on the matter: in an interview with *Paris Match,* he pledged the Rothko to François Pinault's new modern art museum in Paris.

In May 2001, the Bronfman family had taken the first opportunity allowed by the terms of the merger lockup to sell nearly €1.3 billion of Vivendi Universal shares. The sale, which reduced their holding to 6.1 percent but still left them as Vivendi Universal's largest shareholder, was presented in public as simple portfolio diversification. Edgar Bronfman Jr. said, "As executive vice chairman, I am personally gratified that Vivendi Universal is off to a very fast and successful start. I look forward to continuing to work with Jean-Marie and the rest of our very strong management team to realize the enormous potential of Vivendi Universal." Many interpreted the substantial share sale as exactly the opposite: a sign of dissatisfaction. As the months passed, Bronfman found Messier increasingly insecure. Shortly before the acquisition of Houghton Mifflin—which Bronfman considered of marginal relevance to the main thrust of the group's strategy—Steven Spielberg asked Bronfman for an introduction to Messier. The former Seagram chief executive set it up in his suite at the Hotel Bel-Air because he felt it was more conveniently located for the legendary filmmaker than Messier's hotel, the Beverly Hilton. However, when Messier heard that the meeting was to take place in Bronfman's suite, he switched to the Bel-Air and demanded that everyone meet in his suite. In the end, Messier arrived late and found everyone in the restaurant.[3]

On another occasion, Bronfman was surprised to read an interview with Messier in *The New York Times* in which the Frenchman pointed out that although Bronfman's office in the Seagram Building was bigger, his was on the floor above: "I am just over him." Less than six months later, there would be even clearer evidence that all was not well with the relationship. Edgar Bronfman Jr. walked into Messier's office in the Seagram Building one day in late November and confronted him with the news of his plan to resign his operational role in charge of the music division. "He cried when I told him I was leaving," Bronfman said. "He told me, 'I take this as a personal failure.'" The former Seagram chief executive had decided it was time to put some distance between himself and Messier. He had grown increasingly irritated that Messier appeared to be ignoring his advice. He suspected that Messier was marginalizing him to show that, now that he had moved to New

York, he was in sole charge of the U.S. media business. "Up until the USA Networks transaction, he had at least done me the courtesy of asking my advice, but when I wanted to discuss Barry Diller with him his eyes would just glaze over," Bronfman said. "So I said to him, 'The truth is I don't think you did what you could have done to make this work out for the two of us.' But in reality I don't think that mattered. At the time of the merger it was understood in my contract that I had a window after a year.* It wasn't clear to me that I wanted to work for someone else and I am definitely of the belief that businesses need one chief executive to work, not two. This gerrymandered marriage did not work. So I left for reasons that were partly to do with me and partly to do with him."

The Four Seasons restaurant on the ground floor of the Seagram Building, the favored lunch spot for New York power brokers, began to buzz with rumors. The Bronfmans had made this corner of Park Avenue a monument to their drinks and entertainment empire and a symbol of their influence at the interface of Hollywood, Wall Street, and power politics. In the late 1950s Phyllis Lambert had commissioned Ludwig Mies van der Rohe and Philip Johnson to build the modernist skyscraper, which they luxuriously set back from the street and introduced with an ostentatious fountain-covered granite plaza. The restaurant would be a showcase to their taste, its walls graced with works from their art collection. Presidents, ambassadors, movie stars, and bankers all had their favorite tables. Against the backdrop of a Picasso stage curtain made for Diaghilev's 1920 production of *The Three-Cornered Hat,* John F. Kennedy and Marilyn Monroe dined in May 1962, shortly before she serenaded him for the last time with her breathy nightclub version of "Happy Birthday" at Madison Square Garden. Over the years, everyone had come to understand how the Bronfmans had preserved their wealth and power: they were famously unsentimental.

---

*The window in his contract provided Bronfman with a severance package worth three times his annual base salary and target bonus—around $18 million in total—and a consultancy contract that would pay him an undisclosed amount to act as special adviser to the chairman of Vivendi Universal until the end of 2004.

Edgar Bronfman Sr. had often regretted his father's tendency to blur the line between employee and friend. "I watched him form personal relationships with people and then have to fire them. It drove him crazy," he wrote in 1998. "I have avoided such relationships and have never developed an intimate friendship with anybody who works for me."[4] He and his son were in no danger of becoming too fond of Messier. To explain his resignation, Edgar Bronfman Jr. agreed to issue a soothing statement: "My relationship with Jean-Marie has grown over the last two-plus years and we are much more than two executives building a company. It has been a privilege and a pleasure to work with him. Jean-Marie has become a close and good friend, and I continue to have great confidence in his leadership and in an enduring friendship." For his part, Messier said: "I deeply regret Edgar's decision. Edgar has, since the beginning, been my friend and partner in creating this company. Although I will miss our day-to-day interaction, we will maintain our good friendship, and I am pleased that he will remain an active and valued member of our board and a close adviser to me." The fulsome mutual praise confirmed many people's suspicions that all was not well at Vivendi Universal.

Bronfman had urged Jean-Marie Messier not to do the USA Networks deal, telling him the transaction was completely unnecessary. "Look at the actuarial tables. Barry's fifty-nine, you're forty-four. It's simple. Let him get frustrated." By the terms of Bronfman's original deal in 1998, the television businesses reverted automatically to Universal Studios the moment Barry Diller stopped running them. Bronfman had parked the businesses with Diller so that he could develop them for Seagram at a time when it lacked the management talent to do so itself. "I told Jean-Marie that those businesses were not going to be worth more next year with the way the advertising market was going, but he just did not listen." Another senior figure in the media industry told Messier the old story of a turtle who, after some hesitation, agrees to carry a scorpion across a river. As they reach the other side, the scorpion dismounts and stings the turtle. Asked to explain his action, the scorpion says: "It's in my nature; I'm a scorpion." "Barry is brilliant," the executive said. "But if you give him an opportunity to sting, he will. If Jean-Marie was going to let himself be screwed, Barry was happy to do it. He probably felt he had a duty to do it."

Messier would brush aside the warnings. "Barry Diller is someone who, since he left Rupert Murdoch, has never accepted working for anyone. Why would he work for this little French guy?" Messier would ask rhetorically. "Barry has a great ego, true. But he has something greater than his ego, that's his talent. And I prefer to have Barry Diller working with Vivendi Universal than with someone else."[5] Guillaume Hannezo was more concerned about the financial risk than about Diller's ego. "We just don't have the means to finance a transaction of this size," he protested to Messier. The assessment of Goldman Sachs, which was advising Vivendi Universal on the transaction, was that Messier should not proceed if the deal would provoke Moody's into downgrading the group's credit. According to one Goldman Sachs banker, Moody's had been calling incessantly following the news of the Echostar transaction and made it clear that it hated the deal: "He was paying a $1.5 billion market price for an illiquid asset and accepting a lockup. They just could not understand why anyone would do that." When it became clear that Moody's would not downgrade the group's debt in December, Hannezo and Goldman Sachs supported the deal. Nonetheless, many inside the company had major reservations about the price. The financial team from Canal Plus, which had also been involved in the discussions, communicated their anxieties about the transaction: they concluded that the acquisition was far too expensive relative to what it could offer the group.

Maurice Lévy, chairman of Publicis, the world's fourth-largest advertising group and one of Messier's closest advisers, later said that if the deal making had stopped after Houghton Mifflin, Vivendi Universal would still be one of France's most powerful companies. However, as Guillaume Hannezo said in a written submission to the French stock market investigation, that was not the choice Messier made. The finance director claimed he opposed every single one of Messier's deals in 2001, with the fateful exception of USA Networks: "After the profound transformation of our activities through the merger with Seagram and Canal Plus, 2001 was meant to have been dedicated to marking time, to integrating acquisitions, to simplifying the company, and to conserving cash until the markets recovered. Unfortunately, the group did not choose this path and committed a series of errors that are at the origin of the present crisis." According to Hannezo, the finance department of Vivendi Universal throughout 2000, 2001, and 2002 consistently tried to slow the pace of the deal making and sometimes veto acquisitions altogether. He claims that internal documents given to the Commission des Opérations de Bourse (COB), the French stock market regulators, show he consistently recommended that Vivendi Universal sell its stakes in BSkyB or Vivendi Environnement. He claims he even called for Messier to close down Vizzavi, the multiplatform portal once seen as the glue holding together the Vivendi Universal empire, from as early as the summer of 2001.

Hannezo later argued that Messier consistently underestimated Vivendi Universal's debt problem. He felt that the transfer of €15 billion of debt to Vivendi Environnement prior to its flotation on the Paris bourse—"the most that it could carry"—had given the media group a false sense of security. The acquisition of Seagram had added €8.5 billion to its €3 billion to €4 billion of borrowings.* However, Messier promised this new debt would immediately be wiped out with the proceeds from the sale of the Seagram drinks division. The company was not exactly debt-free at birth, as he had promised, but it did not appear unduly stretched. Furthermore, even though regulatory problems delayed the arrival of $8.15 billion of cash until December 21, 2001, a year after the sale to Pernod Ricard and Diageo had been agreed to, Vivendi Universal always knew that it had other liquid assets that it could sell easily if required. Its 63-percent stake in Vivendi Environnement was worth around €8 billion to €10 billion, and its 22-percent stake in BSkyB would produce a similar amount. "If, at this stage, the group had decided to sell before buying other as-

---

*Seagram's net debt of around €7 billion ignored an off-balance commitment of €1.5 billion that Vivendi Universal took onto its books in order to lower the associated financing cost.

sets, it easily had the resources to wipe out its debt and to gather sufficient additional cash to pursue external growth through acquisitions in the media and telecom sector," Hannezo said. "Unfortunately, it decided to do exactly the opposite, satisfying itself that it had the 'potential' wealth on its balance sheet in the form of liquid assets that were worth significantly more than its debt. In a market downturn this decision would necessarily destroy value."

Messier did not explain all this to his directors. He told board members that the purchase of USA Networks was elementary housekeeping. Moreover, he painted a misleading picture of the size of the financial undertaking. He presented the transaction as costing just $10.3 billion, understating it by approximately $2 billion. It ended up costing the company €12.4 billion, according to the new management team.[6] Barry Diller would join the company as chairman of a new entity, Vivendi Universal Entertainment (VUE), which would regroup Universal Studios and USA Networks. When they heard the price that Diller had negotiated with Messier, the Bronfmans blanched. That was nearly three times the amount they had received when they sold the business to Diller three years earlier. Either Messier was overpaying or they had been duped in 1998. They were certain it was not the latter. "Can Vivendi afford to spend this amount? What about our debt level?" asked Jean-Louis Beffa, chairman of the Saint-Gobain building materials group and a member of the board for nearly fifteen years. His relations with Messier were tense: a few years earlier he had unsuccessfully angled to succeed Guy Dejouany as chairman of Générale des Eaux. Messier had his answers ready. The media group was indebted to the tune of only €8.5 billion, he assured them, a perfectly comfortable level. He started to dazzle them with detail. Treasury stock, preferred stock, warrants, convertible debentures . . . it seemed every equity instrument under the sun was being used to fund the transaction. The board members, who had no documents in front of them, were completely lost.

Messier pressed on as fast as he could, even though the details of the deal with Barry Diller were still being negotiated and would not be finalized for several weeks. By the end of the negotiations, Diller had demanded and won complete managerial and financial control of Vivendi Universal's U.S. film and television activities. If Vivendi Universal triggered any tax liability for him personally or for USA Networks by selling the assets USA Networks had just contributed to Vivendi Universal Entertainment, the French company could be forced to pay up to $2 billion in compensation. If any VUE assets were sold, half the proceeds would have to be reinvested in the remaining film and TV business. Finally, VUE would not be allowed to assume more than $800 million of debt. Neither Vivendi Universal's board nor the annual general meeting of shareholders the following April was informed of these constraints on Vivendi Universal's freedom of action that Messier had accepted in order to win Diller's agreement. It was not until September 2002 that the constraints became known to investors. When faced with new directors seeking to unravel the intricacies of the agreements Messier had made, Diller made the contract he had signed with Messier public. It was only then that investors discovered that Diller controlled the future of the group in the United States. The scorpion had stung.

The cost of bringing Diller on board was colossal. The haughty U.S. media executive had declined the offer of a salary. Instead, he settled for a 1.5-percent stake in Vivendi Universal Entertainment, with the right to sell it back to Vivendi Universal for a minimum of $275 million. Universal Studios' existing management team exploited his arrival to renegotiate their contracts. At a meeting in Paris on December 10, just before the group's Christmas party, Ron Meyer and Stacey Snider reminded Messier of the line in their contracts that said they would never have a superior in the group's hierarchy. They threatened to walk. According to sources at Canal Plus, Meyer brought to bear all the negotiating skills he had acquired at Creative Artists during his days as one of Hollywood's top agents and won himself an annual salary, guaranteed for five years, that was said to exceed $10 million. Snider also negotiated herself a rich deal. But what they really wanted was equity. The options they had been granted in 2000, with an exercise price of nearly €80, were now far out of the money.* To prevent a mass walkout of his Hollywood talent, Messier had authorized a new grant of options in October 2001 with a strike price of €48. But now the stock of available options was bare. He promised Meyer and Snider that they would be first in line as soon as he received a new authorization at the annual meeting in April. He planned to ask for the power to give away options of more than 5 percent of Vivendi Universal's share. He promised that 80 percent of the options would be guarded/held back for vital U.S. executives.

None of these hidden costs to the USA Networks transaction were outlined to the board of directors on Friday, December 14, 2001. As the meeting dragged on, continually interrupted by technical problems with the video link to Paris, Messier began to grow impatient, cutting short Jacques Friedmann, Jean-Marc Espalioux, and others when their questions grew too detailed. Time was passing, Messier said. Twice, he told them, he had had to postpone a telephone call with John Malone. Diller too was hopping up and down and needed to know what was happening. It was time to move to a vote, he said. By then, the board members assembled in Paris had learned that the legal documents that had been unavailable at the start of the meeting had just been found. They were on their way to them now. By the time the documents arrived, the decision had been taken. The Vivendi Universal board formally approved the purchase of the entertainment assets of USA Networks. Messier had been forced to push harder for victory than he might have liked, but he had won. Now, with Diller at his side, the conquest of the U.S. media industry could really begin.

---

*Following the completion of the merger with Seagram, Vivendi Universal introduced three stock option programs covering 29.4 million shares and representing around 2.7 percent of its share capital. On December 11, 2000, Vivendi Universal issued 10.9 million share options to 3,681 employees with a nondiscounted strike price of €78.6. At the same time, it started an "outperformance" option plan, issuing 5.2 million options to ninety-one "principal managers," also with a strike price of €78.6. Under the third plan, granted on October 10, 2001, it issued 2,816 employees 13.3 million options with a nondiscounted strike price of €48.2. (See Vivendi Universal 2001 20-F, p. 91.)

CHAPTER SEVEN

# The French Exception

On Monday, December 17, 2001, the lobby of the St. Regis Hotel in New York was thick with television crews. Messier looked radiant. Diller was at his side, looking indifferent to the flashing cameras and burning arc lights, unmoved even at the prospect of becoming the only person ever to run three Hollywood studios. While Messier stood there beaming in the reflected glory of the Hollywood legend, Diller dictated to photographers that there would be no handshake. Too demeaning. "We're going to stand here next to each other, happy, and things like that," Diller said. Moments later, he instructed Messier, "Okay, start and I'll join you."

"At that precise moment, U.S. investors finally recognized Vivendi Universal as a tier one media company," Messier said later that week. Nothing could spoil his triumph. Not even the electricity cut in the middle of his presentation. Not even the French journalist who asked about the risks of the "Americanization of French cinema." He brushed him off: "On your Franco-French movie industry question," Messier replied, "may I just say that as, as we all know and as we all understand, the Franco-French *exception culturelle* is dead. . . . The anxiety underlined there is totally artificial and has no basis."

The exchange between the two Frenchmen appeared to have no resonance at all for the assembled U.S. media, who had little sense of the impact the comment would have on Messier's career and on the stability of the company. The conference had moved rapidly back to Diller, which was where Messier wanted to keep it. The *Washington Post* correspondent welcomed Diller back to the media big leagues: "As a former head of Paramount and Fox, this deal puts you back up at the power level of folks like Michael Eisner [chairman of Walt Disney] and Dick Parsons [who replaced Gerald Levin as the head of AOL Time Warner]. How does it feel to be back?" Diller replied with characteristic charm: "I never felt I went very far away but you can all have your little ideas about that."

Others asked why Vivendi Universal was buying back businesses Edgar Bronfman Jr. had sold just three years before. Diller explained that when he and Bronfman negotiated the original transaction, the intention was for the assets to increase in value, and that when he ceased to be chief executive, Seagram, and Vivendi Universal as its successor, would have a "path to control" that would enable the film and television assets to be put back together. The unexpectedly rapid pace of consolidation in the industry had accelerated the repatriation of the assets, he said. How would Diller both be chairman of VUE and run his own public company, to be renamed USA Interactive after the sale of USA Networks? "The truth is you can't chop time in percentages. . . . That's not real."

Finally, it came to the last question from the floor. "And what about the reporting relationship?" someone asked. The room went quiet. "Maybe I missed this earlier," the journalist continued, "but what is the reporting relationship, Mr. Diller? Who do you report to?" Diller scowled. It evidently pained him to answer. "Who does who . . . ?" he said. "Me?" pointing a finger at his own chest. He then pointed toward Messier. "Him. Directly. Okay." Ignoring the fact that Messier was ready for the next question, Diller motioned for the conference to come to an end. "That's it. Thank you all very much." The room had dissolved into hysterical laughter. "What?" Diller shouted. "Did I do that wrong?" Everyone in the room was aware of what it had cost Diller to admit that he would now be reporting to Messier. "Will Messier be the next media mogul?" the cover of *Fortune* had asked in September. In Messier's mind, they had just been given the answer. Even Barry Diller had bowed to the new king. That was not a press conference; it was a coronation.

"Did you say that? Did you really say that?" Catherine Gros, Messier's director of communications, was waiting at the door of the conference room. Her beehive haircut and childlike face disguised a sharp mind. Someone had alerted her a few minutes earlier. Unusually, she had decided not to stay for the whole meeting. How could she have known that her boss, so accustomed to talking to the press, would make such a mistake? "Did you really say that the Franco-French cultural exception was dead?" she insisted. "I don't know. I can't remember. Don't bore me with it. At any rate, it will help Pierre [Lescure] in his discussions with the government and the French filmmakers," replied Messier, sweeping away her objections with his hands. "I take no responsibility for the consequences," she replied.

Catherine Tasca, France's Socialist culture minister, could not care less about Killer Diller. She did mind intensely that the front pages of all the French newspapers were devoted to hysterical predictions of a crisis in French cinema. "Fear of French filmakers," splashed *Libération* across its front page. Messier's casually uttered death sentence—"The Franco-French cultural exception is dead"—was read by filmmakers and the *gauche caviar* as a declaration of war. At Canal Plus, the mood was bleak. When Pierre Lescure and Denis Olivennes saw the reactions in the papers on Tuesday morning, their worst fears were confirmed. What chance had they now of introducing more flexibility into the system of cinema subsidies that was weighing so heavily on their business? By the end of 2001, the station was funneling nearly €150 million a year toward the French film industry. Over the past few weeks they had been negotiating with the culture ministry and filmmakers' associations to reduce Canal Plus's financial obligations and programming quotas. The chain had to spend 20 percent of its French turnover, amounting to some €1.5 billion in 2001, on buying rights to films, nearly half of which had to be made in France.* In addition, at least 40 percent of all films shown on Canal Plus in 2001 had to be French, and at least 60 percent had to be European, leaving little airtime left for the most commercially attractive movies from the United States.[1]

Even the most ardent cinemaphiles recognized this as a stringent requirement. As a condition of being allowed to merge with Vivendi in December 2000, Canal Plus had reaffirmed its commitment to the support system for four more years. Lescure and Olivennes had been softening the creative community up for the worst. The system could not continue in its present form after 2004. Canal Plus's results had started to deteriorate: subscriber numbers fell in France in 2001 for the first time in the group's seventeen-year history. "You've got to be more aggressive," Messier told Olivennes, reminding him of how he had won a reduction in the cost of Vivendi Universal's third-generation mobile telephone license fee by simply withholding payment to the finance ministry. "Depardieu will chain himself to the railings of the Élysée. Anything can happen when French cinema is at risk," Olivennes replied with some irritation. How often had they explained to Messier the passion with which policy makers would defend the French filmmaking community from dying out like the denizens of Italy's Cinecitta? With more than 70 percent of all French films financed by Canal Plus, the fate of an industry was at stake. Furthermore, the timing of his comment was terrible. It is traditional during preelection periods for the French movie industry to seek promises from the competing Socialist and conservative coalitions that the "cultural exception" will be maintained. In that sense, then, with both legislative and presidential elections taking place in the spring,

---

*In addition, a minimum of 12 percent of its turnover needed to go toward European productions, and a minimum of 9 percent toward French productions. At least three-quarters of the French films should be independent, a restriction that Canal Plus executives argued meant they were being forced to buy low-budget movies few people wanted to see. (See communiqué issued by the ministry of culture on January 4, 2002, titled "Decrees Concerning Rules Applicable to the Different Categories of Television Channel.")

the uproar over Messier's remark served the protectionist lobby perfectly.

Between December 17 and 20, 2001, according to a poll carried out by TNS Media Intelligence, Messier's comment about the cultural exception was cited eighty-two times in French radio and television broadcasts. The cultural establishment had never much liked Messier. It now let fly. Artists, politicians, editorial writers, and intellectuals queued up to denounce the notion that French culture should no longer be protected by the state. They accused Messier of selling out to Hollywood, of being the puppet of Jack Valenti, president of the Motion Picture Association of America, the Hollywood lobby that had for years campaigned against European cultural protectionism. The most vocal attacks came from the artists and film producers themselves. One of their representatives, Pascal Rogard, accused Messier of "spitting in the face of French politicians and cinema professionals" and regretted the "Americanization" of what was once a fine French company. Claudie Ossard, producer of the hugely successful *Amélie,* asserted that Messier's statement was "suicidal" at a time when French cinema was doing well thanks to the system of state support. None of the movies she had produced, Ossard added, including *Delicatessen* and *Arizona Dream,* could have been made without the French cultural exception. Another movie director, Chilean-born Raoul Ruiz, who made *Time Regained* and *Three Lives and Only One Death* in France after fleeing the CIA-backed coup against Salvador Allende, said: "Jean-Marie Messier is behaving like the head of an American studio, and no one should be surprised."

Philip H. Gordon, director of the Brookings Institution's Center for the U.S. and France, argued that the uproar was a reminder of the limits to France's adaptation to globalization. It showed that France was not prepared to sit back and accept all aspects of an Americanized world. The cultural exception did not really ensure the success of French cinema, it just ensured that cinema did not entirely disappear in France, as it more or less had in other European countries. "The real point is not whether French cinema can compete with Hollywood or whether most of the subsidised French films are any good. If a relatively tiny government subsidy for French cinema is what it takes to ensure its diversity—so that films such as *Amélie* or last year's enjoyable comedy *Le Placard* are produced, rather than only US productions—it seems a small price to pay. And if a consequence of this is to reassure the French about the effects of globalisation, even better. Messier, who has probably benefited more than any other French citizen from the country's adaptation to globalisation over the past decade, should know that as well as anyone. *Vive l'exception culturelle.*"[2]

David Kessler, the head of France's National Center for Cinematography, the wing of the ministry of culture responsible for administering the system of financial support, said the French were justifiably upset at Messier's comment.[3] "French people worry a lot about their protection system. We see it with their reaction, even overreaction, to Jean-Marie Messier's comment. But just look at the European film industry: there are some film cultures that were very, very rich that were destroyed in just a few years. There were some tremendous filmmakers in Italy. Now, of course, you have Moretti or Benigni, but you have no more movie tradition in Italy. And it's more or less the case in Germany or England. The only country that was able to protect its movie industry was France because it had this system. When television threatened the movie industry, it was decided that television would give money to save movies. When there are new dangers we must react very quickly because in two or three years, the tissue in which movies can develop can be destroyed. We think quotas are necessary in a world that is not equal. The power and force of the U.S. industry is very dangerous for the others."

Political leaders from the Communists, Greens, and Socialists on the Left, all the way to the Conservative Rally for the Republic and the far-right National Front, condemned Messier.* Defending France from cultural globalization and Americanization was a popular position in the run-up to that spring's parliamentary and presidential elections. Catherine Tasca told parliament, "We all know that French cinema needs Canal Plus, but I would like to

---

*Only the free-market Liberal Party's presidential candidate, Alain Madelin, who then had about 5 percent in the polls, defended Messier.

point out that Canal Plus has become the broadcaster it is today thanks to cinema.* The cultural exception, the defense of cultural diversity, is neither a Franco-French fantasy, an invention of politicians, nor an archaism. It's the basis of public support for the arts to free them from the laws of the market. This is a proposal by a businessman who is developing his group on the other side of the Atlantic and definitely not the policy of this government or of this country." Her rebuke was applauded by the Right, which had defended French culture no less vigorously when it was in power before 1997. President Jacques Chirac also lashed out at Messier: "To consider works of art and cultural goods as ordinary merchandise is a profound mental aberration." The president had been astonished by Messier's breach of the golden rule of French diplomatic etiquette: a French diplomatic position could be criticized at home, but never abroad. Chirac's criticism was all the more devastating for being delivered directly to around five hundred journalists invited to the Elysée Palace to receive his best wishes for the New Year. There were few clearer ways of telling the world that Messier was a marked man.

Tasca, a close ally of Pierre Lescure's and a former executive of Canal Plus, rallied the rest of the government behind her in her efforts to force Messier to climb down. She had not forgotten his faux pas at the Aix-en-Provence opera festival, of which the Vivendi Universal chief executive had recently become chairman. "Be our guest whenever you like," Messier had said to the minister, forgetting that the ministry of culture had supported the festival since its inception. Tasca needed no return invitation from a puffed-up businessman. It now looked as though Messier just wanted to shine in the United States, to rub shoulders with media moguls like Diller, to be more American than the Americans. In the prime minister's office, a number of people felt betrayed. Lionel

---

*Canal Plus describes itself as the "cinema channel" and says cinema "is at the heart of the station." It shows around 400 films a year, of which 350 are in first exclusivity (a year after their theatrical release). Eighty percent of the films shown on Canal Plus have not been previously released on television, and fifty percent will not subsequently be reshown on any other channel.

Jospin sounded out his cabinet. The Socialist government wanted to send a reassuring signal to the filmmaking groups that were whipping the media into an anti-American, anti-Messier frenzy. One week after the meeting in the St. Regis Hotel, on Monday, December 24, the government retaliated. It ordered a probe into whether Vivendi Universal's large number of U.S. shareholders breached French media ownership laws. The French broadcasting regulator said it would ask France's highest administrative court, the Conseil d'Etat, to rule on the matter.

Messier struggled to hold his temper. He had been quoted out of context, he claimed. He confirmed that he had said "The Franco-French cultural exception is dead." But he maintained that he had added: "We are now in a period of cultural diversity. What does that mean? It means we must be both global and national. Vivendi's interest is to be both a major American player and to have Canal Plus and Studio Canal as pillars of the French movie industry." He had been subjected to a "false trial," he claimed in an interview with the left-of-center Paris daily *Libération*. "To describe me or Vivendi as a defender of the homogenization of culture is scandalous. "I know that we are in an electoral period, but even so . . ." The idea of counting Vivendi Universal's U.S. shareholders was nonsense, he spluttered. Vivendi Universal was a French company, domiciled in France, subject to French law. There was no merit in the government's argument, and he could not possibly accept a cap on U.S. investment in Vivendi Universal. To do so would make a mockery of all his attempts to attract the U.S. media investors who best understood the entertainment industry. It would undermine Vivendi Universal's recent listing on the New York Stock Exchange, its laborious adoption of U.S. accounting standards, and its success in attracting investment coverage by the same media analysts who followed the giant American media groups.

"What came over him? How could he make such a blunder?" In early January 2002, over dinner at Siècle, the club patronized by the leading Parisian businessmen, bankers, and media personalities, *l'affaire Messier* was, as ever, the main topic of conversation. Times had changed since the days when few dared voice their worries in the open. Martin Bouygues, chairman of the Bouygues conglomerate, felt vindicated. He had seen an early warning in Messier's attempt to strong-arm the French government into lowering the cost of mobile telephone licenses in September 2001. Messier had withheld a payment toward the €5 billion cost of a license to force the government to lower the fee he had agreed to at the start of the year.* Laurent Fabius, France's finance minister, had already promised the money to the state retirement fund. The former prime minister did not appreciate being forced to negotiate under pressure and gave Messier a choice: pay up by 10 P.M. or suffer a 10-percent fine on top of the fee. Messier backed down. Humiliated by the loss of face, he continued to claim credit for the government's subsequent reduction in the price of the licenses.† He had "shaken the tree," Vivendi Universal said. However, most commentators agreed that it was in fact Martin Bouygues who had persuaded Fabius to lower the price of the licenses by simply refusing to bid at all. After Messier accused Bouygues of a "Stalinlike rewriting of history," the jovial industrialist hit back. He wrote Messier a letter (that happened to find its way onto the front page of *Le Monde*) suggesting he pay a visit to a psychiatrist.

Since moving to New York in September 2001, Messier seemed to have forgotten how France worked. The truth was that he was in the throes of a real love affair with America. On the family's first day in Manhattan, Messier had walked across the Brooklyn Bridge with his children and visited the River Cafe, where they took pictures of each other against the skyline of lower Manhattan. His appearance started to change. The casual loafers that he had worn since the Ecole Polytechnique and the brown suits that had been de rigueur for negotiating local French water contracts were replaced by snazzy ensembles from the smartest New York department stores. Within weeks, he acquired what would become a permanent tan, lost twenty pounds, and abandoned his boyish puddingbowl haircut for a quiff. New York encouraged a princely lifestyle

---

*The license was held by SFR, which was 80 percent owned by Cegetel.
†The license fee was reduced to €619 million flat fee and a 1-percent levy on turnover. Bouygues accepted a license on the revised terms.

unthinkable in France, where public displays of wealth are strongly discouraged. In Paris, a Renault Espace had served the Messiers well, but a New York media mogul needed something with a little more oomph. Like an Airbus. Before long, Messier had ordered one of the larger corporate jets, the A319, to be added to Seagram's fleet of Gulfstream IVs, helicopters, and sundry other aircraft. Messier was soon sprinting up the New York social ladder. The fact that some still associated the Messier name only with the New York Rangers hockey star, Mark, was tiresome, but he turned it to his advantage and it became his stock self-deprecating joke, the perfect icebreaker for his ever more frequent public speeches.

Messier boasted of being the first Frenchman to enter the inner sanctum of American business—the board of the New York Stock Exchange—where he preened alongside domestic goddess Martha Stewart and AOL Time Warner executive Gerald Levin.* He joined that other baron of extravagance, Dennis Koslowski, the subsequently disgraced chief executive of Tyco, on the board of trustees of the Whitney Museum of American Art. He became chairman of the media center of the Museum of Television and Radio in New York and ran a none-too-discreet campaign for a spot on the board of the Metropolitan Opera. Even Messier's wife, Antoinette, picked up a board seat at the New York Philharmonic. As ever, the line between personal and corporate philanthropy was undefined. What was good for Messier was good for Vivendi Universal, and vice versa. As a media group that owned several classical record labels and needed the goodwill of various creative communities, Vivendi's patronage of the arts and philanthropy was certainly consistent with its marketing strategy and corporate goals. Even so, many felt Messier's personal role was excessive. "The breadth of his growing involvement is rare even for the most civic-minded corporate titan," commented *The New York Times.* "Mr. Messier's smooth entrée into New York is one of the clearest examples of how an outsider with financial resources, status and

---

*Martha Stewart resigned from the NYSE on October 16, 2002, following a U.S. Department of Justice investigation into alleged insider trading in the shares of a pharmaceutical company, ImClone Systems.

connections can penetrate the city's inner circle of culture and philanthropy, even as his corporate leadership comes under severe attack."[4]

Even the most cynical of New York media pundits, Michael
Wolff of the *New York Magazine,* was surprised by Messier's delu-
sions of grandeur: "Not long ago, as I was walking on Madison
Avenue in my mogul neighborhood with Steven, my 10-year-old,
who was shopping for an ice-cream cone, we saw a figure who
prompted Steven, not unjaded in the ways of his neighbors' personal
excesses, to exclaim, 'Look at that guy!' There was, languorously
moving up Madison Avenue, a small man, with a coat cast cape-
like over his shoulders, and the most pleased-with-himself expres-
sion I believe I have ever seen on an adult, whom I recognized to
be Jean-Marie Messier (I quite doubt anyone else recognized him).
He occupied a wide swathe of the sidewalk, with a strut to the
left and then a strut to the right, nodding and smiling, or rather
bestowing blessings, on passers-by (who gave him wide and in-
credulous berth). He seemed to see himself as some combination of
religious figure and maestro—his idea, I suppose, of an American
mogul. (Not something, of course, you could see yourself as if
what you are is a CEO of a water and sewer company.) I do not
think he would have considered spontaneous applause to be out
of order."[5]

When the first aircraft crashed into the World Trade Center on
the morning of September 11, Messier was the host of a New York
power breakfast, half schmoozing, half being schmoozed, in the
company of Paul Montrone, chairman of the Metropolitan Opera,
and John J. Veronis, chairman of boutique media investment bank
Veronis Suhler Stevenson and also a director of the opera company. The combination of guests was revealing: a full representation of deal making and philanthropy. Like many other people,
Messier raced to turn on CNN and watched the second plane ex-
plode inside the south tower. The attacks, just days after his arrival, heightened his desire for acceptance in a city suddenly less
welcoming to outsiders, especially those from countries that
chafed at the "You're either with us or against us" ultimatum of
the Bush administration. He started to wear a brooch—not just in

his jacket buttonhole but also in the lapel of his overcoat—that was composed of intertwined French and American national flags, instead of the discreet red pin denoting membership in France's Legion of Honor. He announced he was creating a forum for mutual understanding, based on regular discussions between celebrity intellectuals such as Francis Fukuyama, the U.S. political scientist; Samuel Huntington, author of the fashionable *Clash of Civilizations;* Salman Rushdie, the British writer under *fatwah* since the 1980s; and the French philosopher Luc Ferry. He also commissioned a film made up of eleven shorts—each nine minutes, eleven seconds long and drawn from eleven different countries—to highlight the diversity of national responses to the terrorist attacks.

Back in Paris, the crude anti-Americanism that had greeted the first months of the Bush administration vanished for a while. *Le Monde* ran a headline across its front page saying, "We Are All Americans Now." But the truce did not last, and the high priests of French anti-Americanism soon returned. The Franco-American relationship started to head toward one of its periodic crises. Jean-Pierre Chevènement, a left-wing nationalist who once claimed that the United States was dedicated to "the organized cretinization of the French people" and who, as defense minister in 1991, walked out on President François Mitterrand for supporting George H. W. Bush's Gulf War, was rising fast in the polls for the forthcoming presidential elections. Messier fell victim to the anti-Americanism that burgeoned during the first weeks of the war in Afghanistan that winter. France was having a bad war. The *Charles de Gaulle,* France's only aircraft carrier, conked out with a broken propeller and had to limp back to port. The U.S.-bound shoe bomber Richard Reid dodged the interior ministry's Plan Vigipirate at Paris's Roissy Airport. Between fifty and a hundred al-Qaeda–supporting French nationals were reportedly on the run in Afghanistan. Zaccarias Moussaoui, a Frenchman of Moroccan origin suspected of being the "twentieth hijacker," and other French citizens held at Guantanamo Bay in Cuba, faced a U.S. death penalty whose morality France fiercely contested. Meanwhile, Tony Blair appeared to have seized political and military leadership of Europe.

The French establishment consequently attacked George W.

Bush's "Axis of Evil" speech with gusto. Socialist foreign minister Hubert Védrine dismissed it as "absurd." Lionel Jospin, the only European prime minister to let rip in public, insinuated that the United States did not understand the lessons of its own tragedy: "The world's problems cannot be reduced to the struggle against terrorism, however vital that may be. Nor can such problems be solved by overwhelming military power." The days of France quietly tagging along with the "war against terror" did not last long. The "a bully with a bloody nose is still a bully" camp returned to the ascendant, fortified by daily reports of civilian deaths in Afghanistan. Messier suffered from seeming neither French in France nor American in the United States. "If you were not talking about New York, you got the impression you were wasting his time," one Parisian executive said. Some advised Messier to appoint a deputy to calm things down in Paris, to take the focus away from the overexposed Yankee chief executive. Messier briefly considered promoting either Agnès Touraine, head of Vivendi Universal Publishing, or Philippe Germond, the head of Cegetel, but demurred. He had never shared power and had only just succeeded in dislodging Edgar Bronfman Jr. He would lead Vivendi Universal single-handedly and saw no difficulty in managing a transatlantic group: the headquarters would just have to be wherever he happened to be.

As a consequence, Vivendi Universal's Paris head office started to feel like a provincial outpost of an American company, rather than the beating heart of a global French media company. The investor-relations department and press office in Paris found themselves lacking the most elementary factual information about the company's activities: "Let's wait until after 3 P.M. when we can talk to New York," would be a refrain that infuriated European and particularly French analysts and media. Rumors circulated that Messier intended to redomicile Vivendi Universal in the United States so that it could buy a network like NBC, and that he was contemplating taking U.S. citizenship, just as Rupert Murdoch had done upon acquiring Fox. Messier would deny any such intention: "I'm proud of being a New Yorker—even more so after 9-11—and I'm proud to have my family living here. We are a global group. I'm the French chairman and CEO of a global group." Yet at the same time, his continual gibes at the parochialism of France dented national amour propre: "I love my city of Paris but New York City has been my favorite town for many, many years," he told *The New York Times.* "Paris is where the company is headquartered. But what is for sure is that when I'm attending a French establishment dinner, my reaction is, O.K., it's always the same people, always the same faces. I like very much in New York that you have new faces every time, and I'm really trying to meet with new people."[6]

For Pierre Lescure, everything had changed. For the past six years, since taking over from André Rousselet, the chairman of Canal Plus had enjoyed increasingly close relations with Messier. Their ties grew stronger following the merger. Lescure had thrown in his lot with Messier and had acted as a guarantor of Messier's good intentions in cultural and political circles. Over the years Messier had fallen under Lescure's spell. The son of Communist intellectuals, Lescure had an encyclopedic knowledge of French and American popular culture and had once had an affair with Catherine Deneuve. For the first year following the completion of the merger in December 2000, he had put his network of friends and acquaintances at Messier's disposal. A grateful Messier praised Lescure to all who would listen. "When Pierre leaves, I shall also leave," he would say. Since Messier's move to New York, however, nothing had been the same. Lescure's influence in the introspective New York media community was minimal. At the same time, Messier began to lose confidence that Lescure and Olivennes were serious about turning around Canal Plus's financial performance. In November 2001, Lescure had sent him a budget yet again postponing the group's breakeven. For the first time in ages, it appeared that Messier was focusing on the prosaic, unglamorous problems of one of Vivendi Universal's businesses. Canal Plus was hemorrhaging cash: it would lose almost half a billion euros in 2001. It was unacceptable. He sent the budget back three times before telling them: "Everything has to be renegotiated."

What was only a presentiment in November became reality for

the chairman of Canal Plus in December, when he learned of the purchase of USA Networks and the appointment of Barry Diller. Pierre Lescure wondered what his own role would be. Would he still be responsible for cooperation between the American and European studios, as planned at the time of the merger? Messier remained silent. He did not answer until the press conference of December 17, 2001: Diller would be in charge of U.S. film and television. "What will Pierre Lescure become?" a journalist inquired, noticing the president of Canal Plus in the front row of the auditorium. "I will answer for him," Messier replied. Henceforth Lescure would be limited to Canal Plus in Europe. The next day, Lescure's friends commiserated with him. But none of them could refrain from reminding him of their doubts at the time of the merger: "You see, we were right, Messier has betrayed us, betrayed you." In his office, Messier was enraged: "All this business about the cultural exception is a put-up job," he shouted to anyone who would listen. He suspected Lescure and his friends of whipping up the frenzy. "The filmmakers are such hypocrites," Messier said during a small committee meeting. "They promote cultural problems in order to protect their own tiny financial interests." As for the politicians and businessmen who had also criticized him, they were just jealous of his success. France really was just an "exotic little country," he declared in Los Angeles a few days later.

No one in his circle said a word. Anyone willing to voice criticism had long since been excluded from the management team to make way for courtiers and yes-men. Only the Dream Team had access to Messier: Eric Licoys, Catherine Gros, Guillaume Hannezo, Agnès Touraine, and Philippe Germond. But even they struggled to make him realize he had to step out of the limelight until things calmed down. "The group has a communication problem. We must explain ourselves," Messier said. He asked Maurice Lévy, chief executive of Publicis, to help. The two men had met during the privatization program in 1986, when Messier was still an adviser to Edouard Balladur, the finance minister. Over the years, Générale des Eaux had become one of the French advertising group's largest clients, with a budget larger than that of the car manufacturers Peugeot or Renault. Lévy had become his closest external adviser, but even he felt Messier had stopped listening. Lévy prepared an advertising campaign: "Cultural exceptions? No, exceptional men," proclaimed his billboards, against portraits of Picasso, Dalí, Louis Armstrong, and Mozart. At the beginning of January, Lévy unveiled the prints. Agnès Touraine gave her approval, Pierre Lescure said nothing, and Denis Olivennes vociferously opposed them. "You really have no idea what culture means," he told Messier. His opinion was ignored. Only when Agnès Touraine changed her mind was the campaign shelved.

If there was to be no advertising campaign, at least there would be an interview in *Paris Match*. Messier wanted to reply to his detractors, to explain his move to New York, to affirm his support for French cinema, and to settle his differences with the business community. He also wanted a chance to deny the rumors that he was having an affair with the French actress Sophie Marceau. As Vivendi Universal's shares continued to fall in the new year, the executive suite at the Park Avenue office focused on making sure all was perfect for the *Paris Match* interview. An appointment was made with the magazine's photographers, and on January 8, 2002, the day after a bungled share placement had sent the stock price plummeting and frazzled investor nerves, Messier spent the afternoon ice-skating in front of the *Paris Match* photographers.

After trying a few shots at the Rockefeller Center skating rink, the party decamped to the rink in Central Park, which offered better shots of the Manhattan skyline. There, however, they were frustrated to discover that the operator of the rink wanted written evidence of insurance before he would allow the *Paris Match* cameras. As the afternoon twilight faded, they waited in the park while a search party returned to the office. Faxes flew back and forth between Paris and New York. Messier became incandescent with rage. Finally the precious piece of paper was located, but by then it was too dark to take the photos. The skating rink would be rented again at first light. A fortnight later, just as Vivendi Universal's share price suffered one of its steepest falls, the Parisian business world was amazed to discover Messier once more on the cover of *Paris Match,* twirling alone on the ice, in the pale light of dawn.

"You're going at it too hard. You need less exposure for yourself and for your group. You shouldn't try to be the sole embodiment of Vivendi Universal, particularly just now. The market has shifted. It is not behind you anymore." Once again Georges Ralli, the managing director of Lazard in Paris and a long-standing adviser, was trying to get through to Messier. The interview in *Paris Match* had done him considerable harm, Ralli said. He was turning into a laughingstock. He should stop provoking everyone. However powerful he might be, he still needed support. Messier hardly heard what he said. He had heard it all before. The small world of French business could think what it liked. He did not care. They were always scared of their own shadows, they hated anything that stood out, that showed a bit of spirit. His mind was elsewhere. He was preoccupied with supervising the preparations for the Davos World Economic Forum, which would, exceptionally, be held in New York to help the city recover from the trauma of the September 11 attacks. Messier was one of the coorganizers of the event, and would host the opening party in the Grand Ballroom of the Waldorf-Astoria.

On January 31, in the late afternoon, the area around the Waldorf-Astoria in New York was blue with police. There was an undercurrent of defiant celebration at the gathering, the first large meeting of the international business elite since the September attacks. Barriers barred traffic for blocks around the landmark nineteenth-century hotel, keeping antiglobalization protesters at bay, while guards checked the cameras, laptops, and cell phones of the celebrity participants. Everyone who was anyone was there: Bill Clinton, Dick Cheney, Colin Powell, the German chancellor, the British prime minister, the secretary-general of the UN, Archbishop Desmond Tutu, the most influential investment bankers, the most powerful businessmen, and the cream of the international media. Messier knew them all. It seemed as if it was all for him, a welcome party for a king. He had invited dozens of artists, many of them signed to Universal, to sing for his guests, among them

Bono from U2, India.Arie, Lauryn Hill, Ravi Shankar, and Youssou N'Dour. What a cornucopia of cultural diversity he had provided—there was even a duet by an Algerian and an Israeli. How removed he felt from those small-minded Parisian coteries. If only they could see him now! Sure, Bono had called him a "corporate motherfucker," but he meant it in the nicest possible way. . . .

## CHAPTER EIGHT

# Speeding Up

On December 13, 2001, Guillaume Hannezo felt he had no choice but to write Jean-Marie Messier a personal plea. "I've got the unpleasant feeling of being in a car whose driver is speeding up into the bends and that I'm in the death seat." Unbeknownst to investors and to the board, which would meet the next day to rubberstamp the acquisition of USA Networks, Vivendi Universal had barely escaped being downgraded by credit-rating agencies. Such a step would have made it difficult for the company to borrow money and would have plunged it into a cash crisis. Hannezo knew all too well why this had happened. It had become a habit, almost a drug: every day, Messier would sit in front of his computer and buy Vivendi Universal shares. While the board had approved his purchases of companies, it had no idea of the full extent of his spending spree. This was because Messier never told it about his reckless purchase of Vivendi Universal's own shares at a total cost of over €10 billion to the already highly indebted company. These share buybacks must go down as one of the single most stupid decisions ever made by a major European chief executive.

Strictly speaking, these shares purchases were legal: the annual general meeting of shareholders had authorized buybacks up to a maximum of 10 percent of the company's share capital. The transactions were executed on Messier's personal authority by two mid-level employees in the finance department, Hubert Dupont

Lhotelian and Francois Blondet. "The board delegated this authority to me and to me alone," Messier would later say. "There was nothing illegal about it." Nonetheless, numerous board members have expressed incomprehension as to why they were not made fully aware of colossal gambles on the stock market. At first, Messier justified his purchases by pointing to the need to build up a supply of shares that he could draw on to cover employee stock-option grants, instead of creating new shares that would dilute the existing capital base. However, just a fifth of the shares repurchased would easily have sufficed to meet obligations to employees under stock-option programs. Only 21 million out of the 104 million shares in treasury stock at the end of 2001, then worth €6.3 billion, were destined for this purpose. Most options Vivendi Universal had issued were in any case unlikely to be exercised in the foreseeable future because of the crash in the share price.

The main motive for the buybacks was simply to support the share price. Messier had taken to mopping up Vivendi Universal shares in the market in a vain effort to stanch the flood of selling. The former investment banker had always been obsessed with Vivendi's share price, admitting to checking his Bloomberg and Reuters terminals at least ten times a day. "It's the health bulletin of Vivendi. . . . To face up to the challenges of globalization and new technologies, businesses need to make more and more acquisitions. They can't pay cash for companies which are worth hundreds of billions of dollars. Their cash is their shares. The higher that price, the greater its capacity to develop," he said. The share price, in his opinion, was also a daily vote of confidence in him, his management, and his strategy. From 1994 until mid-2000, the market had voted in his favor. His early years at Générale des Eaux had provided a textbook example of how to set about restructuring an unwieldy continental European conglomerate. Vivendi had been held up as the French equivalent of Nokia in Finland or Mannesmann in Germany, both stodgy conglomerates that had refocused on high-growth industries. The share price anticipated miracles. It had risen from €25 at the time of his appointment as chairman in June 1996 to €150 in the spring of 2000. The former civil servants at the head of other big French groups had looked enviously at the young star, who knew better than anyone how to express himself in the new jargon of "shareholder value," "synergy," and "focus."

But since the merger with Seagram, something had gone wrong. During 2001, Vivendi Universal fared marginally better than its peers in the media and telecommunications sector, but the share price continued to drift downhill. From €115 at the time the Seagram merger was negotiated in June 2000, it had fallen to €75 at the birth of the group in December 2000, and it was continuing to weaken. Managed from Paris, the campaign to attract big U.S. shareholders had failed. In large part, this was because the flurry of acquisitions had raised questions about the group's strategy. Few felt sure they knew in which direction the Vivendi Universal deal machine was pointing or when it would stop. "With Messier, you'd only have to pass him in the street and he'd say, 'I've done a deal,'" said News Corp. chairman Rupert Murdoch. Messier struggled to understand this skepticism. All his experience as a company director since leaving Lazard in late 1994 had been gained during the economic boom and unbridled optimism of the mid- to late-1990s. Now he was wrestling with a bear market that could prove fatal to his plans. If his shares lost their purchasing power, the whole project to transform the group would be jeopardized. By March 2001, the same analysts who months before had valued Vizzavi at €40 billion were sending out research notes saying it was worthless. Cegetel and Canal Plus too were rapidly losing their value as the telecom and media boom faded.

At the start of 2001, Vivendi Universal already owned 5.5 percent of its own shares. In May 2001, the share repurchases started to accelerate. Edgar M. Bronfman Sr. and his brother Charles decided to take the first opportunity to sell some of their shares in Vivendi Universal. "We took a lot of cash off the table," Edgar Bronfman Jr. would later say. Fearing Vivendi Universal's share price would wilt if they sold in the market, Messier agreed to buy back 1.6 percent of the company from the Bronfmans for €1.3 billion. At one level, Messier welcomed their decision: under the terms of the shareholder agreement, the family would progressively lose their rights to board seats as they sold down their stake.

Yet, at another level, he knew that it sent a negative signal to the market that his largest shareholders were dumping their stock. As the half-year reporting deadline approached, Messier on June 28 canceled 22 million shares and sold a further 10 million of the shares he had repurchased. But even after this reduction to its treasury stock, the company still held 6.4 percent of its own shares at the half year. The impact on the share price had been imperceptible. The strain on the group's balance sheet would become clear only later. By mid-2001, Vivendi Universal's net debt had risen to €32.5 billion. Messier was putting on debt at the rate of around €1 billion a month. Yet, as the second half of the year got under way, the share buybacks started again, this time from the other side of the Atlantic.

Messier had arrived in New York on September 2, 2001, to lead a vast seduction campaign targeted at U.S. investors, individuals as well as institutions. The New York media had queued up to welcome the man *Business Week* had hailed as "the most ambitious empire builder since Napoleon Bonaparte." The climax of the first ten days was to have been an appearance on *The Charlie Rose Show,* PBS's flagship program, on September 11. But there would be no show that night. The terrorist attacks, and the swiftly following revelation of massive accounting fraud at Enron, definitively changed the investment climate on Wall Street, ending the decade-long bull market. Of the behemoths of the new economy, Vivendi Universal was the one that continued to flash up all the warning signs: large, complex, acquisitive, and audited by Arthur Andersen. Messier struggled to adapt to the new environment. He was now an object not of adulation but of suspicion. When financial markets reopened following the attacks on the World Trade Center, Vivendi Universal's shares sank to new lows, losing a third of their value as they fell below €40. To revive the faltering investor-relations campaign, Messier hired a top U.S. media analyst, Laura Martin of Crédit Suisse First Boston. Martin would fill the gap that had been embarrassingly created by the resignation of Ariane de Lamaze. The previous investor relations chief had left the company in haste, after declaring her worries about Vivendi

Universal's debt position in a memo to the executive committee with far too much frankness for Messier's liking.

A fortnight after the terrorist attacks, Messier announced that the group would acquire, quite officially this time, 3 percent of its share capital—almost exactly the same amount canceled or sold on June 28. The repurchased shares, he promised, would immediately be canceled, mechanically increasing earnings per share. The market responded well: many companies were taking advantage of the sudden dip in valuations to support their stock prices. The share price went back up above €50. However, to Hannezo's alarm, Messier acquired considerably more than the 3 percent announced to the market. The finance director dismissed the buy-backs as a waste of money: "It's artificial support. You can't fight the market," he told Messier on several occasions. Hannezo was worried that an alarming proportion of the group's cash and short-term credit was being tied up to no purpose. In December, tired of being ignored, he sent a memo to all the directors and the whole of the finance department, imposing bureaucratic obstacles that he hoped would slow Messier down: "Henceforth it is forbidden to buy shares in the group without a written authority from the chairman." Jean-Marie Messier understood the warning. He could no longer dip in and out of the stock as casually as a day trader or nudge the group treasurer to do it for him. Everything would have to be done by the book. Eventually Hannezo decided even to forbid his subordinates from taking the chief executive's phone calls in a last attempt to stop the gambling. "The atmosphere was one of sheer madness," said one insider.

Hannezo's warning came too late. By December 31, 2001, the group held 104 million of its own shares, representing 9.9 percent of its equity capital. According to Claude Bébéar, speaking in December 2002 in his capacity as the chairman of Vivendi Universal's newly created finance committee, "Over two and a half years, the group spent €11 billion repurchasing its own shares, at a loss of €5.3 billion." Messier would later deny that he had taken a speculative gamble on the company's stock. On the contrary, he claimed that the awesome arsenal of shares under his control gave him flexibility in negotiating favorable terms for yet more acquisitions. In the United States, receiving stock rather than cash in exchange for an asset is often more attractive from a tax perspective, enabling the buyer to offer less if he pays in shares.

But this argument was also somewhat spurious. In total, only around €2 billion of the accumulated stock was used for acquisitions. It had been used in the relatively trivial $372 million purchase of MP3.com, which had been half funded in shares. It had also been deployed to pay for John Malone's stake in USA Networks. "This is a man who is famous for never paying a dollar of tax on his transactions," Messier said of Malone. "Without these shares, we would never have reached a deal with him."[1] That was, of course, also untrue. Vivendi Universal could quite simply have created *new* shares to pay for these two deals, thereby avoiding any additional pressure on its balance sheet. But that would have been to break another promise: after the mammoth equity issuance needed to pay for Seagram and Canal Plus, Messier had pledged not to issue a single new Vivendi Universal share.

The steady fall in the share price caused Messier serious alarm. In happier times, the group had offered various important guarantees linked to the performance of the stock. Now he risked being trapped. Most important, Messier had made another massive stock market bet that Vivendi Universal shares would rise. He had sold a huge number of puts that left the company vulnerable to a fall in the share price. The buyers of these puts had the right to force Vivendi Universal to buy back some 23 million shares from them at an average price of €69. At the end of the year, Vivendi Universal's share price had hovered just above €60, but the more Vivendi Universal's share price fell over the following months, the more money the company would lose, with a theoretical maximum loss of €1.6 billion. Every month, cash would be put aside to cover the mounting losses. By mid-2002, when Vivendi Universal's shares had fallen to just above €10, the loss on the sale of these speculative puts looked likely to exceed €1 billion.

Similarly, some acquisitions had nasty claw-back clauses. For example, if Vivendi Universal's share price remained below $37.50 in New York for ten consecutive trading days, Messier would have to pay $250 million in compensation to the former owners of the Rondor Music record company. In good times, such clauses cost nothing. In bear markets, they were ruinous and created a vicious circle. The tumbling share price was also disastrous for Vivendi Universal's employee stock option and company savings plans. "I'll make you rich," Messier had promised Vivendi Universal's senior managers at their first meeting as a group, held in Orlando, Florida, in the spring of 2001. Most had received options in October 2001 with strike prices above €70, or the equivalent in dollars for U.S. employees. As the stock wilted, griping at Universal reached epidemic levels, prompting Barry Diller to lash out at option-obsessed company employees. "Shut up about the stock already," he said. "They literally talk about it all day long. They're depressed about it. Stocks won't rise for another two years."

Messier, however, wanted to keep his promise: he would make them rich. The share price had to recover. In late 2001, in the middle of this massive program of share buybacks, he decided to make a large personal investment in Vivendi Universal shares. He borrowed more than €5 million from Société Générale to exercise options at around €50 and invested a further €20 million of his own. "I put myself into debt to invest in the company because I believe in it," he said. The details of Messier's personal share dealings in late 2001 remain unclear. He has denied attempting to manipulate the share price for his own benefit. Nonetheless, the proximity of his own share purchases to the company's massive share buybacks and the fact that the loan was secured against the value of his own shares would later be a matter of some concern to stock market regulators and other investigators. "Honest, but dumb," claimed one Vivendi Universal insider close to Messier. Either way, at the end of 2001, Messier owned 592,000 shares, worth around €36 million, easily covering the value of the loan. By mid-August 2002, however, they were worth barely €5 million. Messier's personal finances were looking threadbare. Even the low interest rate of 4.6 percent on his €5 million would still require €230,000 of annual interest payments.

Vivendi Universal had spectacularly broken its pledge to make no major acquisitions after the double-headed merger with Seagram and Canal Plus. During 2001, Messier averaged at least a deal a month. Maroc Telecom, MP3.com, Houghton Mifflin, Echostar, and USA Networks alone represented financial commitments of some €20 billion. In the first half of the year significant work had gone into other transactions, notably deals to buy Yahoo!; Belgacom, the Belgian national telecom company; and Club Med, the French holiday group. Messier also considered taking a large stake in Comcast ahead of the giant cable group's merger with AT&T. Hannezo pleaded with Messier to stop, opposing every single one of his deals, with the exception of USA Networks. The finance director also urged him to sell one of the two big minority holdings. At the start of 2001, the stakes in Vivendi Environnement and BSkyB had been worth €8 billion to €10 billion each. Selling either would have eliminated an important part of the debt pile. Messier refused. He would not sell off valuable assets on the cheap. The markets would recover in time. In the event, the 24-percent stake in BSkyB would be sold to Deutsche Bank in October 2001 after the shares had fallen to 650p from a peak of over £22 in March 2000, but even then Messier insisted on retaining exposure to the stock through a complex derivative. A 15-percent stake in Vivendi Environnement would be dumped on the market in a blind panic in June 2002, raising just half of what the same shares would have been worth a year earlier.

Time and time again, Messier would find himself pinched by falling markets. To fund the $2.2 billion acquisition of Houghton Mifflin in June 2001, he had announced the sale of the group's professional press titles. "Everything should go very quickly," he assured the press. "Private equity funds are interested. The sale will bring in at least €2 billion." He spoke too soon. The negotiations were far from complete. Private equity buyers, led by Cinven, exploited his gaffe and slowed the pace of negotiations. To close the deal, Eric Licoys, Vivendi Universal's chief operating officer, threw in the group's medical titles for free, contradicting an earlier statement that had described them as a core business. Only in March 2002, more than seven months after the start of exclusive negotiations, did Licoys finally sell the professional press titles. Even then, instead of the hoped-for €2 billion, the group managed to sell only three-quarters of the business for €1.3 billion. Much more important, Vivendi Universal had to wait throughout 2001 for the $8.15 billion from the sale of Seagram's drinks business. Because of competition issues, the cash did not land until December 21, 2001, a year and a day after the deal was announced. Some other sales were completed more smoothly, notably the holdings in Eurosport, a European sports channel; in France Loisirs; and in AOL France. But such modest proceeds were fast consumed by Messier's voracious appetite for cash. By late 2001, Guillaume Hannezo faced a serious crisis of liquidity.

Hannezo's department was famous for being one of the most chaotic in Paris. The finance director himself set the tone. Even when he was addressing seven thousand shareholders at Vivendi Universal's annual meeting in April 2002, his shirt was untucked and his tie yawned open. While Messier's communications department could boast a staff of eighty, there were barely fifty employees in the accounts department to oversee the activities of more than three thousand subsidiaries. "Anything less than $500 million doesn't interest me," Deputy Finance Director Dominique Gibert would say. The adoption of U.S. accounting standards had taken its toll on Hannezo's staff, whose nerves were frayed with overwork. The department was struggling to cope with the self-imposed burden of dual reporting in French and U.S. accounting standards. After Enron, the demands on their time had also risen exponentially. Investors and the media were demanding an unprecedented level of financial information. Financial markets were punishing any company that failed to provide full and accurate disclosure of all its risks.

Swamped in detail, Hannezo struggled to curb the extravagant spending at the head office, where, following Messier's example, the staff behaved like the investment bankers perennially traipsing through the executive suites. Extravagant use of the Concorde, executive jets, and consultants helped push Vivendi Universal's central costs to over €320 million in 2001, over €1million per head. Yet between them, the activities over which the group had total control—film, music, and publishing—were barely generating enough operating profit to cover the losses of Canal Plus and the Internet division. Shareholders were seeing derisory returns on the €75 billion invested in the media industry. Profit margins were barely over 6 percent, and that thanks only to the full consolidation of the results of minority-owned Cegetel. The financial architecture of Vivendi Universal was looking decidedly shaky.

The banks, however, appeared insouciant about Vivendi Universal's financial position. They fell over each other to lend to the aspirant media giant, which was still able to obtain loans on exceptionally favorable financial conditions, at 40 to 50 basis points above base rates. Exactly how much debt it was carrying at the end of the year would be a matter of considerable confusion. In March, Messier produced full-year results claiming net debt of €28.9 billion at the end of 2001. According to the new management that took over in the summer of 2002, however, Vivendi Universal's net debt had in reality at the time stood at €37 billion, or roughly €8 billion more than the market had realized. Some class-action lawyers would later point to this discrepancy to argue that Vivendi Universal's shares would have been trading at a substantially lower value in the market if the actual debt level had been known at the time.* In other words, they claimed that Messier had created a false market in Vivendi Universal's shares. Even the little that investors did know was enough to be of great concern. Markets had turned against highly indebted groups in the second half of the year, particularly those with significant short-term liabilities: nearly 40 percent of Vivendi Universal's borrowings consisted of bank overdrafts and commercial paper that could vanish at short notice. "In some ways, you could say that our financial management was a little too 'clever' in view of the difficult market conditions," Messier would later admit. "Our teams tried to find cash and financing as cheaply as possible, often at the price of accepting very short-term credits."

Industrially, Vivendi Universal was barely more convincing. It claimed to be a global media powerhouse, but in reality it was little more than a sprawling agglomeration of businesses. The word

---

*The difference would appear to be largely due to the new management's decision to use a stricter definition of net debt that excluded financial receivables.

"synergy" had become a joke. Boston Consulting Group, the U.S. management consultants with an extensive presence in Paris, had been given the task of identifying projects to justify the synergies promised to investors at the time of a merger. "They had just pulled the number out of a hat: the idea that there was €220 million synergies was not just not real. We came up with projects that added perhaps €1 million here or €2 million in ebitda there, never €220 million."

Bronfman complained bitterly that Messier failed to show any operational ability or serious intent to integrate his various acquisitions: "As I proved with my PolyGram merger, value creation is all about execution, not strategy. Messier had no sense whatsoever of how to run the company operationally. This was a merger that required real operational skill. We did not execute the merger. We had decisions made for political reasons." An example of this, according to the former Seagram chief executive, was Pierre Lescure's insistence on running Universal Studios. Bronfman called for the group to be reorganized so that from the outset there was one person in charge of content and one person in charge of distribution. "As it was, if someone wanted to do a content deal, they had to see Pierre for film and me for music," he said. "There was no one person who was able to provide some give and take. Look at General Electric: they don't have a strategy, they just have a religion about execution."

Executive committee meetings, involving the group's senior directors, proved to be pointless. Messier would dominate discussions, rarely showing any concern for whether people were listening. "We would all wonder why we were sitting around the table," said Henri Proglio, chief executive of Vivendi Environnement. "No one knew anything about what anyone else was doing. So we would listen politely and get bored. There seemed to be no possibility of cooperation between the different lines of business. So we only talked about acquisitions." At the end of one of these meetings, Denis Olivennes exploded: "This is Vivendi Frères. We only know how to talk about deals."

At the time of the merger with Seagram, Eric Licoys had been entrusted with the task of overseeing the integration of the various businesses. More a deal maker in the Messier mold than an entre-preneur, Licoys had achieved little. Canal Plus, in particular, had simply refused to play along with trying to weld a cohesive force out of the disparate entities clustered under the Vivendi Universal banner. "The people at Canal were very arrogant and were impossible to deal with," said one Boston Consulting Group project leader. The consultancy struggled to convince Canal Plus of the merit in constructing a database for all the content owned by Vivendi Universal subsidiaries. "They were very pleased with their own business model and past glories." Messier accused Lescure of behaving more like a clan chieftain than the co–chief operating officer of Vivendi Universal.

In the days that preceded Hannezo's "death-seat" memo to Messier, the credit rating agencies, Standard & Poor's and Moody's, expressed serious concern about the group's financial situation. Shaken by the Enron scandal as well as that of electrical equipment group Tyco, the two credit watchdogs had begun to reexamine all major borrowers. When they learned, at the beginning of December, that Vivendi Universal intended to buy Echostar for $1.5 billion in cash and USA Networks for more than $11 billion, of which around $1.8 billion would be in cash and the rest in stock, they objected. They disliked the Echostar deal, questioning the usefulness of paying so much for a small minority stake. Both agencies put the group under surveillance "with a negative outlook," threatening a credit downgrade that would have serious consequences for Vivendi Universal's liquidity. Credit would become more expensive. Some loans would be withdrawn.

The threat had to be taken seriously. Vivendi Universal was increasingly dependent on outside financing, and a lower rating would block its access to the commercial paper market, one of its principal means of raising capital. The finance department pleaded for mercy. While Messier presented the deal with Diller to the press, Hannezo continued to negotiate with the rating agencies. They demanded a precise debt-reduction program in exchange for not downgrading the group there and then. In haste and without informing Henri Proglio, the media group rushed to sell a 9-percent stake in Vivendi Environment for €1.2 billion.

Messier realized that the new hard-line attitude of the rating agencies, who were threatening to downgrade the company ever closer to junk status, meant he urgently needed to raise still more cash. A large amount of short-term debt would fall due for repayment at the end of 2002 and in 2003. In normal circumstances, these borrowings could simply have been rolled over in the commercial paper market. However, if Vivendi Universal were downgraded, that might be impossible. Messier later admitted he failed to act in time: "In the aftermath of September 11, if we had been able to predict the collapse of markets in 2002, the crisis of confidence engendered by the scandals at Enron, WorldCom, and many others, the attempts to destabilize the company, and the reaction of investors, we would have been best advised to issue a €2 billion bond at the end of 2001." A bond would have been a means of borrowing money directly from investors and would have reduced Vivendi Universal's dependency on its banks. In theory, a bond would still have been possible. However, the banks advising Messier insisted on first waiting for the long-delayed $8.1 billion of cash from the sale of Seagrams. But by the time that arrived in late December, conditions in the bond market were deemed too volatile to attempt such a large issue. The €2 billion bond that would have shored up Vivendi Universal's finances was postponed.

The cash would have to come from elsewhere. Only one asset, however, could be sold at such short notice to satisfy Moody's: the shares in Vivendi Universal that Messier had been repurchasing throughout the year. Such was the financial pressure building up toward the end of the year that Messier and Hannezo realized they had no choice but to sell a huge number of these shares on the open market. Messier decided to back out of the undertaking he had made on September 25, 2001, to cancel 3 percent of Vivendi Universal's capital. "He misled the market. No chief executive can afford to do that and especially not at such a tense time," Edgar Bronfman Jr. later said. But Messier had no alternative. The company could no longer afford to cancel its own shares. He now needed to sell them as fast as possible. By mid-December 2001, Messier had grimly accepted that he would have to face the market and admit he had miscalculated. He prepared to sell 55 million shares—5.5 percent of the group's capital—worth €3.3 billion. However, a major obstacle presented itself: shareholders had only authorized him to sell shares at above €60. Notwithstanding all the share buybacks he had undertaken to support the stock, Vivendi Universal's share price had dipped below that level, trading in the mid-50s in the run-up to Christmas. Unless the share price rose back above €60, there could be no share placement. Between Moody's and the market, they were cornered.

Hannezo contacted Hubert Keller at Deutsche Bank and Philippe Altuzarra at Goldman Sachs. At a time of declining deal volumes, both were keen to please a company that was such a rich source of fees. Deutsche Bank had just sold Vivendi Universal's 24-percent stake in British Sky Broadcasting, and Goldman Sachs had just advised Messier on his €12.4 billion purchase of USA Networks. Hannezo and Messier were in no position to delay. The commitments to the rating agencies, who were poised to downgrade the company's credit grade in the absence of an immediate cash inflow, were nonnegotiable. Vivendi Universal was heading toward a crisis of liquidity. They told the banks that the moment the share price recovered above €60, they wanted them to attempt to place the 55 million shares. From that moment, Vivendi Universal undertook not to repurchase any shares in the market or otherwise manipulate the value of its stock. Miraculously, in light trading volumes at the year-end, the Vivendi Universal share price started to recover and passed the magic €60 threshold. Yet Deutsche Bank and Goldman Sachs still hesitated. One senior banker would later say he suspected Vivendi Universal's share price had been manipulated, but he had no means of proving it. It would be one of the many issues probed by the stock market investigations. In any event, both banks declined the business on Wednesday, January 2, 2002, when Vivendi Universal's shares ended at €61.80, and demurred again the following day, even as the shares rose to €64.1. The margin was too tight.

Over the weekend, however, Deutsche Bank changed its mind. The stock had by then stayed above €60 for the previous three trading days. Before the market opened on Monday, January 7, the German bank took the plunge, taking on the whole placement itself. Piqued at the lost opportunity, Goldman Sachs decided it too wanted a piece of the action and was awarded around 40 percent of the €3.3 billion placement. Vivendi Universal had succeeded in raising its cash. The threat that the rating agencies might downgrade the group to near junk status had lifted. The Christmas crisis was over. As the market opened on Monday, however, the relief proved short-lived. "It was too tight, and in a placement, there's no such thing as a 'half success,'" Messier later said. "It's black or it's white." The two banks found themselves unable to sell the shares for more than the €60 they had paid for them. That morning, Vivendi Universal's stock had crashed back below €60. The stock closed at €59.20 on Monday and €58.20 the next day. Their sales forces tried frantically to flog the stock to as near €60 as possible. In the end, they offloaded around two-thirds of the shares, almost all of them at a loss, and were stuck with the balance on their own books. By Wednesday the shares had fallen to €57, and the banks confirmed that they had been left holding unwanted stakes in the company. Deutsche Bank was believed to have lost €400 million and Goldman Sachs €500 million, although neither would ever confirm the amount. "Let's just say it was sufficiently serious to merit a line all of its own in the first-quarter results," was all one Goldman Sachs banker would say.

For Vivendi Universal, the ramifications of the failed share placement were serious. It had succeeded in raising €3.3 billion, but at a huge cost. By dumping such a volume of shares on the market, Messier had broken an important promise. Investors were furious that he had told them he was going to cancel the shares and then instead turned around and sold them. The market smelled panic. Why was Vivendi Universal suddenly selling shares at €60 that it had been purchasing in bulk the previous year at an average price of €73? The haste with which the operation had been conducted and the tight pricing around the €60 minimum alerted the market to the risk of a cash crunch. Furthermore, the overhang of stock in the hands of the two investment banks set a ceiling for the group's share price. To avoid crystallizing a loss, the banks would sell Vivendi Universal shares whenever the stock price started to move back up toward €60. The share price, how-

ever, would never regain that level. Within three months it would
be down to €40. Messier tried to minimize the damage. It was
plain bad luck, he said, that AOL Time Warner had announced a
profit warning at just that moment. Vivendi Universal's main com-
petitor and fellow pioneer of convergence had announced that its
annual losses could reach $60 billion. Once again, Messier trotted
out his favorite homily: "The market is right, but not all the time."
Vivendi Universal had begun its season in hell.

The finance department was still worried. The €3.3 billion had
immediately been absorbed in the repayment of loans. "We have
to think right now about issuing a bond for between €2.5 billion
and €3 billion to strengthen the financial structure of the group,"
insisted an internal memo from the treasury department. Once
again, Hannezo's team started to examine whether it would be
possible to issue a large bond. After taking the temperature of the
market, the finance department decided it would be better to wait
a few weeks rather than return immediately to the market in the
mistrustful atmosphere that prevailed after the bungled share sale.
Vivendi Universal had become an object of suspicion. Some analysts were speaking openly of a "Messier discount," others of a
"credibility issue." Executive committee members pressed Messier
to explain his strategy to investors, but he refused. The man who
had once delighted in meeting analysts and investors, who had
once been the darling of financial markets, withdrew to his tent in
a titanic fit of petulance. The market no longer liked him. He no
longer liked the market.

Hannezo, meanwhile, needed to find €4 billion in cash. He
needed money to pay for the acquisition of Stream, an Italian pay-
television platform that had long been engaged in ruinous competition with Canal Plus's subsidiary Telepiu. He needed to find
nearly $2 billion to pay the cash component of the USA Networks
deal and a further $1.5 billion to pay for the 10-percent stake in
Echostar. Even more urgent matters were demanding his attention,
particularly the purchase of a further 15-percent stake in Maroc
Telecom for €1.1 billion, planned for February 2002 but hastily
deferred. It was apparent that all was not well in the House of

Messier. The constant arbitrage between French and U.S. accounting standards, the ever-shifting perimeter of the group, and the growing complexity of its financial structures had made its accounts all but incomprehensible to even the smartest analysts.

Back in June 2000, Terry Smith had been one of the first analysts to conclude that Messier was wasting tens of billions of dollars in capital by setting himself up as a transatlantic media mogul: "The economics of the movie industry seems to represent the ultimate triumph of hope over experience," he had written at the time of Vivendi's purchase of Seagram. A year later, Collins Stewart skewered Messier again with a research note that was headlined "Vivendi: Dangerous Eurotrash." Smith said: "Four-year-olds can build quite complex structures with Lego but you wouldn't call them architects. We could get enough from the published numbers, even if they were incomprehensible, to know they were pissing money against the wall."

Guillaume Hannezo puts forward several explanations for why his department failed to produce accounts that anyone could hope to understand. From the outset, he argued, Vivendi Universal faced a fundamental mismatch between its European investors and U.S. assets. As its strategy was to become a world leader in the media and entertainment sector, it needed to be evaluated alongside AOL Time Warner, Viacom, News Corp., and Disney, all of which were American and covered by analysts based for the most part in New York and Los Angeles. Vivendi Universal needed to attract new shareholders in the United States. Yet for technical reasons, the merger with Seagram achieved exactly the opposite effect, generating substantial flowback of Vivendi Universal shares across the Atlantic, back to France.

Hannezo and Messier decided to fight against the flow with a double project, which retrospectively can be seen as having accelerated the downward spiral. This consisted of moving the management to the United States, which, along with mistakes of communication and style, provoked incomprehension, anxiety, and a growing gulf between the management and the French grass roots; and of presenting all financial data according to U.S. accounting standards, rather than just reconciling net income as did most other European companies seeking access to the American capital markets.

Hannezo argued that it was a mistake for Vivendi Universal to adopt U.S. accounting norms before it had completed its transformation into a focused media group that had shed all its traditional and extraneous businesses. U.S. investors wanted a simple story, he said, which Hannezo and Messier could not yet tell. "A conglomerate stuffed full of minority interests, whose revenues and cash flows mostly came from business units (telecom and water) with a completely different economic logic, which required days and days of analysis before anyone could have an informed opinion on it, which produced two sets of completely incompatible accounts (French and U.S.) . . . had at the end of the day little chance of interesting American investors, who were free to choose from an infinite number of simpler media companies," he said, claiming further that it was plain bad luck that the group moved to U.S. accounting norms just as these norms lost a good deal of their credibility in the wake of the Enron affair. This meant that what appeared at the start to have been the choice of an extremely rigorous accounting standard, which penalized the company on a number of key indicators (debt, net profit, ebitda), was seen as suspect by investors. "Post-Enron, all complexity became suspect, and Vivendi Universal, with its two sets of accounts, minority interests, seven or eight business lines, permanent 'deal machine,' fiscal acrobatics, and Arthur Andersen as its auditor, appeared more suspect than others," Hannezo said.

Until the start of 2002, the various stock market authorities had shown little concern at the complexity of the group's financial disclosure, still less made any objection. That changed after Enron. The COB, the famously toothless French stock market watchdog, stirred itself into action. Philippe Danjou, the head of their accounting division, felt it was time to become a little more proactive, if only out of self-protection. When Vivendi Universal's auditors—some from the small firm of Salustro Reydel and others from Arthur Andersen—came to discuss the group's full-year accounts with the stock market authorities, Danjou was especially attentive. One item in particular caught his attention: the breath-takingly complex operation involving BSkyB shares. In essence, the transaction amounted to Vivendi Universal borrowing money against the value of its 22-percent stake. However, the tax-driven structure was so arcane that no one knew how to account for it in the 2001 results. Was it a sale or a loan? "A sale," insisted the representatives of the two auditing companies in February. Salustro Reydel, however, was internally divided. "A loan," argued Xavier Paper, Salustro's head of methodology. This would mean Vivendi Universal was unable to book a profit on the sale and its debt would increase. Anxious that the transaction be treated properly, Paper sent his conclusions directly to the COB on February 21.

On March 1, when Vivendi Universal learned of the COB's decision to accept Paper's interpretation, the reaction was swift and angry. "I am furious to learn, on rereading the COB's memo, that they have received advice from Xavier Paper. . . . I therefore want you to send me a copy of Paper's memo and to let me know what action the practice intends to take to avoid repetition of this kind of problem, which could be highly prejudicial to VU," wrote Dominique Gibert in an e-mail to Bernard Cattenoz, one of the Salustro Reydel auditors charged with Vivendi Universal's accounts. Two hours later, Guillaume Hannezo fired off his own e-mail: "There is a real problem in the way that Salustro functions and I hope that it will be dealt with one way or another as soon as possible." At nine that night Messier himself protested: "I am extremely shocked to learn all this: it raises a real ethical problem in terms of the professionalism of Salustro." Salustro Reydel could ill afford Messier's wrath, as Vivendi Universal represented around 10 percent of its revenues. Relations between the two companies had been exceptionally close; they had even established a joint venture that produced accounting software. Salustro Reydel's international expansion had been driven by the overseas expansion of the Messier empire.

Salustro's senior managers begged Messier's pardon and promised immediate retribution against Paper: "We wish to express our regret over the incidents provoked by one of our associates. On receipt of your letter we brought forward the board meeting to today, Sunday, March 3. During the meeting the board members unanimously decided to suspend Xavier Paper from his function as head of accounting methodology, with immediate effect," wrote Jean-Claude Reydel, chairman of Salustro Reydel's board, and Bernard Cattenoz. Only after the COB itself intervened did the auditing firm revoke its decision and reinstate Paper in his position. Messier had again been cornered. Vivendi Universal was stuck with Salustro Reydel because French law requires public companies to use two auditing firms, whose independence is theoretically guaranteed by making their appointment fixed for six years. Reports of Messier's apparent attempt to put pressure on Vivendi Universal's auditors further damaged the company's reputation for transparency. Not only was Vivendi Universal audited by Arthur Andersen, but it had been caught red-handed bullying a small French auditing firm, which was unhealthily dependent on its business, into sacking one of its employees. The echoes of Enron were growing louder.

Internally, the tension between Hannezo and Messier was becoming intolerable. Messier had already blamed his finance director for mishandling the share placement in January. He also raged at Hannezo for mishandling relations with the stock market regulator and the accounting firm. Hannezo fought back, firing off an angry e-mail to the chief executive on Monday, March 4: "The problem isn't our businesses, it's us. Or, more exactly, it's you. The problem we need to solve is your credibility, which you are in the process of losing." The following day, the French company's board reacted with considerable surprise when they read the figures Messier had placed before them. Once again, the news had been heavily leaked to the press over the previous few days to help manage expectations in the market. The board had assumed that the figures had been exaggerated to make the reality a pleasant surprise, but the opposite was true. The company's 2001 results were worse than all the newspapers had predicted. Messier was proposing to announce the largest loss ever recorded by a French company. The first year of Vivendi Universal's existence would end in ignominy: it would report a loss of €13.6 billion, more than the worst deficit ever recorded by Crédit Lyonnais, the benchmark for all French financial disasters. Vivendi Universal would write off nearly €16 billion of goodwill attached to the overpriced assets sitting on its balance sheet.

Shocked by these figures, the board members began to look at the details. Once again, Messier had juggled with the differences between French and American accounting standards. Since the merger, all of Vivendi Universal's board meetings had been held in English. Several of the French board members, who had been directors of the old Générale des Eaux, struggled to follow and tended to shy away from asking questions. But the scale of the losses prompted them to speak out. The doubts that several of them had started to hold at Christmas, at the time of the acquisition of USA Networks and the stake in Echostar, came out into the open. "Jean-Marie, what is our debt position?" asked Jacques Friedmann in hesitant English. Like all the board members, one figure struck him above all others: the level of indebtedness. Many remembered the assurances that they had been given throughout the previous year: Vivendi Universal has zero debt, Messier had stated in January 2001; even at the last board meeting in December, he had reassured them that it had only €8.5 billion of net debt. Yet now they were being told that Vivendi Universal's net debt was actually €14.6 billion at the year-end, excluding Vivendi Environnement, or €28.9 billion in total. Nor did this take into account the acquisition of USA Networks, which had not yet closed. Where had this debt come from? Several directors felt uneasy at Messier's evasive responses, as if they were in the presence of someone who was too clever to lie, but was not telling the truth.

Bronfman would be more blunt: "He lied to you, he lied to me, he lied to everybody, and that's putting it charitably. But his lies were invariably lies of omission. I heard someone describe him as Clintonesque, and that's about right. He would tell you something that would be technically the truth, but would leave a misleading impression." Often Messier had embellished the facts or neglected to tell the board of specific financial undertakings. This time it was different: either he was hiding something or he was no longer in control of the group. Something was evidently wrong.

Only Samuel Minzberg, the lawyer representing Charles Bronfman on the board, dared to say so openly. As ever, it was felt that to criticize a chairman at his own board meeting was to display the height of bad manners. French boardroom etiquette dictated that anyone who objected to the way a company was being run should simply resign and without fuss. The presence on the board of Marc Viénot, the former chairman of Société Générale and author of France's two main corporate-governance codes, had a reassuring effect on the other French directors. In all probability, few gave the company more than a moment's thought from one board meeting to the next. Most important for the outside world, as chairman of Vivendi Universal's audit committee, Viénot gave much-needed credibility to the opaque company's accounts. "For some reason, he did not do his job," said Bronfman. "There was a complicity between him and Messier which I did not understand."

For several weeks, Samuel Minzberg, who had taken to signing memos "SlM" in imitation of Messier's grand alphanumeric, had been expressing his disbelief at what Messier was telling them. He began to think that Messier was manipulating the information he was giving to the board. The other Bronfman family members on the board, the two Edgars, at first paid little attention. They only started to listen closely to what Minzberg was saying after the board meeting to approve the 2001 results. They then followed his lead. "He just did his homework," Edgar Bronfman Sr. would later say admiringly of Minzberg, a lawyer who runs Claridge Inc., Charles Bronfman's family investment firm. "He went through the figures and said what he [Messier] said wasn't true. I paid very little attention to it at the beginning and suddenly realized: 'Oh my God, we've got to get this guy out.' "[2]

Around the time of that March board meeting, three directors indicated to Messier their wish to resign from his board. Minzberg had taken aside Jean-Louis Beffa, chairman of Saint-Gobain, to explain his worries. The board needed to rein Messier in or find a replacement. Beffa agreed, but was reluctant to risk a confrontation. After all, Messier sat on the board of Saint-Gobain, just as he sat on the boards of companies chaired by several other Vivendi Universal directors: LVMH, BNP Paribas, and Alcatel. The industrialist chose the easy way out and told Messier of his intention to resign. René Thomas, the septuagenarian honorary chairman of the Banque Nationale de Paris, and Bernard Arnault, the billionaire chairman of LVMH, also saw their opening. They too would be resigning their mandates, they told Messier.

The Vivendi Universal chief executive pleaded with them to stay. But Beffa and Thomas were adamant: they would leave the board after the annual shareholder meeting on April 24. Messier turned all his powers of persuasion on Arnault, appealing to their friendship in a time of need. After several minutes of emotional blackmail, Arnault reluctantly agreed to renew his mandate at the forthcoming shareholder meeting. He told Messier he nonetheless planned to leave the Vivendi Universal board after the summer. The situation was too hot for his liking. A new law had just been passed that broadened directors' responsibilities: his personal fortune, large enough for him to be frequently described as France's richest man, could be at risk if things ended badly. Vivendi Universal was his only outside directorship, and Messier was an old friend, but he would have to leave the board.

In the subtle language of the French boardroom, Messier had been sent a clear message. Other warnings would follow. Philippe Foriel-Destezet quietly told him he too would be leaving. Like Arnault, the billionaire founder of the Adecco temporary-employment agency worried that his personal fortune might be at risk from lawsuits if he stayed. Messier went in search of replacements. To his amazement, others refused to join his board. To reject an invitation to join a French board is a personal insult to the chairman. Michel Pébéreau, chairman of BNP Paribas, was just one to turn him down. The snub from France's leading banker underlined the suspicion with which Messier was by then held by the French establishment. The rebuff was all the more embarrassing for the fact that Messier himself sat on the board of BNP, which was one of Vivendi Universal's main lending banks. Pébéreau attempted to soften the blow by claiming he had too many directorships.

In reality, Pébéreau was acting on advice received in January following the botched share placement: on no account should he accept any invitation to join the Vivendi Universal board or in any way put his credibility at risk by bolstering that of Messier. The message filtered down the BNP Paribas hierarchy: it was time to reduce the bank's exposure to the opaque media group. Keen to smooth over Pébéreau's rejection, Messier approached Baudouin Prot, the number two at the French bank. The message was confirmed: Prot too turned down the opening on the Vivendi Universal board. Not until June 25, 2002, would Messier succeed in appointing a BNP director to his board, and then only its number three, Chief Operating Officer Dominique Hoenn, who was two years away from retirement.

Messier had kept up appearances, but he knew that the board meeting had not gone well. The strain was evident at the press conference late that afternoon. He gave every impression of not wanting to be there. The results were terrible, and no amount of presentational legerdemain could disguise it. The mammoth loss took him back to his arrival at Générale des Eaux in 1995, when he had had to announce the first loss in the 150-year history of the company. Then, however, it was a question of drawing a line under other people's mistakes. This time, the €13.6 billion deficit he was about to announce was not just the largest loss in French corporate history, it was all his own doing, the culmination of seven years of his management, the fruits of the great transformation of Générale des Eaux into a twenty-first-century wonderstock. Defensive and irritable, he dismissed any suggestion that the loss signaled that he had destroyed value for shareholders. "Anyone can destroy value in falling markets. No need for a merger to do that," he would say glibly. "The loss is a simple question of accounting. The group is in great shape. It's going better than well."

"Plan B, change of management," announced Edouard Tétreau and Eric Ravary, both analysts with Crédit Lyonnais in Paris. On March 20, 2002, in a hard-hitting thirty-eight-page study of Vivendi Universal titled "The End of an Exception," they said there was a 10-percent chance Messier might be dismissed by the board. Like many analysts, Tétreau distributed his research to clients by e-mail, making it available shortly afterwards to the media. The report was soon making headlines as wire agencies such as Reuters and Dow Jones seized on the tightly argued research. Months of frustration at the company's evasiveness and obvious attempts to manipulate the media found a perfect outlet. At last someone had said in public what everyone had been privately feeling for weeks: that Messier's halo had slipped. The small section in Tétreau's note that discussed the slender chance of Messier's being fired was quoted and requoted for several weeks. According to Tétreau and Ravary, the "Messier discount" afflicting the share price was more than 30 percent, meaning that they thought Vivendi Universal's shares would rise by that amount if he were fired. The probability of that happening might remain small, but no one had ever dared even hint at it before. The man still widely considered as the most powerful businessman in France had become a liability.

The research note was as much a shock to Messier as it was to the French establishment. The idea that a chairman of a major French company could simply be fired was risible. The cultural dislike of confrontation meant that it simply did not happen, or at least not in the same brutal way as in the United States or the United Kingdom. Most changes at the tops of companies occurred for political reasons and generally coincided with a change in government. Shareholders seldom had any influence on such decisions. At worst, when things had been going badly for a long time, the French establishment would take charge. Chief executives would be eased out with a quiet word from a senior figure charged with the delicate operation. There would be no resistance. Discretion was the rule. The all-powerful *président–directeur-générale* would be allowed to preannounce his departure, or to bring in a competent chief executive to run the company—Messier had performed this task for Dejouany between November 1994 and June 1996—while he continued to chair the board.

The indignity of the Crédit Lyonnais research note was intolerable. It crystallized Messier's feeling of growing alienation from the financial community and confirmed what many had been telling him: his own credibility had suffered terribly over the previous six months. Messier would not forgive Tétreau. When a second note from the Crédit Lyonnais analyst suggested that Vivendi Universal might even face bankruptcy, Messier decided he would have Tétreau's head. He ordered a probe into Tétreau's past and soon found material he hoped would discredit the thirty-four-year-old analyst. It turned out that Tétreau had been fired from his previous job as an adviser at France's media watchdog, the Conseil Supérieur Audiovisuel, for some fairly eccentric behavior that culminated, one drunken night, with him being caught red-handed urinating into the fridge of the CSA's president, Hervé Bourges.

Armed with such trivial tales, Messier wrote to Dominique Ferrero, chief executive of Crédit Lyonnais, letting it be clearly understood that he wished the bank to dispense with the analyst's services. It required the intervention of Jean Peyrelevade, the independent-minded head of the French bank, to dissuade Messier from continuing with his bluster. "Why don't you go fuck yourself," Peyrelevade is said to have told the Vivendi Universal chief executive, according to versions of the story circulating within Crédit Lyonnais.* Like Xavier Paper at Salustro Reydel, Tétreau kept his job. Messier, nonetheless, won a partial victory. Tétreau admitted that the dispute between him and Messier might be seen to color his independence of judgment: he pulled back from following Vivendi Universal on a daily basis, delegating the responsibility to one of his colleagues. However, a taboo had been broken, and Messier's life expectancy became a subject of morbid discussion as rumors of regicide rebounded across Paris.

---

*In French, Peyrelevade's reported words were "Allez-vous faire foutre." Attempts to confirm this story with his office were unsuccessful.

## CHAPTER NINE

# Claude and the Boys

Once again, in 2002 Claude Bébéar, the sixty-seven-year-old founder of the giant French insurance group AXA, had invited a handful of France's leading chief executives to join him as he followed the French rugby team around Europe for the annual Six Nations tournament. The faces varied little year to year. Like Bébéar, who hailed from the Dordogne, they tended to come from the rugby-loving southwest and to enjoy fine wine, food, and jokes that were a bit on the heavy side. The "old crocodile," as Bébéar was known behind his back, liked to hunt in a pack. There would be Jean-René Fourtou, vice chairman of the Franco-German pharmaceutical group Aventis; Henri Lachmann, chairman of Schneider Electric; Serge Kampf, chairman of consulting firm Cap Gemini; Thierry Breton, chairman of consumer electronics group Thomson Multimedia; and Christian Blanc, former chairman of Air France and an independent presidential candidate in the forthcoming poll on April 19. To provide his friends and guests with expert commentary, Bébéar liked to bring along Jean-Pierre Rives, the forty-nine-year-old former captain of the French rugby team.

On Saturday, March 23, 2002, they had arranged to meet at Le Bourget Airport to travel to Murrayfield in Edinburgh. There they were to see France play Scotland. For Rives, this game always had a special significance. Eighteen years before, he had made his final international appearance for France at the home of Scottish rugby. Claude Bébéar's guests were astounded at the sumptuous Airbus that had been provided for them: beige fitted carpets, matching leather armchairs, pale wood, fine porcelain and crystal, and a bedroom at the back. Even though they were company chairmen, accustomed to a certain lifestyle, they were embarrassed at the gratuitous opulence. They wondered whose shareholders were paying for this little baby. Their astonishment increased when Bébéar revealed the identity of the owner: Jean-Marie Messier. This was his Airbus A319—the plane whose existence he had always denied.*

As they flew to Edinburgh, the businessmen were thrilled to have discovered Messier's secret. "Claude, you don't know how to live properly. Look at what it's like to be a billionaire," shouted Rives as he lorded it in an armchair. Everyone had a story to tell about Messier and his princely lifestyle: invitations to Méry-sur-Oise, Vivendi's château northwest of Paris, elegantly redecorated by Jean-Michel Wilmotte; the trips by private plane to the opera at Aix, sponsored by Vivendi Universal; dinners at the group's head-quarters that were invariably accompanied by Messier's favorite *grand cru,* the ruby-colored Château Ducru Beaucaillou from the aristocratic St. Julien vineyards of the Médoc; the $17.5 million Park Avenue apartment bought for him by the company in New York and redecorated by Wilmotte at a cost of nearly $3 million to his shareholders; and, of course, his €5.2 million annual pay package that made him one of the best-paid chief executives not just in France but in the whole of continental Europe. They all admitted to being impressed by his panache but also ill at ease with his conspicuous extravagance. He behaved more like a man who owned his own company than a hired manager. They agreed that he had lost all sense of reality.

In those feverish spring months, even the smallest piece of news about Jean-Marie Messier would receive lavish media atten-

---

*In defending the Airbus in his book *My True Diary,* Jean-Marie Messier repeats a factual error made in the original report of the episode in *Le Monde* in September 2002. Messier's account wrongly claims that Bébéar et al. were flying to Cardiff to watch Wales play France on February 18, 2002.

tion, but for these company chairmen the discovery of this Airbus was in fact a highly significant turning point in their relations with the chairman of Vivendi Universal. After the merger with Seagram in June 2000, Vivendi Universal had decided to buy a large jet so senior executives could travel easily between Paris and New York or onward to the West Coast of America without stopping. Vivendi Universal entered into discussions with Airbus, the European aircraft manufacturer, which proposed an A319, one of the largest corporate jets on the market. The contract was duly signed by Messier himself and Noël Forgeard, the Airbus chairman. The plane was fitted out to the highest specifications. Indeed, the question had arisen over whether or not to fit a shower. With a shower, and the hundreds of liters of water required to supply it, the aircraft would be unable to fly from Paris to Los Angeles without refueling, which was the whole point of the acquisition. Nevertheless, it was finally decided to fit the shower.

Inevitably, to Messier's embarrassment, word of the extraordinary aircraft and of the decision to fit a shower soon filtered into the gossip columns of the French press. The affair caused such a stir in Paris that even Jacques Chirac got wind of it. Making an appearance at the Le Bourget air show, he told his entourage that he wanted to see whether Messier's Airbus was more luxurious than even the presidential airplane. It looked as though Messier might have committed the same lèse-majesté as Nicolas Fouquet, Louis XIV's finance minister, who had angered the monarch by entertaining ideas above his station. The brilliant financier had hired the finest designers of the day to build Vaux-le-Vicomte, then the finest house in France. Speculation that Fouquet had been pilfering money from the treasury grew in the run-up to his moment of triumph on August 17, 1661, when the king and his army of courtiers came to inspect the magnificent château at a lavish housewarming. Nineteen days later, Fouquet was arrested by d'Artagnan, fabled Gascon captain of the King's musketeers, charged with embezzlement, and thrown in jail for the rest of his life.

In panic at the idea that his conspicuous consumption might have slighted Chirac and aghast at the message more unwanted publicity about the now much-regretted Airbus might send to investors, Messier decided that not only would he never use the plane, but also deny its existence altogether. Accordingly, it was parked inside a specially-created aircraft-leasing company called Aéro Services. In reality, this changed nothing, as Aéro Services was 98 percent owned by Vivendi Universal. So even if the plane could now be rented out by other companies as a means of spreading its fixed operating costs over a larger number of users, there was no hiding that Vivendi Universal was still its legal owner. Extraordinarily, Messier continued to deny any such thing. He first formally denied that Vivendi Universal owned an Airbus in his interview with *Paris Match* in January. More seriously, he would do so again in April at the company's annual shareholder meeting. He even went so far as to tell the company's sovereign body: "It is time to kill all these ridiculous rumors. Vivendi Universal does not have an Airbus."

The disavowel was an extraordinary lapse of judgment: the Airbus would come back to haunt him. As ever, the bungled cover-up was far worse than the original crime. For Edgar Bronfman Jr., the bald denial in front of the shareholders was a pivotal moment in their relationship. He and his family had harbored doubts about Messier's credibility for some time, but to them this was a straightforward deception: "The big turning point for me, the final turning point, in fact, was at the annual shareholder meeting. He was under a lot of pressure, in front of a lot of shareholders and the press too. I thought that if he was ever going to sober up and fly straight it would be here. Someone asked him a question about our operating expenses. He answered by saying that he had sold two G4s and that, no, contrary to the rumors that he read in the newspapers, VU did not own an Airbus. For me it was over at that moment. Because VU does own an Airbus. There he was, when he really needed to play it straight, lying and over something no one had even asked him about."

Messier would later admit in *Mon Vrai Journal* that Vivendi Universal did indeed own an Airbus. However, he denied responsibility for buying it, saying that Airbus had persuaded Aéro Services that it would be a good investment. He also said that he had never actually flown in it. "Not a single hour. Many French and European companies did rent it, on the other hand, but who cares: the accusation was so easy to make, the answer so long. I paid a heavy price." Ironically, Messier would liken Bébéar and his circle to the world of d'Artagnan immortalized by Alexandre Dumas: "This club rallied all those French entrepreneurs who would swear an oath of loyalty and mutual protection to its charismatic leader, in the Gascon manner, in the manner of the musketeers. . . . 'Claude for all and all for Claude.'"[1] Claude Bébéar was certainly the most scathing in his criticisms of Messier during that flight to Edinburgh. The chairman of AXA had stopped trusting Messier long ago. He felt Messier had broken his word back in 1994. After promising to join the electrical equipment company Schneider, at that point within AXA's sphere of influence, Messier had opted for Générale des Eaux without letting Bébéar know.

Since then, the rift had continued to widen. The right-wing insurance chief was endlessly irritated by Messier's homilies on capitalism and globalization. To Bébéar, it seemed that Messier's average day consisted of a series of self-promoting stunts: meetings with José Bové, the symbol of French farming resistance; Horst Köhler of the International Monetary Fund; or antiglobalization rock group Noir Désir. He felt that Messier's desire to appear in the newspapers and on television verged on a sickness. They found themselves in opposing camps on a number of issues. The AXA chairman objected strongly to Messier's attempt to play the role of Ambroise Roux, godfather of French capitalism during the 1980s and 1990s. He watched with irritation as Messier involved himself in the battle to succeed Roux at the head of the powerful French private-sector employers' lobby, acted as a peacemaker in the luxury-goods war over Gucci between François Pinault and Bernard Arnault, and then telephoned the whole of Paris to give the impression that he carried some weight in the battle between Société Générale and BNP over the fate of Paribas. Watching him at close hand during a dinner in September 2001, Bébéar finally concluded that the Vivendi Universal chief was suffering from an acute and dangerous megalomania.

Could this have been simply the jealousy of a man with similar ambitions to dominate the French business world, whose fame had been eclipsed? Jean-Marie Messier advanced this thesis many times: "Bébéar no doubt wishes to be the only Frenchman of his generation and the next to succeed in the USA," he would say. "It would have been better if he had stayed out of Vivendi Universal." Messier believed Bébéar represented a throwback to an earlier era of French capitalism, when the fates of companies were decided not by shareholders but by backroom horse-trading between unaccountable power brokers in hock to various political and financial interests. The chairman of AXA would swear this was far from the truth. Bébéar's credibility stemmed from the fact that he was a genuine entrepreneur—a relative rarity in France's administrative corporate culture—who had risen to the top of his industry without spending time in government. From the outset he objected to the word "godfather," too close, in his eyes, to the world of the Mafia or even the Florentine practices of Ambroise Roux. But the primary-school teacher's son acknowledged that he liked being a man of influence. One of the world's leading insurance companies, AXA controlled nearly $1 trillion of assets, giving Bébéar the ability to influence not just the managements of companies eager to attract stable long-term shareholders, but also the shape of European banking and finance.

Like Messier a generation later, Bébéar attended the Ecole Polytechnique. Unlike Messier, however, he graduated toward the bottom of the class, despite coming in fourth in the entry exam. He had spent too much time playing rugby and, in his capacity as elected class representative, organizing frat-house-style parties to keep up with the country's most ambitious aspiring technocrats. Instead of following his peers into government service or the high echelons of France's most prestigious industrial companies, Bébéar allowed himself to be recruited by a classmate's father, André Sahut d'Izarn, an ultra-Catholic monarchist, with the intention that he would eventually succeed him at the helm of his obscure insurance company in the suburbs of Rouen.

There could hardly be a less glamorous prospect for an aspiring "X." But that was not how Bébéar saw it. He rapidly learned the trade and secured his actuary's diploma, the qualification of which he often appeared most proud. By 1975, he had become chairman of the company, which he renamed AXA and launched into a frenetic acquisition spree. By 1988 it was second only to UAP in the French market. At this point, Bébéar managed to crack the U.S. market—a feat that had eluded the majority of French and European businessmen across a range of industries—with the 1991 acquisition of Equitable, the fifth largest U.S. life insurer. Five years later, with the takeover of UAP, he doubled AXA's size in the French market, and then gave the group a substantial presence in the UK with the purchase of Guardian Royal Exchange.

In short, Bébéar felt it was he, not Messier, who had best demonstrated how well-managed French groups could become world leaders through careful and controlled acquisitions.

For a time, Bébéar toyed with a career in politics. He flirted with a reactionary Catholic and aristocratic fringe, becoming close to Count Jean de Beaumont, the owner of the Rivaud empire, from whom he acquired a passion for hunting, before moving toward Valéry Giscard d'Estaing's Union for French Democracy (French acronym UDF), the non-Gaullist, center-right party of the time. In 1978, when Giscard was at the Elysée, Bébéar served as national treasurer of the UDF before handing over responsibility to Jean-René Fourtou, his closest friend and another rugby-loving Girondin. Like Ambroise Roux, Bébéar created his own club, Entreprise et Cité, which assembled France's thirty or so most powerful businessmen. To join Entreprise et Cité was a sign of respect to Bébéar, an almost feudal recognition of his status in the place de Paris.

Since handing over day-to-day responsibility at AXA to Henri de Castries, another bright young énarque, in 2000, Bébéar had found he had time on his hands. He had edited a book lamenting the slow pace of French economic reform and run Paris's unsuccessful bid to host the 2008 Olympics, but then once again found his attention starting to wander. The crisis of confidence in global capital markets was starting to do grave damage to the value of AXA's massive investments in the stock market. It even held 0.5

percent of Vivendi Universal's shares directly at the end of 2001. Bébéar feared, above all, a repetition of the Enron and WorldCom scandals in the French market. Bébéar zeroed in on Jean-Marie Messier as the weakest link.

In his eyes, the Airbus was another sign that not all was well within the Messier empire. Worried that the board was failing to supervise the chief executive, Bébéar decided to put Messier under his personal watch. One after another, Messier's closest colleagues and advisers came into his office: Eric Licoys, his chief operating officer and old colleague from Lazard; Agnès Touraine, head of publishing; Guillaume Hannezo, his finance director; and Catherine Gros, his director of communications, as well as outsiders such as Georges Ralli, managing director of Lazard; and Maurice Lévy, chairman of the Publicis advertising group. All gave him the same advice.

"You must recover your credibility." "Stop talking to the press all the time." "You're overexposed." "Try showing you have a team and that you're running a group." After hearing these criticisms repeated over and over again, Messier decided he had made mistakes. He would recognize that he had overpersonalized the group's image, that he had been "maladroit" with his comment about the death of the French cultural exception and the interview in *Paris Match*. A public apology would restore calm. To explain that he intended to put himself less in the limelight, he launched a campaign of lunches and meetings with the editors and relevant reporters of all the leading newspapers. Not everyone was convinced. After seeing Messier at a breakfast in May 2002, the editor of the *Financial Times* bet his counterpart at *Les Echos* a bottle of champagne that the Vivendi Universal boss would lose his job by the end of 2002.

In his desire to win back the support of the market, Messier made it his highest priority to put Canal Plus back on track. His relations with the pay-TV channel had worsened since December, when he had been attacked by filmmakers and politicians alike for pronouncing the death of the French cultural exception. Pierre Lescure and Denis Olivennes accused him openly of doublespeak, of imposing unrealistic objectives, of denying reality. They knew they would take the blame for Vivendi Universal's poor results. Their anger grew when they discovered that Messier was doing all he could to set them against one another, one day telling Denis Olivennes, "Pierre's tired. He lost the desire to win," and the next confiding to Lescure: "You need someone more creative by your side. A real media professional." When the two directors realized what was happening, they closed ranks.

Faced with this solidarity, Messier decided to take the battle to them. As soon as the group's catastrophic results were announced on March 5, 2002, he launched his attack, blaming them for the largest loss in French corporate history. He continued to deny that the Seagram part of the double-headed transaction had destroyed any value for his shareholders, even though he had written off €3.1 billion relating to the music division and €1.3 billion relating to Universal Studios. He focused the blame on Canal Plus. Almost half of the write-down in the group's assets—€6 billion out of the €12.6 billion impairment charge—was due to the plunge in value of Canal Plus, he explained. Vivendi Universal's bad operating results? Those too were the fault of the pay-TV platform, which, for the first time in its history, had lost subscribers even in France and was still hemorrhaging cash in Italy. Then he delivered his ultimatum: "The management team at Canal Plus must ensure that the station breaks even within two years." This message was repeated two days later in an interview with the newspaper *La Tribune.*

Messier knew that this was an impossible demand. Given Canal Plus's existing commitments, the 2002 results would be even worse than those of 2001, when it had lost nearly €400 million at the operating profit level. To Lescure and Olivennes, this was Stalinist management. The target he had set them was impossible in the absence of a complete reversal of the strategy he had approved months before. They would have to close down or sell all of Canal Plus's loss-making international operations, and, in particular, Telepiu, the Italian pay-TV platform whose expansion Messier had fully supported just three months before. Over Christmas, Messier himself had even agreed that Telepiu should buy Stream, a rival owned by Rupert Murdoch, whose ferocious competition for sports and movie rights explained much of the Canal subsidiary's losses. Stunned that they were being set a target that everyone knew they could not possibly meet, Lescure and Olivennes wrote an e-mail to Canal Plus's four thousand employees, explaining that they had told Messier that if he wanted Canal Plus to break even within two years they would have to sell Telepiu, and that buying Stream would in the short term only worsen Canal Plus's losses, but that this strategic choice was rejected by Vivendi Universal. The next day their e-mail, which effectively laid responsibility for Canal Plus's losses squarely at the door of Jean-Marie Messier, was in all the papers. Canal Plus had declared war on Vivendi Universal.

On March 19, the three hundred most senior executives of Vivendi Universal met in Normandy, at the coastal resort of Deauville, to begin a three-day brainstorming session. The managers of the different subsidiaries were to share ideas and create "synergies." Everyone had to come up with at least one idea of how the different divisions of the sprawling empire could collaborate. It rained incessantly. Fifteen months into Vivendi's merger with Seagram, the annual get-together had revealed ebbing confidence in the transatlantic alliance. Hollywood executives, including Barry Diller and Ron Meyer, itched to leave the rain-swept Normandy resort. Messier seemed at a loss over how to motivate his U.S. executives, puzzling them by continual references to the United States' role in the Normandy landings of 1944 and his decision to organize a rose-laying ceremony at the graves of the servicemen who had died on the beaches. At one lunch event, the U.S. executives were surprised to find themselves being waited on by people dressed in GI uniforms of the 1940s. The morale of the Hollywood executives was directly correlated to the declining share price. Barry Diller had rallied to Messier's support, rebuking them in a newspaper interview. "Shut up about the stock already. They literally talk about it all day long. They're depressed about it."

Messier felt the time had come to tackle the cancer at the heart of the group. He summoned Lescure and Olivennes for dinner at Chez Miocque, the town's best brasserie. On Messier's orders, half the tables in the small restaurant were kept empty to provide them with privacy. Their e-mail had displayed "unacceptable disloyalty," he told them. He accused Lescure of being the "king of rumors." The two men were far from contrite. Olivennes had become exasperated with Messier's overbearing style and inconsistency. He repeated to Messier's face the contents of the e-mail they had sent to all of Canal Plus's staff and much of the media. Of course, Canal Plus was heavily loss-making: how could it not be when they had decided to expand so fast into Italy? If you want to see financial results, we have to sell Telepiu to Murdoch. Olivennes told Messier he could no longer flip-flop on decisions, set contradictory targets, blame others when they were not achieved, silence dissent in the executive committee, and run the company through *Paris Match*. Messier ignored him, criticizing their management, "indeed lack of management," Canal's crony culture, its absence of team spirit, and the "constant provocation of *Les Guignols.*" Olivennes lashed out again: "Vivendi Universal shows all the failings of a totalitarian system: personality cult, distribution of propaganda, conspiracy theory of history, and now the physical elimination of all opposition." Back at their hotel, Lescure and Olivennes went over the discussion and agreed that if they did not know the date, they knew the outcome: they were condemned. They decided to strike first.

It was a perfect New York spring morning as Jean-Marie Messier walked down Park Avenue toward the Seagram Building. But by 8:30 A.M. on Friday, April 12, 2002, his day would already be ruined. The Vivendi Universal chief executive had been looking forward to his family vacation in the Bahamas, not least because he hoped to take up an invitation to spend some time on Barry Diller's yacht. His induction into the inner circle of Hollywood media moguldom was about to begin. That Christmas, Messier had paid for his entry ticket by buying half of Diller's media company for over €12.4 billion. Diller had agreed to replace Pierre Lescure at the head of all Vivendi Universal's U.S. film and television operations. Messier's credibility had soared in New York, but the reaction in France to the humiliation of Lescure, an icon of French broadcasting, had been as frosty as the season. To the

French establishment, Diller's arrival was fresh evidence of the worrying Americanization of their national champion. At the time of the merger with Vivendi, Canal Plus had been promised that it would have responsibility for Universal Studios. That promise had been broken. The backlash had been under way for several months, but that morning it was to gain a new intensity. An e-mail from Denis Olivennes, one of his most senior French executives, changed Messier's mood in an instant. In three short lines, Olivennes tendered his resignation.

After reading the e-mail, Messier immediately called Olivennes on his cell phone. Across the Atlantic, the forty-year-old was having lunch at Pierre Lescure's airy penthouse apartment on avenue Raphael, one of the smartest addresses in Paris's chic Sixteenth Arrondissement. They had spent the morning discussing the dysfunctionality of the Messier empire: the unhappiness of the Bronfmans, the arrival of Diller, the accelerating deal machine, the mounting debt, the lack of focus on day-to-day operations, and the paranoia of the chief executive. Olivennes had barely finished the Frisbee-sized steak specially prepared by Lescure's chef to suit his all-protein diet when Messier's number flashed on his display. "It's him," Olivennes said. Lescure motioned to his deputy to take the call in his study, before cutting the end off a Cohiba and offering another to the Paris correspondent of the *Financial Times*. The show was about to start. The lunch guests puffed ruminatively on their seven-inch Esplendidos while Olivennes unloaded his anger. There had been a "global misunderstanding," Messier said, volunteering that he would see Olivennes's departure as a "personal failure." Why not think about it for a few days? If he really wanted to go, then Messier said they should wait and announce his resignation at the annual meeting. Olivennes refused. Minutes later, Olivennes's cell phone rang again. This time it was the French minister of culture, Catherine Tasca. A long-standing friend of both Canal Plus executives, she had been kept informed of the impending showdown. She offered them her full support. Within a few minutes, the news was out.

On putting down the telephone, Messier decided to return to

Paris immediately to confront Pierre Lescure. Although his holiday would have to be canceled, Messier welcomed the now inevitable confrontation with the French establishment. He no longer valued Lescure. Since moving to New York in September, he had hired real entertainment industry executives, such as Barry Diller, whose achievements made Lescure's mastery of the backwaters of French broadcasting seem paltry by comparison. Edgar Bronfman Jr. and Barry Diller would almost certainly support the move to tackle the major source of losses within Vivendi Universal's film and television operations. If Canal Plus were any normal business and Pierre Lescure any regular chief executive, the decision would have been simple. The pay-television operator had been losing money for five years, draining €500 million from Vivendi Universal's cash resources in 2001. It was jeopardizing the entire Vivendi Universal project, holding back his plans to expand in the United States. Moreover, Lescure and Olivennes were clearly not tough enough to reform the system of expensive handouts to the French film industry that cost Canal Plus nearly €150 million in 2001 for little commercial benefit.

The leaks were multiplying in all the newspapers, and Messier saw the handiwork of the "king of rumors" behind all of them. On Monday morning, the *Financial Times* had devoted its lead front page story to the rift within the Vivendi Universal boardroom. French directors opposed Messier's plan to grant senior managers a huge quantity of share options, covering up to 5 percent of the group's capital. Shareholders were mobilizing in protest ahead of the vote on the options at the annual meeting in ten days' time. Messier summoned Lescure to his office the following afternoon. With his disarming habit of mixing friendship and business, he opened the conversation by asking for news of Anna, the three-year-old Vietnamese girl Lescure had adopted. "You haven't called me in to talk about Anna." "Pierre, I propose that you take over the chair of the supervisory board of Canal Plus." "Who will be chairman of the executive committee?" "Xavier Couture. You've got three minutes to accept. Yes or no?" Messier was proposing to deprive Lescure of all responsibility for the company he had co-founded eighteen years before. "It's no," Lescure responded. Only three months before, Lescure had envisaged hiring Couture simply as the director of a lowly Canal Plus subsidiary. He had no desire to work in close daily contact with an obvious Messier aparatchik "Well, you'll have to accept the consequences," retorted Messier. "It's up to *you* to accept the consequences. I'm not resigning," concluded Lescure. The Vivendi Universal chief executive informed Lescure that he had no choice but to demand his resignation.

As Lescure left the room, Messier blanched when he saw the copy of *Le Monde* in the older man's hand. His own name leaped out at him from the headline that ran across the top of the afternoon newspaper's freshly printed front page: "Qui vent la chute de Jean-Marie Messier?" ("Who wants the fall of Jean-Marie Messier?") A vicious cartoon by Plantu, *Le Monde*'s main cartoonist, depicted the Vivendi Universal chief executive lying on the ground with his head in the jaws of a guillotine. The violence of the sketch stopped him short. For Messier it provided further confirmation of the conspiracy being woven by his enemies in the French establishment. Lescure, after all, sat on one of the newspaper's supervisory councils. For years, Messier had claimed that Jean-Marie Colombani, editor of *Le Monde,* which he dismissively referred to as "the *Evening Lescure,*" had been pursuing a personal vendetta against him. He alleged—falsely—that Colombani in 1998 had threatened to hunt him down for twenty years after Vivendi refused to sell him *L'Express,* the leading weekly newsmagazine. Right-wing politicians, and the magazine's staff, had opposed the sale to left-leaning *Le Monde.* Socialist politicians had been keen to see a left-of-center media group emerge as a counterweight to the right-wing families such as Lagardere, Dassault, and Bouygues that controlled many of France's most influential media outlets. In the end, Messier withdrew the magazine from sale.

Messier argued that the sacking of Pierre Lescure would finally put an end to the group's troubles. He had good reason, he said, to shake up the management of Canal Plus, which had been hemorrhaging cash—€500 million in 2001. Whatever the cultural significance of the pay-television company, Vivendi Universal could hardly be expected to carry such losses for long. Investors would welcome the move to take Canal Plus in hand, he said. He issued a statement: "For the first time in 17 years, Canal Plus lost subscribers last year. . . . If Canal Plus were not part of Vivendi Universal, its financial situation would be extremely precarious and its existence threatened. . . . As Vivendi Universal's role is not to continue to bankroll Canal Plus indefinitely, vigorous strategic and operational measures need to be taken. In the absence of proposals for any such measures from Pierre Lescure, it was decided to appoint Xavier Couture to the executive board and to offer Mr. Lescure the chairmanship of the supervisory board in place of Jean-Marie Messier. This would have enabled Mr. Lescure to remain the guardian of the spirit and the culture of Canal Plus. This refusal led to conclusions having to be drawn. . . . The departure of Pierre Lescure was not taken for personal reasons, but for business reasons."

The reaction to the departure of the chairman of Canal Plus was nonetheless swift and hysterical. The entire staff of Canal Plus went on strike as soon as they heard of the dismissal of their heroic boss, interrupting normal programs to broadcast furious personal attacks against Messier. Pierre Lescure's emotional farewell speech to his employees, made on his return to his riverside office, was televised live, his tears and passionate denunciation of Messier endlessly repeated on all news bulletins that night. As *Variety* would note the next day, the intensity of feeling at Canal Plus made for award-winning daytime drama. *Les Guignols,* the satirical puppets modeled on *Spitting Image* in the United Kingdom, were unleashed live on air and spent the evening hurling ever more abusive epithets at the "Master of the World." As Canal Plus entered a paroxysm of rebellion against Vivendi Universal, Messier ordered his press officers to pump out another press release. "It is extremely shocking that the chairman of a television channel should use airtime to his own means, without condemning a program during which customers were asked to cancel their subscriptions. Such a move would endanger the entire channel. . . . Vivendi Universal once again confirms in the strongest way possible that it will respect all of its commitments on editorial freedom for Canal Plus and funding for the French film industry." The statement was released to no avail: Messier's voice was drowned out in the noise.

Over two hundred actors and directors—including Johnny Depp, Isabel Adjani, and David Lynch—sent messages of support to the ousted chairman of Canal Plus. Filmmakers once again proclaimed the death of French cinema. "Canal Putsch" ran the front-page headline in *Libération*, the left-wing newspaper. Presidential candidates lambasted Messier as the unacceptable face of globalization and "American capitalism." He was treated as a traitor to French culture and France's civilizing mission in the United States. After proclaiming the French cultural exception to be dead at Christmas, he had then slaughtered Pierre Lescure, one of the guardians of the temple, and replaced him with Barry Diller, the spiritual father of Bart Simpson. Only one candidate out of sixteen in April's presidential race, the ultraliberal Alain Madelin, rose to Messier's defense. Jean-Marie Le Pen branded President Jacques Chirac "the candidate of Jean-Marie Messier," even though the latter had publicly described the Vivendi Universal chief executive's views on French culture a "mental aberration." Messier made a perfect whipping boy for Lionel Jospin, who was eager to win support from the antiglobalization voters on the left of his party. The Socialist prime minister demanded a formal probe into whether Canal Plus and Vivendi Universal conformed with media laws limiting non-French ownership of national broadcasters to 20 percent. The threat that had been brandished in December was put into action. Jean-Marie Messier succeeded where sixteen French presidential candidates failed. He added late sparkle to an otherwise pedestrian election campaign.

Shareholders thanked him for neither the timing nor the style of the move. Messier would doubtless have been wiser to wait until after the elections to stamp his authority on Canal Plus. In a consensual culture, his courageous appetite for open confrontation with the government, and his provocative attitude to *l'exception française*, looked likely only to hinder progress in reforming the system of state protection for French cinema. The government made it clear that his blunderbuss approach had wrecked any chance of renegotiating Canal Plus's obligation. He had contrived to turn a management dispute into a row about France's very cultural survival. Vivendi Universal was showing signs of a tumultuous identity crisis. Just a year before, Messier had been feted as the conquering hero of French capitalism who had planted the Tricolore in Hollywood. But Vivendi Universal's depressed share price, a controversial stock option plan, and his overbearing style had all taken their toll. To many in France, especially on the left, the media mogul had become the unacceptable face of global capitalism. In America, events in France were watched with some bemusement. Barry Diller described the reaction as "a storm in a French teacup." He told Fox News, "The things that are going on in France are of France, and I don't think we can really figure them out anyway."[2] Peter Bart, editor of *Variety*, said, "Lescure is a figure the French know and trust. The messianic Messier is still an unknown who even had the temerity to move to New York City in his new duties. The French feel they have a big stake in the outcome of this struggle. Hollywood has a lot riding on it as well."

One of the legacies of the French Revolution is a grim interest in the death throes of the rich and powerful, and on April 17, 2002, several hundred Parisians blocked one of the roads leading to the Arc de Triomphe as they stood outside the headquarters of Vivendi Universal calling for the blood of Jean-Marie Messier. They threw eggs at the windows and waved banners depicting Messier as either the devil or a giant phallus. The day before the presidential vote, several thousand people of all ages, many wearing T-shirts saying "Je n'aime pas les Jean-Maries" ("I don't like Jean-Maries") and "Super-menteur" ("Super Liar") rallied at an anti–Vivendi Universal rock concert in a Paris park. The Messier saga generated such passion that week that it pushed from the headlines what should have been the main event.* The election re-

---

*Le Monde,* the long-standing newspaper of the French elite, devoted its front page to Vivendi Universal on April 17, 18, and 19. That week, the *Financial Times* splashed with the Vivendi Universal saga for six consecutive days in its European edition.

sults would see France stunned by the victory of Jean-Marie Le Pen over the incumbent Socialist prime minister, Lionel Jospin; while the French chattering classes had been talking about only Messier and the cultural exception, they had failed altogether to notice the welling of support for the extreme Right across the south and east of France. The political earthquake had caught France unaware.

At the Elysée presidential palace and at Matignon, official residence of the prime minister, tempers flared. The political establishment felt Messier had gone too far. Many politicians half blamed Messier for the shocking election result that had called into question France's republican and democratic credentials. By suddenly presenting the unacceptable face of capitalism to the nation days before the election, Messier, they argued, had boosted the appeal of Le Pen, a man who wanted to roll back the clock of French economic history. In addition, politicians knew that Messier was desperate to sell Vivendi Environnement. They worried about all the secrets buried in its vaults. For decades, the old Générale des Eaux had played a role in the funding of political parties: it was imperative that Vivendi Environnement stay in friendly French hands. Laurent Fabius, the French finance minister and a former prime minister, was the first to warn Messier.

The day after the sacking of Lescure, Maurice Lévy, chairman of Publicis, had invited Fabius and Messier to attend his investiture as an officer of the Legion of Honor. At the end of the ceremony, Fabius took Messier to one side. His message was short and clear: "One does not sell a French number one." Even President Jacques Chirac, whose own political machine had long benefited from the largesse of the old Générale des Eaux, entered the fray, thundering into the television cameras: "Vivendi Environnement must remain French." Messier sent countless ingratiating signals to the Elysée palace. He failed, however, to obtain an appointment with the president, or even with one of his top advisers. "The guy's a pain in the ass. I don't want to see him anymore," Chirac had told his entourage. Messier, with whom Chirac had talked for an hour at the Elysée following his acquisition of Seagram, was reduced to communicating via third parties: he promised the president that although he still planned to reduce his holding in Vivendi Environnement, he would not do anything before the end of the French elections in June.

If there was one thing that had never frightened Messier, it was adversity. He showed an almost inhuman capacity to soak up punches. In the days that followed the sacking of Lescure, a seminal moment in French business history, he went on a massive public-relations counterattack to defuse the row. He tried to stifle every rumor of a crisis in his leadership. Thierry Breton was being suggested as a possible candidate to replace him at Vivendi. Opportunely, members of Messier's team remembered an agreement under discussion with Breton's electronics company concerning digital decoders. The negotiations were rushed to completion, and Breton was surprised to be invited, as soon as he stepped off a flight from Tokyo, to sign the hastily reached agreement. Messier could thus announce that he was on the best of terms with the man who had been suggested by the media as his likely successor. He also sought to neutralize the threat from Claude Bébéar. Messier fixed a meeting for April 17 with the AXA insurance boss at his office on avenue Matignon. The insurance chief's office was something of a legend in Paris, not just for its gilded ceilings and rich fabrics, but because Bébéar kept several hunting rifles in a cabinet behind his desk. On arriving in the imposing building right by the Elysée presidential palace, Messier played his best card first. He immediately offered Bébéar a seat on the Vivendi Universal board. Bébéar, however, refused out of hand. He did not want to lend his credibility to Vivendi Universal in order to save Messier.

Bébéar told Messier he needed to articulate a clear strategy to his board. If he needed to sell Vivendi Environnement to raise cash, he should have a proper debate with the Vivendi Universal board. "Either you obtain a majority and get rid of all the directors who vote against your project, or you find yourself in a minority and should leave." He reproached Messier for his excessive exposure in the media. In his own defense, Messier explained that there had been a need for a high media profile to introduce a new company to U.S. investors, but that he now intended to keep a much lower profile. He acknowledged he had been maladroit, saying that he had been introverted when he was twenty and had been living out the adolescence he never had. Unamused, Bébéar replied: "At the age of forty-five and with responsibility for a group like Vivendi Universal, it's too late to play out an adolescent crisis. No one has confidence in you anymore." Bébéar felt he had made his views perfectly plain. However, on leaving the insurance chief's offices, Jean-Marie Messier rang his closest associates straight away and reported, "Everything's OK. Claude agrees with me. I've convinced him." In *Mon Vrai Journal,* Messier would claim Bébéar told him that day that he had found Vivendi Universal's strategy well articulated and convincing.[3]

Messier reserved his best performance for his shareholders, of whom nearly seven thousand had gathered at the Zenith, a vast, overheated concert hall in the northeast of Paris, in the late afternoon of April 24. It had been a year of "paradox," he claimed. "Our strategy is showing its impact but not in our share price." To remedy this problem, he continued, "the only answer is—" "Resignation!" shouted one shareholder. After the applause and cheering that swept the room died down, Messier managed to finish the sentence with the word "transparency." Bouncing back, though, he flattered and cajoled his shareholders, defusing much of their anger with carefully crafted gambits. He promised to forgo his share of the €2 billion stock option program they were about to vote on if the shares had not recovered that year's 35-percent fall by September, when the new options were to be granted. He said Vivendi Universal's executive committee had promised to reinvest their annual bonuses in the company's shares as a sign of their commitment and confidence. He admitted to "excessive and maladroit personal communication."

As his pièce de résistance, Messier promised his shareholders a €1 billion dividend. This large cash outflow had worried several of his board members at the lunch that preceded the annual shareholder meeting. "The board meeting which sacked me was the first proper one in the company's history," Pierre Lescure would later say. "People actually asked questions for the first time." Bernard Arnault joined Samuel Minzberg in posing pertinent questions.

"Have we really got the means to pay so much?" Arnault had asked after following the cash flow in the accounts with his finger. The lack of a proper response to his question left him dissatisfied. His presence on the board was doing little for his precious image and was a waste of time if no one even listened to him. "If we don't pay the dividend, it will be the last straw for the shareholders," retorted Jean-Louis Beffa, a fervent believer, like Edgar Bronfman, that shareholders should at least enjoy some reward in these lean times. After starting the year at €61.50, Vivendi Universal's shares had dropped to €38.20 by the time of the annual shareholder meeting.

The storm over Canal Plus swept all before it during the shareholder meeting open session. The station's employees monopolized the floor as they demanded explanations for the sacking of Lescure, who had decided to attend the shareholder meeting in person and was sitting with the other Vivendi Universal directors in the front row. Bruno Gaccio, star of *Les Guignols,* berated the chief executive for his treatment of Lescure and the collapse in the share price. Messier looked icily at him: "I find that you talk a lot about money, Mr. Gaccio." Shortly afterward, a man sitting close to the sound equipment and cameras stood up. "I'm sick of people at Canal Plus abusing this group!" he shouted. The mood of the meeting changed. The auditorium, filled with small shareholders who had hitherto allowed themselves to be dominated by the Canal Plus employees, started to applaud heartily. The group's employees and union representatives could not believe their eyes. One person claimed the angry man was nothing but a stooge: "This was the man assigned to Messier's autocue. The communications department pushed him into speaking." Genuine shareholder or not, his intervention proved to be decisive. "With a quick, piercing glance along the first row, filled with his managers and board, Messier did not turn a hair, didn't even make a gesture. He knew that he had won," reported *Le Monde* the next day in its account of the AGM (annual general meeting of shareholders).

There was only one tough question from the hall. Did Messier have the support of his board? someone asked. Messier signaled to

Marc Viénot, the oldest French director on the board, to speak on its behalf. Explaining by way of preamble that he found himself in an unusual position, the chairman of Vivendi Universal's audit committee said: "We would have reduced the powers of the chairman if we had been unhappy. His strategic choices have, in my opinion, the unanimous backing of the board." Sitting in a line along the front row of the hall, the other board members were surprised. The U.S. directors were furious. Samuel Minzberg was shaking with anger, according to Pierre Lescure, who was sitting right by him. What right did Viénot have to speak for them in this way? No one had been consulted in advance about any statement from the board. In fact, at the board meeting just a few hours before, the American members had explicitly stated their opposition to any statement of support for Messier. "You'll know when you don't have my support," Minzberg had said earlier that day. He and Edgar Bronfman Jr. had argued that a statement of support for Messier from the board would raise more questions than it answered. They were outraged at being presented with a fait accompli by Messier and Marc Viénot. That was not how a board was supposed to work.

Messier faced just one last hurdle: the vote. Every shareholder in the room had been given an electronic handheld device, like a remote control, with three choices. Shareholders could vote for a resolution or against it, or they could abstain, which had the same impact as voting against, but was less confrontational. In the polite world of French business, it is exceptionally rare for large shareholders to vote against a chairman's resolution. On the rare occasions when there is dissent, it is expressed through abstention. Seldom does the result go against the will of the chairman. As was usual, most big shareholders had delivered their votes to Messier well in advance of the meeting itself. To guarantee a resounding victory, Messier had hired Georgeson Shareholder, the vote-gathering organization that had just played a key role in Hewlett-Packard's takeover of Compaq. These hired consultants had secured the vast majority of the votes Messier needed; yet the shareholders in the room, who represented 20 percent of the total votes that would be cast that evening, would still be crucial for success on the most important resolutions. In particular, Messier was worried that shareholder activists would try to vote down his proposal to grant share options of more than 5 percent of the company's capital, at that time worth around €2 billion, to senior executives. For several weeks, the campaign against the share option proposal had been growing in strength. Inside the company many thought the proposal insensitive given the fall in share price; outsiders judged it scandalous.

The first votes—to approve the 2001 accounts and put the largest loss in French history behind them—passed smoothly. The results had immediately flashed up on the huge screen behind Messier and Finance Director Guillaume Hannezo, who were sitting at a table on the stage. To his irritation, however, Messier noticed an unusually high abstention rate of almost 21 percent. In previous years, just 3–4 percent had dared to abstain from supporting his management of the company. This was a worrying sign. The hardest votes were still to come. The result of the fourth vote stopped him short. The resolution to revoke Pierre Lescure's mandate as a Vivendi Universal director had barely been approved: nearly 45 percent of his shareholders abstained. In other words, shareholders had almost voted to overrule both him and the board by demanding the retention of Lescure as a director of Vivendi Universal. If just 5 percent more had abstained or voted against the resolution, Messier would have had no choice but to offer his resignation. His authority would have been wholly undermined by such a reversal. The minds of the Vivendi Universal directors were all whirring. There was something strange happening. They had never seen a result quite like it.

Pierre Lescure was delighted at the result, but was nonetheless left perplexed. He suspected something had gone wrong. Many people had told him they had voted against his dismissal, yet none of their votes had registered in the "against" column. Not a single shareholder seemed to have voted against Messier's resolutions. The Vivendi Universal chief executive pressed on with a look of foreboding. The vital resolution—authorizing him to grant share options of more than €2 billion of Vivendi Universal stock to the company's senior executives—was still to come. Uniquely, because it related to the capital structure of the company, this resolution would need a two-thirds majority to succeed. In normal circumstances, that would be easily achievable. Most votes at French shareholder meetings tend to pass with approval rates in the high nineties. As shareholders voted on the stock option resolution, number sixteen, Messier tensed his shoulders and began to perspire. The result flashed up on the huge screen behind him. An enormous number of shareholders had abstained. He flinched as he read the data. "Resolution sixteen, rejected," he announced. Shareholders had voted down the controversial option plan: 41 percent had abstained or voted against, leaving Messier short of the two-thirds majority needed. "We must reward talent," said an ashen Messier. "We will come back with a modified proposal."

Colette Neuville, a French shareholder rights activist, whose organization, Adam,* had long campaigned for better corporate governance at Vivendi Universal, could scarcely believe it. In all her years of campaigning against overmighty French bosses, she had never won such an unexpected victory. It was a real coming of age for French capitalism, she thought. The shareholder meeting ended after eight in the evening. That same night, at Siècle, the discreet Parisian private club, Jean-François Dubos, general counsel of Vivendi Universal, rounded upon Jean-Louis Beffa. The chairman of Saint-Gobain had resigned from the Vivendi Universal board the previous day and had not attended the shareholder meeting which forced the directors' hands. "We've checked. It's you who caused the measure to fail. You voted against." Beffa, whose company owned just over 1 percent of Vivendi Universal's shares, was irritated at the threatening tone. He had not voted against, he insisted. On the contrary, he had ordered all Saint-Gobain's votes to be cast in support of Messier. In front of Dubos, Beffa telephoned Saint-Gobain's senior legal officer, who confirmed that he had supported all of Messier's resolutions. The next

---

*Adam = Association pour la defense des actionnaires minoritaires.

day, the scene was replayed at Vivendi Universal's headquarters at 42 avenue Friedland. Messier was hosting a reception for Antoine Zacharias, the chairman of Vinci, Vivendi's former construction subsidiary, to celebrate his entry into the One Hundred Club, a gourmet dining club that gathered together many of the country's leading business figures. Messier and Beffa found themselves face to face, next to Zacharias. Messier had still not come to terms with the previous day's vote. He took Beffa to task, accusing him of voting against the resolutions and of wanting him to lose face in front of the AGM. Once again, Beffa defended himself, reminding Messier that his votes alone would have been insufficient to block the resolution. Furious at the insinuations, Beffa demanded that they check the voting machine used by Saint-Gobain's legal officer. The examination, however, showed that the votes had been recorded as abstentions, exactly as Messier claimed.

After further investigation, Messier discovered that it was not just Saint-Gobain that, accidentally or not, had voted against his resolutions. Three big banks—BNP Paribas, Société Générale, and Crédit Agricole—had their votes recorded as abstentions. Either they were all lying about the way they had voted or there was some skulduggery at work. Two nights later, Messier rushed out a press release claiming "corroborating indicators of the systematic malfunction of the voting machines of the main shareholders." With his heightened sensitivity to conspiracy, Messier immediately declared there had been a fraud: his spin doctors implied that the piracy was more likely to have been the work of technicians at Canal Plus, familiar with electronic handsets, than of any of the many antiglobalization groups that had been demonstrating outside the Zenith. Without discussing it with his board, Messier declared all the votes null and void. The dividend would be paid into an escrow account, pending the organization of another vote. The apparently arbitrary verdict that hackers must have fixed the result met with incredulity. It seemed that Messier was behaving like a petulant child unable to accept defeat. "Pirates ahoy!" exclaimed "Breakingviews," the business comment column of the *Wall Street Journal Europe,* in an article heavy with irony. The *Financial*

*Times'* "Lex" column was even harsher: "We can only hope that his outrageous options plan is defeated once again."*

Messier was relieved to have found a palatable explanation for the rejection of his stock option plan. However, he was under no illusion about how weak his position had become. The day after the annual shareholder meeting, he had had breakfast with Albert Frère, the Belgian financier, and Bernard Arnault, the chairman of LVMH. The two entrepreneurs co-owned Château Cheval Blanc, one of the great vineyards of St. Emilion. He considered them among his closest friends in the French business world. That morning Arnault and Frère were honest with a man they still regarded with a great deal of affection. It would not be too late for him to save himself, they felt, if only he realized the danger that he was facing. Their tone was blunt. "You're screwing everything up and losing all your credibility. Stop making an exhibition of yourself like a fairground monkey," Frère said, before relaying to Messier in the frankest terms how people now saw him, stressing his megalomania, overexposure, manipulativeness, and paranoia. "The house is burning," he concluded. "Don't go back to New York. Stay in Paris. This is where things are happening."

---

*In the end, Vivendi Universal's board, irritated at not being consulted over the decision to call a new meeting, decided instead to ask the Paris commercial court to investigate. After months of investigation, the expert was unable to find any evidence of fraud. The investigation was hampered by the fact that the memory of the voting devices had been erased. The investigation concluded that there had been a malfunction of the voting system, but Vivendi Universal did little to disabuse the market of the notion that there had been a fraud perpetrated by Canal Plus employees in protest of the sacking of Pierre Lescure.

## CHAPTER TEN

# Vivendi vs. Universal

Since the start of his torment in December 2001, Jean-Marie Messier would shut himself inside his Park Avenue office for hours on end, staring into the depths of the Rothko as he racked his brains for a solution to the deadlock with the markets. The crisis of trust was so acute that his every utterance and action had become suspect. Removing Vivendi Universal from the front pages had become impossible. He spent hours on the telephone to trusted advisers: Maurice Lévy, the chairman of Publicis; British politician Peter Mandelson; Valérie Bernis, his old friend from the days of Edouard Balladur's cabinet; and Patricia Barbizet, the powerful executive at the head of François Pinault's fashion and retail empire. The faithful members of the old Dream Team—Eric Licoys, Guillaume Hannezo, Agnès Touraine, Philippe Germond, Catherine Gros—still dared to enter his office, bringing him the latest news from the city. They were shocked at how isolated he had become from the outside world. His employees no longer saw him. It had been a long time since he had visited any of the subsidiaries or French operations to see how work was going or to listen to people's expectations. He had succumbed to the "limousine syndrome" he had warned about in *j6m.com*.[1]

Smiling and affable, Messier let none of his distress show to the outside world. The bankers who oiled the wheels of the Vivendi Universal deal machine were astonished at his resilience and self-control as the media attacks grew ever fiercer. Yet, with one or two exceptions, few offered him moral support. A wall had erected itself imperceptibly between Messier and the business world. In New York, high society still welcomed his generous support for philanthropic and humanitarian causes. But behind his back, the comments were harsh. "He'll never be one of us," said Felix Rohatyn. The former American ambassador to France and onetime Lazard rainmaker had once dated Phyllis Bronfman, Edgar M. Bronfman Sr.'s sister, and remained close to the family. He confided his doubts about Messier to several French acquaintances. In public, most chief executives pretended nothing was wrong, yet in private, many believed Messier had joined the living dead. Little things—handshakes a bit softer, less eye contact, unanswered calls, fewer invitations, the intolerable impertinence of the media—indicated that he was no longer the coming man.

Messier continued to benefit, however, from the formal support of his board members. To the French directors, Messier had explained that Vivendi Universal was the victim of an obnoxious smear campaign started by the Bronfmans. Most of the French board members backed him out of a feeling of national solidarity. They too disliked the idea that a chief executive could be sacrificed just to please the whims of the stock market. That was not the French way. Meanwhile, he put it about in the American press and among his U.S. board members that it was French chauvinism that was holding up the transformation of Vivendi Universal into a pure-play media group by preventing him from selling Vivendi Environnement. Messier played both ends against the middle, presenting himself to the French as the last line of defense against the predatory Yankee hordes, and to the Americans as the champion of globalization and shareholder value. For several months he succeeded in achieving total paralysis, delaying the moment at which French and American board members would realize they shared common interests. Knowing little about each other, mutually suspicious, and encouraged by Messier to harbor the worst imaginable prejudices, the French and U.S. board members were failing to act as a coherent supervisory body.

The strange apathy of the Vivendi Universal board did little to reassure Amir Jahanchahi. Son of a former finance minister under the shah, the Iranian was well known in a small circle of wealthy and discreet international investors. Like many others, he had been seduced by Messier and the Vivendi Universal project in 2000. Collectively, he and his partners reckoned themselves among the biggest private investors in the ambitious French media group, with just under 2 percent of the capital. The falling share price and Messier's increasingly erratic behavior worried them. As the board appeared to offer little means of remedying the situation, Jahanchahi turned to Claude Bébéar. At the end of March, the Iranian financier sent him a message, outlining his concerns about Messier in some detail. Since the Six Nations tournament, Henri Lachmann had also told Bébéar, a close friend and patron, of his concerns and of those of Jean-Marc Espalioux, another Vivendi Universal board member. But those conversations had been vague. If Bébéar had long held definite ideas about Messier as an individual, he was not so sure about the corporation. He barely understood anything of the entertainment industry and the Internet. So he listened to the financier but promised nothing. Instead, he gathered information. Now that he was no longer running the day-to-day operations of AXA, he had time to take an interest in current affairs. It took him no time to reach a conclusion.

On Wednesday, April 10, 2002, less than three weeks after the trip to Murrayfield in Messier's Airbus, Claude Bébéar, Henri Lachmann, and Thierry Breton found themselves in the foyer of the Opéra Bastille during the intermission of *The Barber of Seville*. They were the guests of Philippe Villin, an old friend of Messier's from the Ecole Nationale d'Administration, who had become head of Lehman Brothers in Paris. The conversation turned to Vivendi Universal. Bébéar was unable to be diplomatic as he addressed Lachmann: "Henri, the situation is becoming dangerous. As a board member, it's your responsibility. If you don't do something, it's the whole Paris stock market that's going to suffer." These words were uttered in front of only three people, but the next day everyone who mattered knew that Bébéar was squaring up for a fight with Messier. Bébéar had decided to go public. Normally afraid of confrontation, the business world was nonetheless relieved that he had shown his hand. In private, company chairmen would admit that Messier was doing the image of French business more and more harm, but none had dared throw the first stone. Half willingly, half under duress, the old crocodile put himself at the head of the posse that Messier would nickname the "grand-daddy gunslingers."

On May 22, in an interview on a French radio station, Radio Classique, Bébéar for the first time voiced his worries about Vivendi Universal. He declared that the company had "a strategy problem" that in the United States would generally be solved by a change in management. "The board must define a strategy," Bébéar said, "agree with the management on how to apply it, and, as often happens in the U.S., change the management if necessary." A musket shot rang out across the Atlantic. Although it had been known for a month that Bébéar was lobbying Vivendi Universal board members to tackle the crisis of confidence in the group, his direct intervention raised eyebrows. American investors found it bizarre that a leading businessman who was neither a board member nor a major shareholder of Vivendi Universal should have found it necessary or appropriate to go over the heads of the board to the public in this way. What had happened to the French corporate governance system? "Imagine Maurice Greenberg of American Insurance Group publicly criticizing Steve Case's performance as chairman of AOL Time Warner and hinting that Case should be fired. That would be bizarre, right? Not in France," wrote *Forbes*. "Bébéar is a prominent member of that informal group of business leaders, bureaucrats and politicians that basically runs France. This club obviously finds Messier too internationalist in attitude, so it has voted to expel him from its ranks. And Bébéar is the designated messenger of doom."

The radio interview created a frenzy of speculation. While some, notably Amir Jahanchahi, pressed Bébéar to move in for the kill, the insurance chief hesitated. Marc Viénot was lobbying the banking community and the powerful network of *inspecteurs des finances* to rally around Messier. He was not to be thrown to the wolves, but helped through the crisis that was engulfing the group. The whisper went around that Bébéar was bored in premature retirement and jealous. The Vivendi Universal chief executive suggested that Bébéar was irritated because Messier had founded his Club of 40 for talented executives under the age of forty without first paying allegiance to the AXA chief executive by joining his club, Entreprise et Cité. He hinted that Bébéar was doing the bidding of self-interested politicians anxious to preserve the "Frenchness" of Vivendi Environnement. In the end, Messier decided that Bébéar was motivated by "his ferocious desire to be seen as *the* godfather of French capitalism. The one who makes and unmakes chief executives, who decides which strategies are good and which are bad."[2] He claimed that Bébéar was seeking to become the next Ambroise Roux, for thirty years the éminence grise of French business, who had died in 1999; he also suggested that Bébéar would do better to look after AXA, whose results had suffered since September 11, 2001.

As Vivendi Universal's financial condition worsened, Bébéar steeled himself for direct action. For several weeks Guillaume Hannezo had again found himself embroiled in negotiations with Moody's. The rating agency argued that Vivendi Universal now looked even riskier than before and that its credit rating deserved to be downgraded. Messier and Hannezo struggled to persuade Moody's to soften its stance, but on Friday, May 3, it told Hannezo that the group's rating would be lowered to just one notch above junk status. The long communiqué from Moody's announcing the bad news culminated with a bombshell: "The company is unlikely to achieve meaningful excess cash flow during the current financial year once the outflow for its 2001 dividend is taken into consideration." In other words, it was entirely dependent on the goodwill of the banks to roll over its short-term borrowings. That goodwill was ever more in doubt. With this downgrade, moreover, the odds of Vivendi Universal's being able to issue a long-term bond would lengthen. The commercial paper market—its main source of cheap short-term debt—could close in an instant if its credit rating deteriorated further. The company was teetering on the verge of disaster. As word of Vivendi Universal's impending liquidity crisis reached the market, the shares dropped to below €30 for the first time. They had fallen more than 50 percent since the start of the year and now stood at a fifth of the level reached in March 2000.

The pressure on Hannezo was becoming intolerable. On May 7, he wrote two e-mails, one to Messier and one to Dominique Ferrero, chief executive of Crédit Lyonnais. He urged Messier to confront his board with the need to sell Vivendi Environnement. "Looking for a consensus is the surest way to lead us to a real disaster: liquidity spiral, etc. To back the majority viewpoint against that of the minority is a defensible line to take. It's honorable and not systematically catastrophic." Messier replied, "I am not looking for consensus, I assure you. I am looking for a solid and sustainable majority on many fronts." The memo to Ferrero complained about the work of Edouard Tétreau, the analyst who ran the bank's media research unit and who had crossed swords with Messier in April. Tétreau had issued a perceptive note to clients speculating about the possibility of a liquidity crisis. "Until today, I have never complained to a bank's management about the work of an analyst," the finance director wrote. "When this analyst calculated the impact on our share price of various different scenarios, including a change of management, we treated it like any other question. This is totally different, a research paper, which we were not sent and to which we cannot reply, that constructs bankruptcy scenarios on the basis of wholly imaginary off-balance-sheet commitments and spreads totally libelous rumors."

A week after the downgrade, on Monday, May 13, Deputy Finance Director Dominique Gibert sounded the alarm. "We've got no more money," he said simply. A week earlier, the group had disgorged nearly $1.8 billion to pay for the cash element of the USA Networks acquisition and more than €1 billion to pay shareholders the dividend that Bernard Arnault had tried to question. The till was empty. The company needed to sell assets fast. For several months, Vivendi Environnement had been the obvious solution: it was worth around €6 billion and was highly liquid. Yet the sale had been bedeviled by French politics, and financial markets had become bewildered by the welter of contradictory statements about the water group's status within the corporation. On March 6, Messier had told analysts the stake would be sold, before changing course in the run-up to the elections and denying any such intention at the annual general meeting on April 24. Three weeks later, he had no choice. He needed the cash. The majority stake in Vivendi Environnement had to be sold. That Monday evening, Messier met Henri Proglio at avenue Friedland to plead for his support in effecting a sale the moment the elections were out of the way on June 16. He told Proglio there was no longer any question of his being replaced by Eric Licoys. He promised Proglio he would construct a *noyau dur* of friendly French institutional shareholders, just like in the good old days of privatizations.

An article questioning the group's financial strength and titled "The Mysteries of Vivendi Universal" appeared on the front page of the evening edition of *Le Monde* on Tuesday, May 14. When he saw it, Messier gave every impression of being outraged. The dismissal of Pierre Lescure had incited the paper to further "bad faith," he claimed. The evidence was plain. "Ten front-page headlines in two years, of which seven in three months, in 80 days to be precise, between April 17 and July 3."[3] This time, Messier wanted to hit back hard. To let the article pass would signal that Vivendi Universal had sunk below the water line. Reminding everyone "that responsibility goes with independence," he filed a libel suit against the paper that sought €1 million in damages, an unprecedented and terrifying sum.* In the meantime, he ordered all advertising in *Le Monde* to be stopped. It was a warning shot to other newspapers to watch what they wrote. Later he offered to withdraw the legal action and the advertising ban on condition that the author of the article—Martine Orange—stop writing about the group. Inevitably, in a world conditioned by memories of the litigiousness of Robert Maxwell and other businessmen who have abused libel laws, the attempt to muzzle *Le Monde* raised suspicions further.

Messier saw the *Le Monde* article as the latest development in the manhunt, "with all that is special in France: underground networks, lies, and deceit."[4] A climate of fear spread among the per-

---

*The suit was later dropped by the new management, and the veracity of *Le Monde*'s story was confirmed by testimony given to the various investigations.

sonnel and beyond. A week later, a female manager in the finance department was sacked after speaking to *Le Monde* (the conversation had taken place over private mobile telephones) Other employees believed they were followed, their phones were being tapped, and their e-mail was placed under surveillance. Even Claude Bébéar believed his phones were being tapped. Colette Neuville received a strange visit from a person purporting to work for Radio France who gave his name as Yves Ilvinec. "I'm just back from Colombia. There, people are killed for less than this," he said without preamble. She could later find no trace of any journalist at Radio France of that name. Similar threats were made a few days later in the editorial offices of *Le Monde*. All Paris played at frightening itself. Meetings started to be arranged in more and more unlikely places. Mobile-telephone conversations over the SFR network run by Vivendi were avoided. Some people even dispatched their secretaries to purchase pay-as-you-go unidentifiable mobile phones to ensure that their conversations would not be overheard.

Messier ended up frightening himself, concluding that he was living in the amoral world of J. R. Ewing. "*Dallas* . . . Your ruthless world exists. I have encountered it," he later wrote.[5] He claimed that journalists told him they had received frequent visits from motorcycle couriers who would drop off documents containing damaging allegations about Vivendi Universal and then take off at high speed. "Welcome to the little world of intrigue, secret investigations, and shadowy networks, of which one—let us call it 'A'—is based in London and has the delicacy to count among its members a former officer of a foreign country fired for torturing prisoners! Surveillance; espionage of my smallest deeds and acts, of my most insignificant human relations; tapping of my telephones; manipulation of taped recordings; photos or purported photos; rumor-mongering and the passing of documents to my board or to newsrooms: the complete amateur James Bond was there. I was spared nothing. My mistake was to have put up with these thuggish methods in the name of the group and not to have warned my directors while there was still time. A weakness of pride or honor."

Jean-Marie Messier's world had evidently become a strange and frightening place. But how much was real and how much was imaginary? Were there really these shadow networks of intrigue and subterfuge? Certainly, no journalists encountered by the authors have ever mentioned any anonymous dossiers relating to Messier or Vivendi Universal being dropped off in newsrooms by helmeted motorcycle deliverymen. None were delivered to either the *Financial Times* or *Le Monde,* the two newspapers whose correspondents Messier feels were most engaged in his "little world of intrigue," his *"Dallas."* The idea that everyone had an angle obsessed him. Just as he appeared convinced that *Le Monde* was the agent of Pierre Lescure, so he seemed certain that the *Financial Times* was the agent of the Bronfmans. Edgar Bronfman Jr. recalls Messier coming up to him in New York on one occasion early in 2002 and accusing him of leaking information to Jo Johnson of the *Financial Times.* "I've never spoken to her," Bronfman promised.* His genuine confusion over the gender of the *Financial Times* journalist was sufficient, on that occasion, to convince an increasingly suspicious Messier of his good faith.

If it was not Bronfman, then it must have been Samuel Minzberg. Messier was convinced that Minzberg was behind his own loss of credibility in financial markets and the prime force motivating journalists to probe Vivendi Universal for wrongdoing. In *My True Diary,* Messier lashes out at the *Financial Times* for asking questions, which he suggested were planted by Minzberg, "more worthy of a tabloid rag than a business newspaper." There appears to have been a coincidence of timing: at exactly the moment that Minzberg was demanding to have Messier's bank accounts checked and asking pointed questions about the cost of his apartment in New York, the *Financial Times*'s Paris correspondent sent an e-mail with questions on the very same subject. The idea was to find out exactly what shareholders would end up paying for this famous apartment: Vivendi Universal never deigned to make

---

*That was true at the moment it was said. Edgar Bronfman Jr. subsequently met Jo Johnson for two interviews at the Ritz in Paris.

any disclosure on the subject. In the end, it would emerge that the cost of furnishing the $17.5 million Park Avenue apartment exceeded a $1.75 million budget by almost $1 million. Overall, the company spent more than $20 million for Messier not to feel outclassed by other Park Avenue moguls. Was that reasonable? Did anyone have a right to know?

No matter what the cost, there is nothing illegal about companies owning luxury apartments or assigning them for executives' personal use. However, if use of the apartment is granted as part of a chief executive's remuneration, the SEC requires that the perk be disclosed to shareholders, along with salary, bonuses, share options, and so on. However, few such luxury apartments are ever disclosed in SEC filings. Companies tend to claim that the apartments are not perks, but normal business expenses incurred "for the convenience of the company," even if they are used exclusively by one person. The argument goes that these apartments are close to work (Messier's at 515 Park Avenue was perhaps ten minutes from the Seagram Building at number 375) and save the valuable time of highly paid executives. Much the same argument used to be wheeled out for corporate ownership of executive jets. The reality is that these apartments tend all too often to stretch far beyond simple expedience and become genuine monuments to chief executive greed. Shareholders in Tyco were similarly outraged to find that they had paid $16.8 million for Dennis Kozlowski's apartment at 950 Fifth Avenue, then thrown in another $3 million for improvements. His duplex included a $6,000 shower curtain, coat hangers valued at $2,900, two sets of sheets for $5,960, and a $445 pincushion. His office boasted a $15,000 dog umbrella stand, although it was never clear whether this was a stand for his dog's umbrellas or one in the shape of a dog.

The French board members found themselves in a novel situation. In the past, it had generally been the state that decided when to terminate the mandates of underperforming chief executives. Vivendi Universal, however, was a rarity in France in that it was neither state-controlled, like France Telecom, Renault, and Air France, nor dominated by family shareholders, like LVMH, L'Oréal, and Michelin. Rather, with its shares widely held by a million small investors, Vivendi Universal was more like most U.S. or UK companies. International investors regarded the reaction of the Vivendi Universal board as an important test of the capacity of the French economy to apply Anglo-American rules of corporate governance in the interests of shareholders.

"Resign now. You'll be able to come back in two or three years. Everything will have been forgotten then. You'll be able to start a new career," advised Alain Minc, the consultant who was acting to some extent as spokesman for the captains of industry. Messier immediately rejected the advice. He would fight right to the end if necessary. He was sure no French board would adopt crude American practices and dismiss him. Anyway, how would they justify doing that? The situation was much less serious than people were saying: "There are two difficult years to get through," he confided to those closest to him, "but I am there for fifteen years." Once again, he called on Maurice Lévy for help. The lobbying machine ground into action. Yves de Chaisemartin, chief executive of the newspaper group that controlled *Le Figaro,* was prevailed upon to write an editorial in the right-wing newspaper: "Private Messier must be saved," he argued at length.

Messsier's stubbornness was making a smooth resolution of the boardroom problem impossible. He was forcing his French board members to defend him against five U.S. board members who now clearly wanted him to resign. Every day the Vivendi Universal boardmembers discovered in the press new details of financial commitments of which they should have been made aware by the company's management. They realized that they had never been given a full set of financial statements for the first quarter, replete with balance sheet, cash flow, and a detailed assessment of the liquidity position. They requested a full briefing on the group's cash-flow situation at the next board meeting, due to be held in New York on May 29.

Some board members were frightened, particularly in light of the new legislation that had come into force at the beginning of 2002. Henceforth, they were personally liable for damages if they failed in their supervisory duties. This simple fact, invoked time after time by Claude Bébéar, proved counterproductive to his efforts to galvanize them into action. Instead of taking steps to address Vivendi Universal's problems, several directors preferred to resign, abandoning shareholders to their fate. Philippe Foriel-Destezet, who had been a member of the board since 1997, discovered a conflict of interest that compelled him to resign. According to Messier's desperate communications department, Foriel-Destezet had suddenly realized that the French media group was one of his employment agency Adecco's largest clients.

Following the resignations of Jean-Louis Beffa and René Thomas in April, the departure of the Adecco chairman unsettled investors. It seemed that the smart rats were jumping ship. Messier knew it; but in one way he no longer cared. The departures would give him an opportunity to even up the board, to introduce new and younger directors who were favorable toward his strategy and less hesitant about selling Vivendi Environnement, the old core of the company. In his eyes, it was not the indebtedness, the collapse of the share price, the cash flow, and the strategic deadlock that was the problem with Vivendi Universal. It was the split among the board members, some of whom were now questioning his decisions.

He had several names in mind to replace those who had left. At the March board meeting, he had proposed Agnès Touraine and Philippe Germond, but both members of the Dream Team were rejected. Messier also asked two close friends to join the board: Maurice Lévy and Georges Ralli. It required the personal intervention of Elisabeth Badinter, leading shareholder in Publicis, to dissuade Lévy from accepting the post. Although Ralli was delighted at the suggestion, his candidacy was also rejected by the board. He was already a board member of Vivendi Environnement and was far too closely associated with Messier to be a credible independent director in their eyes. Messier's attempts to take advantage of the slew of resignations to put in place people who would be loyal to him had failed.

It was thus in a climate of mistrust that the board met in New York. The media buildup to the meeting had been vast. Some thought Messier might follow Minc's advice and resign; most agreed that if he decided to stay, the odds of him actually being fired were low. Investors hoped at the very least for a signal that the board was taking matters in hand. Confidence in the existing management team had all but disappeared. Like a veteran politician, Messier had counted and recounted his forces. He knew he could muster at least five votes, including his own, out of fifteen.* He knew the five North American board members had now lined up against him. The question was whether they would choose to pounce before they were certain of victory. If they demanded a vote of confidence in his management, he would need to be able to call upon the support of at least three of the remaining five: Henri Lachmann, Jacques Friedmann, Jean-Marc Espalioux, the increasingly distant Bernard Arnault, and Esther Koplowitz, the billionaire owner of a Spanish construction company. It would be tight.

Once again, chance smiled upon Messier. Samuel Minzberg overplayed his hand. His insistent questioning, which in Messier's mind reflected a "pathological disorder or mania," made the meeting drag on for eight hours. The French directors had never seen such aggression. "This hostility expressed in the heart of the board extended inexcusably the length of our board meetings while at the same time limiting their quality," Messier said. "At exactly the moment that the board should have been working elbow to elbow to focus on the short-term problems caused by the fact that financial markets had become totally irrational, every session turned into an inquisition. The only thing that was missing was the Anglepoise lamp in the eyes and someone shouting: 'Answer yes or no!'"[6] Realizing that the attacks were proving counterproductive, Edgar Bronfman Jr. decided against pushing for a motion to dismiss Messier. Even the international directors had been upset by Minzberg.

Simon Murray, in particular, recoiled at Minzberg's affront to the chairman. Apart from being the only Englishman, the financier stood out from the other board members. Inspired by Gary Cooper in *Beau Geste,* he left home at the age of nineteen to join

---

*Apart from his own vote, he could count on the support of Eric Licoys, Simon Murray, Serge Tchuruk, and Marc Viénot. Bernard Arnault, formerly very close, no longer came to any board meetings, but allowed Messier to vote on his behalf.

the French foreign legion. His account of five years of sun, sand, and slaughter in the Algerian desert, *Legionnaire*, had sold more than a million copies and in 2002 was being made into an action film called *Simon: An English Legionnaire*. "Simon was a vociferous supporter of Jean-Marie's. It was more emotional than rational," said Edgar Bronfman Jr. "He took offense at Sam's style, which unfortunately sometimes obscured the substance of his comments." At the end of the meeting Messier found a handwritten note to Minzberg from one of the Bronfmans: "Sam. Watch out. You're doing too much. It's obvious that your strategy is above all just making the French stick together."[7]

It was after one in the morning in Paris by the time the board finished and the exhausted French board members, who had participated by videoconference, bade each other good night. Nothing had been decided. The only sop to the market was an announcement of a special corporate-governance committee that would review the way the board had been functioning. A representative from each of the opposing camps would sit on the new committee: Marc Viénot from the French side and Edgar Bronfman Jr. from the U.S. camp. The arrangement impressed no one. "Why is it only now, when Vivendi is in such a parlous state, that the board appears to be waking up to its responsibilities?" said Colette Neuville of Adam. "The governance of this company is a catastrophe and the problem won't be solved by committee." Delighted to have survived the meeting, Messier downplayed the significance of the new board-level committee, cockily announcing, "I have in no way been placed under supervision."

The following day, Vivendi Universal's share price started to wilt again: hedge funds had bet there would be a bounce if Messier looked more likely to be pushed out than before. The Messier discount was by this stage estimated to be almost 50 percent. It appeared the funds had miscalculated. The nonsense with the corporate-governance committee indicated that the Bronfmans would be unable to force Messier out if he still had the French on his side. Messier could rule Vivendi Universal with a divided board, relying on the cozy French system of mutual support that he had once derided. If Messier stayed in power, they argued, there was little hope of a change in strategy. Once again, Claude Bébéar found himself the subject of shareholder pleas. Samuel Minzberg, having recognized his tactical error at the board meeting in New York, had contacted Bébéar directly to propose that he become chairman of Vivendi Universal. Bébéar rejected the idea but assured Minzberg that he was following the situation closely. Further impetus to remove Messier had come from the revelation that the Vivendi Universal chief executive had been awarded a massive bonus in 2001. Investors had been outraged to learn in May that Messier had received a 250-percent bonus, taking his income to €5.12 million, even though he had delivered the largest loss in French corporate history.

The vultures began to circle. Investment bankers had realized that untold fees could be generated from a breakup of Vivendi Universal. Given the drought in mergers-and-acquisitions fees, the banks would have much to gain from the arrival of a new chairman intent on breaking up the sprawling empire. Industrialists too started to run their slide rules over the parts of the Messier empire. Jean-Luc Lagardère, chairman of the Lagardère media and defense conglomerate, was interested in several of Vivendi Universal's businesses. Many in Paris felt that the only resolution for Vivendi Universal's problems would be a breakup of the empire into its constituent parts: Vivendi Environnement, Cegetel, and Canal Plus in France, and the entertainment assets and Houghton Mifflin in the United States. That would at least resolve the Franco-American impasse within the boardroom. But to get to that stage required the deposition of Messier.

Messier's position continued to weaken in line with Vivendi Universal's financial situation. With the fall in the share price, the guarantee mechanisms kicked into action. The former owners of Rondor Music demanded to be paid €230 million. The puts Messier had sold at €68 were now out of the money to the tune of €1 billion. Alerted by their bankers to the financial crisis at Vivendi Universal, Messier's partners in Cegetel took fright. BT Group, the former UK telecommunications monopoly that owned 26 percent of Cegetel, demanded to examine the accounts of the telecom joint venture. It realized that contrary to its understanding of the shareholders' agreement, Cegetel was lending money to Vivendi Universal. BT demanded and won the immediate repayment of €720 million. Messier rued the day, back in 2000, that he had treated the British company haughtily. BT's senior managers had not forgotten how Messier had ignored their complaints at being unfairly shut out from his alliance with Vodafone to create Vizzavi. The shoe was now on the other foot.

Under pressure, Hannezo and Messier rushed to sell what they could, raising a pitiful €27 million from a few property assets, and announcing the sale to Rupert Murdoch of Telepiu in Italy for €1.5 billion.* But Messier knew that this cash would take months to arrive. The board meeting in New York had failed to agree to Hannezo's request to sell warrants in USA Networks, leading to a row between the finance director and the two Edgar Bronfmans. Two days after the meeting, on May 31, Edgar Bronfman Sr., who rarely intervened in the day-to-day affairs of the company, wrote to Hannezo: "It worries me that you write to Edgar Jr. telling him that he should either fire you or let you do your job, because that makes me think you do not understand what your prime responsibility is. Your job is to restore the credibility of the group which has been lost as a result of saying one thing and doing its opposite. To restore our credibility we must be beyond suspicion, like Caesar's wife. Complex transactions that will take us before the courts and guarantee us unflattering headlines will not restore our credibility. On the contrary they will damage it further. You should never even have suggested such a sale."

On Wednesday, June 12, however, the two executives realized they had no choice but to sell a substantial portion of Vivendi Universal's 63-percent stake in Vivendi Environnement. The problem was that the board was not scheduled to meet to approve such a sale until Monday, June 17, the day after the last of the votes for the French parliamentary elections. They both knew the group could not wait that long and so set about constructing yet another

---

*Murdoch exploited this premature announcement of his purchase of Telepiu to ratchet down the price to just €873 million.

complex financial transaction that would bring some quick cash into the depleted coffers. That Wednesday, Deutsche Bank agreed to swap €1.4 billion against a 12.7-percent stake in Vivendi Environnement. When the loan eventually fell due, Vivendi would have to repay the loan and take back possession of its shares. This mechanism allowed the group to get hold of the money quickly without selling shares on the market before it had secured the board's approval. It also enabled Vivendi Universal to avoid a large tax bill from the French government. In 2000, at the time of the merger with Seagram, the group had undertaken to keep its entire holding in Vivendi Environnement until the end of 2003 in return for a total exoneration from capital gains tax. This was the type of highly complex transaction that investors simply would not tolerate in the charged environment after Enron. It was rushed and poorly disclosed, and reeked of panic.

As agreed with Henri Proglio and numerous French politicians, on the morning of Monday, June 17, the day after the legislative elections, Deutsche Bank prepared to launch the sale of the Vivendi Environnement shares it had bought from Vivendi Universal on the twelfth. Suddenly, however, the offer disappeared from the market. The French company had ordered that everything be stopped. In the panic to raise the funds, no one had stopped to talk to Esther Koplowitz. If Vivendi Universal's stake in Vivendi Environnement fell below 50 percent, which it would the moment the water group proceeded with a planned rights issue, the construction magnate, one of the world's richest women, would have the right to force the media group to buy back her half of a joint venture. Around €900 million was at stake, enough to bring down the entire group, given the state of its finances.* Her lawyers, bankers, and friends all advised her to activate this clause, take the money, and regain her freedom. As if overcome by a death wish or subconsciously wanting an end to his long struggle to stay in power, Messier made not the slightest attempt to convince the

---

*Vivendi Universal's 63-percent stake would fall to around 40.8 percent following the sale of a 15-percent stake and a simultaneous capital increase by Vivendi Environnement to which it would not subscribe.

Vivendi Universal board member to do the opposite. Esther Koplowitz held the fate of France's largest private-sector employer in her hands. Messier and his 380,000 staff were at her complete mercy.

At 11 A.M. on Monday, June 17, Proglio took it upon himself to negotiate with the tall and imposing Spaniard. They held each other in high esteem. Proglio had offered his sympathy the previous August when she had been the victim of one of the largest international art heists in history. Nineteen paintings valued at $30 million and including masterpieces such as *The Fall of the Burro* by Goya and *Guitar on a Chair* by the cubist Juan Gris had been stolen from her Madrid mansion. By June, Spanish police had recovered ten of the paintings, and it was just conceivable that the partial return of her precious art collection had left Esther Koplowitz in a charitable mood. But would that be enough to counterbalance the attraction of hundreds of millions of euros?

"Think, Esther. You're holding a bomb. You can exercise your option. But are you sure Vivendi has the means to pay? You run the risk of blowing everything apart without even getting your stake back. If you stay with us, Vivendi Universal will be able to sell Vivendi Environnement. That will save us. I need to get away from Vivendi Universal very rapidly. For the moment I haven't got much to offer you in exchange, except the strengthening of our commercial agreements." Koplowitz agreed, but only on the condition that she would have nothing further to do with Vivendi Universal.

At 3 P.M. the board assembled at avenue Friedland for what would be Messier's penultimate meeting as chairman. It was another dysfunctional session: the directors were spread across five different locations. The videoconference screen once again had turned into a shuddering mosaic. From the outset, Samuel Minzberg resumed where he had left off in New York at the end of the previous month. He refused to vote on the sale of Vivendi Environnement until he had had time to read the documents, which, as usual, had only just arrived in front of them.

Simon Murray, showing a soldier's loyalty to his captain, bridled at Minzberg's manner: "Fine. Let's all vote. Sam, you can vote later." "Fuck you," answered Minzberg. He then asked Hannezo if he knew of any financial relationship between Messier and Murray that might be affecting Murray's judgment. According to Messier, Minzberg even asked if Hannezo had checked their bank accounts. "As a lawyer, he doubtless frequently encounters instances of personal conflict of interest, fraud, corruption! . . . But here, at Vivendi Universal, we are not part of that world. . . . Yet this man, for whom no blow was too low, who would insinuate anything, finally succeeded in influencing the weakest and most fragile of my French board members. We are choirboys in the face of such methods."[8]

Distracted by the furious rows between Minzberg, Murray, and Messier, the board learned nothing of the financing agreement that had been set up with Deutsche Bank five days earlier. Eventually, the board agreed in principle to sell a 15-percent stake in Vivendi Environnement. Yet, just three days later, on Friday, June 21, evidence that Vivendi Universal had already sold a 12.7-percent stake to Deutsche Bank leaked into the market. Under French law, the bank was obliged after five working days to declare any holding of more than 5 percent of a company's shares. Vivendi Universal's description of the share pledge as a "classic financing operation" did nothing to allay investor anxieties. News of the "grim repo," further evidence of a cash crunch, sent the share price down 7 percent, to below €25. "There is no problem of financing. The group used this mechanism simply because it allows us to raise money at an advantageous price," Messier tried to explain.

The damage to Messier's reputation was severe. Even Marc Viénot now recognized the extreme threat to the chief executive's position and rallied to his assistance yet again. The former Société Générale chairman allowed himself to be quoted in the *Financial Times* denying there was a liquidity crisis and saying he did not believe that any directors would ask for Messier's resignation at yet another board meeting, scheduled for June 25. "He has a strong position within the board and is doing the job for which we hired him. If there were a change of strategy and he were not in a position to execute the new strategy, things might be different, but that is not the case. The strategy is the same." Even Viénot, however, admitted that Messier had lost "quite a lot of credibility with the capital markets."

Other board members, speaking on condition of anonymity, said they feared that Messier would come under mounting pressure from U.S. directors to resign, and doubted whether the French establishment could save him. "I think Messier knows he is finished, but does not understand," one said. "He is still a member of the establishment and it will rally around against any organized U.S. attack. But it seems to me as though the campaign against him will not stop until he negotiates his exit package."

CHAPTER ELEVEN

# The Last Days of J6M

Jean-Marie Messier looked at the Reuters screen, aghast at the 23-percent fall in the morning session. By lunchtime on Monday, June 24, 2002, Vivendi Universal's shares had slumped to €18, their lowest level since May 1989 and far below the €23 they had been worth at the time of his arrival as chief executive of the old Générale des Eaux in November 1994.* For two years he had battled against this wave of selling. Since the $42 billion acquisition of Universal Studios in June 2000, his biggest deal of all, the declining share price had been the sole constant in his universe.

That morning's fall, however, was something different: the violence of the market's reaction stopped him short. It was the clearest of messages: investors wanted him to resign. Everyone was selling: American pension funds, French banks, offshore hedge funds, even the loyal army of small French shareholders. Standing in his office with Eric Licoys, Messier blamed Guillaume Hannezo for the panic in the market. The finance director's latest ruse to raise cash from the markets had backfired. Investors were panicking at the rumors of an imminent liquidity crisis at the conglomerate.

---

*Générale des Eaux's share price was €23 at the start of November 1994, when Messier became chief executive.

When Hannezo joined them, Licoys and Messier could barely contain their anger. The market's reaction to the revelation of the media group's surreptitious plan to raise cash against the value of its water business was the culmination of weeks of suspicion. For several months, Messier had felt that the unkempt forty-year-old had failed to explain Vivendi Universal's strategy and reassure investors of its financial solidity. To restore his own credibility with financial markets, he would have to sacrifice Hannezo, a man he had long regarded as one of France's most intellectually gifted financiers, just as he had knifed Lescure and Olivennes.

Nine months earlier, he and Hannezo had moved to New York to introduce the new French media giant to the Wall Street investors who really counted. The original plan had been for Hannezo to return to Paris in September, leaving Messier to represent the company in New York, but now the chief executive wanted a new finance director, someone who could speak to Wall Street. Hannezo could not disguise his bitterness. He felt that for three months it was he who had held the company together and prevented its financial collapse. He had negotiated sudden loans, produced cash from the most implausible sources, and prevented Messier from pursuing any number of ruinous acquisitions. He had tried so hard to rein in Messier's ambition. How many times had he said "No"?

Back in December 2001, at the start of Vivendi Universal's descent into hell, it was Hannezo who had sent Messier a personal plea by e-mail: "All I ask is that all this doesn't end in disgrace." He had tried again on several occasions. On March 4, 2002, he had attempted to alert Messier to the fact that only he could save them: "Our jobs, our reputations are at stake. What investors want to know right now is the following: Is VU a total fraud like Enron? Is VU threatened by its debt? Has J-M-M completely lost it?" Messier had ignored him, swatting him away like a fly, as if it were the natural role of finance directors, masters of caution and timidity, to be ignored. Like so many others, Hannezo worried constantly that Messier had stopped listening, but he remained fundamentally loyal to his colleague and chief executive of six years.

Messier, however, preferred Agnès Touraine, chief executive of Vivendi Universal's publishing arm, and Philippe Germond, the head of the telecommunications wing to Hannezo. They were less argumentative, less intellectual, and less threatening. Hannezo, first in his class at the Ecole Nationale d'Administration, training ground for the French ruling class, was too brilliant. Known in Paris as the "Mozart of finance," he was the only person at Vivendi Universal whose technical skills were better than Messier's, whose deal-making artistry surpassed that of the former Lazard wunderkind.

Moreover, he was maddeningly popular with the company's employees. Everyone liked to share jokes with Hannezo. He cultivated a mad professor image, wandering the corridors with his shirttail dangling, his tie wrenched to one side, and a cigar hanging from his mouth morning to night. Messier saw that it was time for a change. Although he had opposed Hannezo's departure earlier in the year, he now wanted him to leave as soon as possible. Once again, Messier sought a scapegoat who would allow him to win back the confidence of the markets.

For Bernard Arnault, Vivendi Universal no longer belonged in his stable of luxury brands. The image-conscious entrepreneur, nicknamed the "wolf in cashmere" for the cold manner with which he had constructed the world's leading luxury goods empire and the largest private fortune in France, had decided to resign from Messier's board. The risk to his personal fortune had increased since the start of the year: a new French law left board members personally liable for failures of corporate governance at publicly listed companies. Arnault had told Messier he would resign his mandate as an independent director in September, once the storm in the capital markets had blown over. But in light of Vivendi Universal's worsening liquidity crunch that June, his trusted adviser, Pierre Godé, told him he no longer had any choice. He had to drop Messier as fast as possible.

As Vivendi Universal's shares plunged that Monday morning, the Vivendi Universal chief executive pleaded with Bernard Arnault to change his mind, or at least to delay the announcement. Arnault's timing, so soon after other board-level resignations and the calamitous plunge in the share price and so near the next board meeting, could not be worse. On the one hand, it would look as though insiders had got wind of an undisclosed accounting problem; on the other, it would leave Messier ever more exposed to the attacks of the Bronfman family's representatives and other U.S. directors who were threatening to seek his dismissal at the forthcoming meeting in Paris.

Messier's appeals went unheeded. The following day, hours before Vivendi Universal's board was to meet for its third formal session in four weeks, the news bulletins flashed the news of Bernard Arnault's resignation from the board of Vivendi Universal. "A knife in the back," Messier later told the board member, claiming ignorance of the urgent necessity that might have pushed him to resign just ahead of a vital board meeting and the day of a "major stock market accident." With characteristic sangfroid, Arnault replied that the timing was certainly not perfect, but would never have been.

There could have been no worse atmosphere for the last board meeting before the summer holidays than that created by the 23-percent share price fall and Arnault's resignation. The precise causes of the collapse in the share price remain mysterious. There had been little fresh news since Friday's 7-percent share price fall on the back of market anxiety at the indecent haste Vivendi Universal had displayed in raising cash against its shares in Vivendi Environnement. Word of stresses in Vivendi Universal's financial situation were spreading throughout the banking community.

The Vivendi Universal board had decided a few weeks before to take the rare step of bypassing Jean-Marie Messier in order to get a clearer picture of the group's financial situation. Edgar Bronfman Jr. solicited the views of Citigroup and of Goldman Sachs. Citigroup's analysis was much more pessimistic than that of its rival and, in hindsight, much more accurate. It estimated that the gulf in Vivendi Universal's finances was as much as €5–7 billion. In the end, however, it was Goldman Sachs that won the mandate from the board. Bronfman commissioned the bank to undertake assessment of the group's liquidity position. On Monday night, after the markets closed, Goldman Sachs reported the grim news to

Vivendi Universal's senior executives and to Bronfman. Reeling from the 23-percent collapse in the share price, Messier and Hannezo listened in fury to the three managing directors of Goldman Sachs as they described the pitiable condition in which they found the company.

Philippe Altuzarra, supported by Eric Coutts and Glenn Earle, outlined four scenarios for Vivendi Universal, with the most probable being that, in the absence of a major bond issue, the group would have to file for bankruptcy as early as September or October. It was a simple question of mathematics: the amount of available resources in cash and credit lines, divided by the burn rate, and adjusted for the likelihood of Messier and Hannezo being able to raise fresh funds through asset sales or a bond issue. Even though the other scenarios were less bleak, at the end of the meeting, Bronfman had heard quite enough. He accompanied Jean-Marie Messier back to his office at 42 avenue Friedland, where he asked the chairman and chief executive of Vivendi Universal to resign. Messier declined.

Over a private breakfast the next day, Bronfman repeated his request that Messier step down at that afternoon's board meeting. Once again, Messier refused. A few hours later, the fifteen directors of Vivendi Universal gathered for a pre–board meeting lunch, just as they had done before the annual shareholder meeting in April. The atmosphere was unrecognizable. The five Americans on the board—Edgar Bronfman; his seventy-three-year-old father; Samuel Minzberg; Marie-Josée Kravis, the wife of Kohlberg Kravis Roberts founding partner and *Barbarians at the Gate* protagonist Henry Kravis; and Richard Brown, chairman of Electronic Data Systems—knew their moment had come. It was time for regime change, with or without allies. As the lunch drew to a close, Minzberg approached Messier loyalist Simon Murray. The craggy sixty-two-year-old flinched as the lawyer clutched his arm. Minzberg apologized for swearing at him at the board meeting in May: "Will you vote with us?" he asked. With a soldier's stiffness, Murray said he would make a decision based on the presentations to the board.

A few minutes later, in the boardroom on the penthouse floor of the avenue Friedland offices, Messier barely looked at Edgar Bronfman Jr. and the four other American directors as he opened the session. Bright sunshine entered the room through the French windows onto the lush roof garden created by Sir James Goldsmith, the British raider who had owned the old *L'Express* building in the 1980s. Messier had arranged the order of business to ensure a smooth start. He was sure the Americans would approve the appointment of Dominique Hoenn, the chief operating officer of BNP Paribas, France's largest bank, to replace Bernard Arnault on the board. It would signal that the place de Paris fully supported both him and the Vivendi Universal project in these volatile markets.

Right from the outset, the fifteen board members split along national lines, leaving the North American board members dated. Once again, Sam Minzberg refused to vote, for procedural reasons, haranguing the chairman: Vivendi Universal's human resources committee had not yet discussed the appointment, he argued. At the time of Seagram's merger with Vivendi, the Bronfmans had insisted that they had the right to chair the committee that selected new board members. As the committee had not approved the appointment, the board should wait. Messier countered that a plenary session of the board was nonetheless entitled to validate the appointment and pushed for a vote. The result left Messier in no doubt of what was to follow: without hesitation, the five U.S. directors opposed the appointment of Hoenn. The ten Europeans were in favor.

Edgar Bronfman Jr. read a long indictment of Messier's management that highlighted the collapse of investor confidence in the group. After dwelling on the origins of the Messier discount, he invited Philippe Altuzarra to present Goldman Sachs's findings to the full board. It was one of the most difficult moments of the elegant banker's stellar career: Messier and he had both studied at the Ecole Nationale d'Adminstration, had been friends for many years, and also enjoyed a close working relationship. Although Messier's closest investment-banking relations remained with his former colleagues at Lazard, he had used Goldman Sachs's services on numerous occasions. The firm had advised Messier just six months before on his €12 billion acquisition of USA Networks from Barry Diller and had also handled the January share placement.

Yet Goldman Sachs had also been the long-standing adviser to the Bronfmans at Seagram, helping the U.S. company with most of its acquisitions and disposals of businesses since the 1960s, including the merger with Vivendi in June 2000. The request from Edgar Bronfman Jr. put Altuzarra in the most difficult of positions, requiring him to choose between his professional duties and his personal loyalty to Messier. Yet like so many other of Messier's close advisers, Altuzarra had come to feel his counsel was no longer being heeded by the Vivendi Universal chief executive. After some reflection, he accepted the unusual mandate from the Vivendi Universal board to second-guess the company's own management. "We were in a very strange and difficult position," one Goldman Sachs banker would later say.

Messier lashed out at the three bankers, interrupting them at every opportunity to claim they were overstating the risks of default. He said the company could issue a bond that would neutralize all of the cash-flow concerns. However, U.S. board member Richard Brown asked Altuzarra whether, in his opinion, a bond was actually feasible in current market conditions. Before the head of Goldman Sachs in Paris could respond, Messier cut him short. Some accounts of the meeting have it that Messier snapped at Altuzarra like a judge ruling evidence inadmissible in a court of law: "You're not here to give market advice. You're here for a specific assignment and you can keep your responses to that assignment only." Others present remember it differently. They say Messier tried to prevent Goldman Sachs from answering Richard Brown's question by arguing that the U.S. bank, as a mergers-and-acquisitions specialist, was simply not qualified to offer such advice.

"Well, I don't care. I still want to know," replied Brown, a silver-haired fifty-three-year-old who sat on the boards of some of the largest companies in the United States, including the Home Depot domestic improvement group. The U.S. bank repeated that in its view Vivendi Universal had only a small chance of launching a bond. It concluded that the company would face a material risk of bankruptcy as early as September, just three months away, if it did not swiftly sell another large stake in Vivendi Environnement.

After all that had just been brought to its attention, Edgar Bronfman Jr. decided that any responsible board would now support a motion to dismiss the chief executive. Yet even as he called for a vote, he realized he had miscalculated. The French board members hesitated, again regrouping along national lines, while Simon Murray rushed to Messier's rescue. He spoke fervently in Messier's support for several minutes and concluded that those who did not agree with his strategy should leave the board if they found themselves in a minority.

Serge Tchuruk, chairman of Alcatel, a company whose plunging share price left him equally exposed to shareholder unrest, and Marc Viénot also backed Messier, rejecting the idea that a chief executive could be jettisoned at the whim of the markets. Everyone at the table knew the impasse was unsustainable: either the U.S. directors must leave the board or the French must suggest a new chief executive. But lacking a candidate of their own to replace Messier, and with their ears still ringing from his stirring warnings of an American putsch, the nine French board members banded together to save him. Exactly as Messier had hoped, the board split. He had slipped from the Bronfmans' clutches.

With the next board meeting not due to be held until September, Messier had bought himself three months. Edgar Bronfman Jr. determined not to be outmaneuvered: the U.S. board members, even though they had found themselves in a minority at the meeting, would on no account resign. With 6 percent of Vivendi Universal's shares, the Bronfmans had too much of their wealth invested in the Franco-American media group to walk away from the problem. The board had just been informed that the company would within weeks be in the throes of another liquidity crisis. Only a bond—which the world's leading investment bank had just told them was almost impossible in current market conditions—stood between them and bankruptcy.

It seemed unbelievable to Edgar Bronfman Jr. that the French board members were planning to head off for the long summer holidays without seriously confronting the fact that Vivendi Universal was heading for the rocks. In private, however, several French board members faced the reality of the situation: no chief executive ever survived for long with a divided board. Jean-Marc Espalioux, chairman of Accor and former deputy chief executive of Vivendi Universal, privately divulged that in his opinion the matter would be dealt with quietly over the summer. Away from the glare of the television cameras, the Parisian business world would make Messier understand that he would have to leave the group once a suitable successor had been found. But he would leave with honor. It would happen by the end of the year.

However, even as the French board members emerged from Vivendi Universal's headquarters on avenue Friedland into the beautiful summer evening, their complacency was shattered. That night all Vivendi Universal's hopes of escaping a liquidity crisis would die with the revelation that WorldCom had perpetrated a massive accounting fraud. The news of the $3.8 billion fraud triggered a 75-percent fall in the telecommunications group's share price in after-hours trading in New York and pushed it, within days, to file for the largest bankruptcy in history. The next morning, President George W. Bush himself made a statement deploring the latest "outrageous" development in the crisis of corporate America. "Those entrusted with shareholders' money must strive for the highest of standards," he intoned.

For Vivendi Universal, any prospect of issuing a bond vanished. The latest corporate scandal caused havoc in the debt markets, not just raising borrowing costs, but actually making it inconceivable that a high-risk company such as Vivendi Universal, already the object of considerable suspicion, could tap the markets for any fresh loans. For Messier, it signaled the end: "The bankruptcy of WorldCom ruined our plan for a bond issue, which would have been sufficient to eliminate all risk to our cash position until the end of the year and beyond."[1]

WorldCom unsettled the French board members. The hope

that the bond markets would calm sufficiently to allow the group to raise cash had been their last excuse for doing nothing, the only justification for brushing aside Goldman Sachs's dire predictions. The situation at Vivendi Universal also unnerved the French stock market regulator. The next morning, Wednesday, June 26, at the request of the Commission des Opérations de Bourse, Messier put out a lengthy statement to clarify the group's financial position. As ever, he described it in the rosiest light: "Owing to its strong free cash flow, combined with the execution of the disposals program and potential bond issues, Vivendi Universal is confident of its capacity to meet its anticipated obligations over the next twelve months."

For Edgar Bronfman Jr., the comment was typical of the "Clintonesque" pattern of misrepresentation that he had come to loathe. "He was aware there was a liquidity crisis, but could always argue he was getting advice that he could do a bond. It has to be said that that is anyway only a crappy lawyer's kind of argument—a company is in bad shape if only a single bond stands in the way of its going bankrupt—but there it is. The bond markets were certainly getting tighter and tighter, but at no moment did it actually become impossible for him to do a bond until after WorldCom on June 25."

The French directors received a further impetus to address the crisis at Vivendi Universal from reports that Edgar Bronfman Jr. and Claude Bébéar planned to call an extraordinary shareholder meeting to oust Messier. It was also (incorrectly) suggested that Bronfman might propose himself or Barry Diller, the newly appointed head of Universal Studios, as a possible replacement at the helm of the company. Messier had long held out the bogeyman of a Bronfman taking control of Vivendi Universal as a means of uniting the French directors in his support, but now the threat was working against him. Suddenly, out of fear of seeing hard-nosed American management take over Vivendi Universal, the French board members screwed up their courage and decided that it was time to act.

The business world that had created Messier, put him on a pedestal, and presented him as the symbol of France's ability to adapt to the challenges of the global marketplace decided to destroy its masterpiece. As Alain Minc, the author of *www.capitalisme.fr* and ubiquitous philosophe of French corporate affairs, put it: "France Inc. took over." The first move came that Wednesday, the day after the board meeting. Just as Messier was telling a conference of skeptical media analysts that he planned to run Vivendi Universal "for fifteen years," Michel Pébéreau, the imperious chairman of BNP Paribas, the largest French bank and second most exposed lender to the French company, decided to give the thumbs-down.

At the end of the previous week, on learning of the rushed attempt to raise money from Deutsche Bank that had panicked already frazzled investors, Pébéreau had asked once again to be briefed on the Vivendi Universal situation. On discovering the facts, he lost his temper: what had the board been doing? he raged. What had the audit committee been thinking? Pébéreau ordered that no new loans be granted. His decision freed Daniel Bouton, chairman of Société Générale, the largest lender to the Franco-American media group, who also decided to freeze fresh funds for Messier. Bouton summoned Messier the next day to deliver his ultimatum: resign or risk seeing the company forced to file for insolvency. Messier sent Hannezo in his place, but the banker's message was duly transmitted.

The refusal of the two French banks to extend new loans to France's largest private-sector employer sent the clearest of signals: Messier was finished. According to one banker involved in Messier's last desperate attempts to raise cash to keep his empire running, the banks were determined to use their leverage to force management change. Messier did not give up. Later that day negotiations with Barclays Bank to roll over a huge loan collapsed. Over the weekend, Bayerische Landesbank, the German bank that had been heavily exposed to Kirch, the stricken Bavarian media group, also decided to back away from a new €1 billion loan. "I think by Saturday morning, Messier knew it was over," one banker said. Either way, the banks played a vital role in pushing French board members toward showing Messier the door.

The lending bankers, long regarded as the plodding work-horses of the financial community, were the new masters. They held the most crucial ingredient in the postbubble economy: cash. Cash mattered to Vivendi Universal because other sources of short-term finance were fast disappearing. The debt markets, both commercial paper and bond markets, had started to close to Vivendi Universal following the downgrade delivered by Moody's in May. Moreover, the Franco-American media group had practically no more assets that could be sold at short notice. Even its stake in Vivendi Environnement was subject to a lockup agreement that prevented it from being sold for another eighteen months.

The day after the board meeting, Bronfman and Sam Minzberg had a long discussion with Claude Bébéar. The two Americans told the head of AXA that they would accept any candidate of his choice, but pleaded with him to hurry. Still unsure that they would be able to convince the French board members to take action against Messier, Bébéar and the American directors decided to gather the 5 percent of Vivendi Universal's votes that would enable them to bypass the board and demand an extraordinary shareholder meeting.

Bébéar told Bronfman and Sam Minzberg that he had a candidate in mind: Jean-René Fourtou, vice chairman of Aventis. Fourtou had all the right qualities. First, because he was a friend, one of Bébéar's circle of southwestern wine and rugby lovers. Also, at the age of sixty-two, his career was behind him. He would not be tempted to pursue the Messier dream. He was a no-nonsense, stolidly anti-intellectual businessman. For two months, however, he had rejected the invitation: he was semiretired and was looking forward to lowering his golf handicap. He had already run a major French company, Rhône-Poulenc, and created a European champion by merging it with Germany's Hoechst to create Aventis. In sum, he felt he had nothing to prove.

Yet over a dinner in Brussels that evening with former French president Valéry Giscard d'Estaing, Fourtou changed his mind. "You must do it for France," the president of the European Convention told him. With the statesman's words ringing in his ears, Fourtou, who had once acted as treasurer of the elder statesman's centrist political party, agreed to accept an unpaid mandate as a rescue chief executive. He decided he would do it for the *"gloire,"* he later said.

By a quirk of fate, the next day Fourtou and Bébéar would find themselves at the same table as Messier at the One Hundred Club. That Thursday, June 27, it was the turn of Alain Ducasse, the first-ever "nine-star" chef (three of his restaurants had received the Michelin Guide's ultimate accolade), to showcase his talents for Paris's biggest lunchers. A man who had assiduously cultivated his networks for twenty-five years, Messier had been too proud to pull out of the One Hundred Club meeting. Alongside him at the top table were several more of the actors in his own drama, including Jean-Louis Beffa, who had resigned from the Vivendi Universal board in April, and Jean-Marc Espalioux, another of Messier's board members. The atmosphere was glacial, but not a word was said of the storm that had engulfed their lunch companion. There would be a time and a place for everything.

That evening, Espalioux would join the key French board members—Jacques Friedmann, Marc Viénot, Dominique Hoenn, and Henri Lachmann for an informal meeting in Serge Tchuruk's boardroom at Alcatel. Informed by Bébéar that Fourtou was waiting in the wings, Lachmann proposed that they ask Messier to resign. One by one, the board members gave their assent to a maneuver that would be virtually without precedent in French history. Serge Tchuruk had little fondness for Fourtou, who had replaced him at the head of Rhône-Poulenc in 1986, but eventually he gave his consent. Marc Viénot, who had nurtured Messier's career for many years, resisted the longest, but even he capitulated.

They had no need to ask for the views of Arnault. In the charged atmosphere that had followed his resignation, Messier and Arnault had launched savage attacks on each other through the media. Arnault had let it be known he had given up trying to gain influence within the boardroom, found Vivendi Universal "dysfunctional," and no longer believed Messier to be the right person to restore the group's credibility with investors. Punch-drunk, Messier lashed back at Arnault's criticism that he had failed to keep the board informed of major financial undertakings, including the sale of shares in Vivendi Environnement. "Bernard Arnault didn't attend the last three board meetings before he resigned from the board," Messier said. "If he was not aware, it's because he was not at the meetings where the transaction was discussed." Arnault's claim that Messier treated his board with disdain was absurd. "If he thinks it's a rubber stamp, he should have resigned years ago. He has been a board member since June 1996 after all. What has he been doing all this time?"

From the Arnault camp, the response was equally barbed: "Ask Mr. Messier how many board meetings he has attended at LVMH recently. I think you will find the answer is close to zero. If they continue like this, I think you will find Mr. Messier may not last the summer." There remained one last board member to consult: Simon Murray. After defending Messier on Tuesday at the board meeting in Paris, the British financier had already returned to London. Edgar Bronfman Jr., who had decided to stay at the Ritz in Paris until the situation was resolved to his satisfaction, flew across the Channel to discuss Vivendi Universal with him face to face. By the end of the meeting, the Bronfman heir had Murray's proxy. "He did a total one-eighty. How did I do it? You underestimate my powers of persuasion." Bronfman told Murray to look beyond Sam Minzberg's style and listen to what he was saying. Murray said that the honorable thing for him to do would be to resign as a director immediately. Murray's decision sealed Messier's fate. Even his loyal foreign legionnaire had abandoned him.

During the evening of Thursday, June 27, everything was finalized. The French board members agreed that Messier should be asked to resign. Edgar Bronfman Jr. was informed. Two board members, Henri Lachmann and Jacques Friedmann, both close to Claude Bébéar and to President Jacques Chirac, were chosen to explain to Messier how things stood and to suggest that he resign. For Friedmann, the mission evoked memories of an earlier era in French business history. In the 1980s he had been given a nickname by the bosses of public companies: the "undertaker." It had been the job of this powerful public servant to inform the chairmen of companies within the state's then far-reaching sphere of influence that they had fallen from favor with the Elysée palace or with Matignon, official residences respectively of the French president and his prime minister, and were "to be resigned."

On Friday, June 28, Jacques Friedmann found himself in a familiar situation. That morning, he had alerted the Elysée palace and Matignon to what was to come. He had then called Messier to fix an appointment for the afternoon. Messier realized that the meeting could mean only one thing. The two men knew each other well. It was, after all, Friedmann who had spotted Messier when he was at the Ecole Nationale d'Administration, had opened doors to ministerial staffs, had placed him with Edouard Balladur, then finance minister, and had subsequently supported him right through to his assumption of the reins of power at the influential and secretive Générale des Eaux. Friedmann was quick to deliver the message. The man they called the undertaker explained to his protégé that it was in his own best interest to resign. He could leave with honor, but he would have to leave now.

Messier received Friedmann and Lachmann in his office. They talked for two hours. "You should resign; if not, the board or even an annual shareholder meeting will force the issue. Nobody supports you anymore. The markets want you to resign. You know it. Go before someone is obliged to humiliate you," repeated the two board members. They asked him to summon the board on Sunday, June 30, for a special session during which he would announce his resignation as chairman and chief executive.

"All this is nothing but a huge plot. I'll never resign," replied Messier. He showed them letters he had received from Sam Minzberg, whom he said had been harassing him. He explained that in his eyes there were three groups of people who shared an interest in pushing him out: one was led by Claude Bébéar, who wanted to establish himself as "*the* godfather of French business"; there was the political ambush by the Elysée palace, Jacques Chirac never having liked him since his days as an adviser to Edouard Balladur, his onetime rival on the Right for the French presidency; and last, there were the Hollywood moguls, who had never accepted that he should come and challenge them on their own ground and had encouraged the Bronfmans to deploy their "bootlegger" methods to retake control of Universal Studios.

"You're not the victim of a plot, you're a victim of yourself and your errors," retorted Lachmann. The Vivendi Universal chief executive again complained that to hand over control of the group to new management would be tantamount to a takeover, but without a premium, and that shareholders should have a right to express an opinion on what would amount to a complete reversal of the group's strategy. It was not Vivendi Universal's shareholders who were trying to force him out but self-interested cliques of "granddaddy gunslingers" from the French business establishment of the 1970s and venal politicians clustered like flies around Chirac. Why should he submit to that?

Shareholders deserved at the very least to receive either a full-takeover bid or the chance to vote on an alternative strategy for the company at a shareholder meeting, he argued. Yet his logic failed to convince: there was not to be a change of economic control and ownership at Vivendi Universal, just a change of management. The two men said that they would have no choice but to convene an extraordinary shareholder meeting that would vote him out if he did not resign. Messier did not jump at the opportunity to defend himself in front of his shareholders. His reply was dry and abrupt: "Let them do it if they dare," he said defiantly, bidding the two board members good day and refusing to shake Lachmann's hand on the way out.

Straightaway, Messier convened all the staff working in the avenue Friedland headquarters. He acknowledged and apologized for his mistakes. "The group has two difficult years ahead, but we'll succeed," he said. His staff were touched by the confession, made in the best Catholic tradition. He knew the financial crisis was deepening. That morning he had ordered the sale of Vivendi Universal's remaining stake in Vinci, its former construction subsidiary, even though the securities were already pledged for a bond issue that was repayable in those same shares.* Nevertheless, he had no choice but to sell, and fast. The transaction raised €353 million.

The sale left a twitchy Moody's unmoved. That afternoon the

---

*Simultaneously, Vivendi Universal bought calls to hedge the outstanding bonds that were exchangeable into the Vinci shares.

credit rating agency told the finance department that it would probably be forced once again to lower the group's credit rating. This time it would be the end. A further downgrade would mean that Vivendi Universal fell to junk status—many institutions and pension funds would be legally barred from holding its shares. Billions of euros of borrowings would immediately fall due for repayment—money that the company simply did not have. Just two days earlier Messier had promised the market that the group could meet its cash-flow deadlines over the next twelve months with equanimity. It now faced bankruptcy.

Throughout the weekend, directors pressed him to call a board meeting. He refused. According to the company's statutes, only the chairman had the right to call a board meeting within ninety days of the previous one. He could see no need for one, he told them: the next meeting would be held on September 25. By then, he was confident, everything would be better, the summer squall forgotten. Moreover, he let it be known that he was ready to make concessions to the markets: why not split his role as chairman and chief executive? He offered to make Agnès Touraine chief executive, leaving him as chairman of the board. This gambit would have been accepted with relief just months earlier, but was now rejected.

The moment for stalling maneuvers had passed. The whole of Jean-Marie Messier's famous network—énarques, Polytechniciens, *inspecteurs des finances,* members of Siècle, of the One Hundred Club, of the Club of 40—which once made him the most powerful businessman in France had evaporated. His friends recommended he leave with dignity. His wife, Antoinette, a sensible former physics teacher, telephoned board members to express understanding for their situation. "I'm not phoning to defend Jean-Marie," she said on that Saturday to Lachmann. "You have to do what's best for Vivendi," she concluded. Only when the French board members, who gathered at Henri Lachmann's house in the Sixth Arrondissement on the morning of Sunday, June 30, threatened to issue a communiqué explicitly stating their loss of confidence in him did Messier show the first sign of accepting his fate. At 7 P.M., he agreed to call a board meeting to announce his abdication.

One crucial stumbling block, however, remained: Messier refused to call a meeting until Vivendi Universal, which was represented in the final negotiations by Edgar Bronfman Jr. and Marc Viénot, agreed to pay him a €21.7 million severance package, worth more than four times his total remuneration in 2001 of €5.12 million. "His attitude was 'Unless I get my money, I'm not going to call a board meeting,'" said Bronfman. "But we couldn't wait until September. The company would have been gone by then. My view was that, however repugnant it may be to give that cocksucker anything, it was more important to save the company. It was blackmail, and any agreement negotiated under duress would of course not be valid. But it was my duty to agree to it. It was €20 million or so to save a company with a €13 billion equity value. I take that deal any day."

The board members were white with fury. Not only had Messier attempted to hold the company to ransom, but he had revealed himself to be guilty of extreme hypocrisy. All Paris remembered how two years earlier he had condemned Elf Aquitaine for awarding its chairman, Philippe Jaffré, a pay-off of some €18 million–€19 million. "If I was an Elf director, I would not have voted in favor of the golden parachute given to Philippe Jaffré," he had written in *j6m.com*. "The possibility of being fired by one's shareholders, whether as a result of a takeover or for any other reason, is one of the risks of being a chief executive. We are paid for that. And well paid. These special payments—the golden parachutes that we hear so much about—cannot be justified for executive directors. My contract has no such clause. I promise my board never to negotiate one."

# EPILOGUE

At 7 P.M. on Sunday, June 30, after a weekend of protracted negotiations, Jean-Marie Messier finally agreed to call a board meeting
to announce his abdication. He had one last demand. He wanted
an assurance that the €21.7 million severance package that Edgar
Bronfman Jr. and Marc Viénot had just agreed to would not be
subject to board approval.

At this, however, the American and the Frenchman both bridled. "It was impossible," said Bronfman. "He was still chairman
and therefore the agreement of the board was necessary for any
payment. So I refused to sign and so did Marc Viénot." However,
Eric Licoys, loyal member of the Dream Team, did sign on behalf
of the company.

With the paper in his pocket, on Monday, July 1, Messier duly
called a board meeting for that Wednesday. The promise of compensation did not last long. At the meeting, the board members
decided to refuse him a single euro. The legal wrangles over the
golden parachute that Messier had promised never to seek would
remain unresolved at the end of 2002.

Messier chose not to attend that last meeting. On Tuesday, July
2, he convened all the headquarters staff for an emotional farewell
address. For a man who had always liked Napoleonic compar-
isons, the scene had about it something of the farewell address to
the Old Guard at Fontainebleau.

"To restore peace and calm to Vivendi Universal, I have decided to step down. For me, it is a heartbreaking decision: I wanted to create this company. I built it because I believed in it. And I still do. I am leaving so that Vivendi Universal can continue. I leave with a heavy heart in the hope of easing the tensions between the members of our board and ending the constant suspicions of the market.

"Vivendi Universal must go on. Partial disposals are necessary but the core must be preserved: a major media and communications company, the only truly global and multicultural company," he declared with tears in his eyes.

Emotions ran high, notwithstanding the financial collapse of the group and the decline in the share price to its lowest level since the mid-1980s. People cried, hugged each other, denounced the political cabal against the group, and admired their chairman's apparent spirit of sacrifice. The scene of Messier leaving the Vivendi Universal headquarters crying and receiving the embraces and applause of his employees was broadcast repeatedly over the television networks that night.*

While he was staging his departure, Vivendi Universal's board members were working to choose a replacement. Jean-Louis Beffa was sounded out but declined on Friday, as did Jean-Marc Espalioux. The financier Vincent Bolloré offered his services, arguing

---

*On April 20, 1814, the emperor of France and would-be ruler of Europe said good-bye to the Old Guard after his failed invasion of Russia and defeat by the Allies, with strikingly similar words: "Soldiers of my Old Guard: I bid you farewell. For twenty years I have constantly accompanied you on the road to honor and glory. In these latter times, as in the days of our prosperity, you have invariably been models of courage and fidelity. With men such as you our cause could not be lost; but the war would have been interminable; it would have been civil war, and that would have entailed deeper misfortunes on France. I have sacrificed all of my interests to those of the country. I go, but you, my friends, will continue to serve France. Her happiness was my only thought. It will still be the object of my wishes. Do not regret my fate; if I have consented to survive, it is to serve your glory. I intend to write the history of the great achievements we have performed together. Adieu, my friends. Would I could press you all to my heart."

that he would not be afraid of standing up to the banks, but he was rejected.

There remained Jean-René Fourtou. Several board members objected. They balked not so much because of his age, proximity to Bébéar, or lack of knowledge of the media industry; the semi-retired vice chairman of Aventis had a more serious defect: he was not an *inspecteur des Finances,* the ultraexclusive group of civil servants composed in large part of those who had finished at the top of the graduating class at the Ecole Nationale d'Adminstration.

A caste within a caste, monopolizing many of the top jobs in the public services, large corporations, and banks, they considered the chairmanship of Vivendi Universal theirs by right. Messier had been an *inspecteur des finances,* so Vivendi Universal was now part of their fief. Their representatives on the Vivendi Universal board—Viénot, Friedmann, and Espalioux—firmly intended to see the job pass to one of their own.

They agreed on a name: Charles de Croisset. Chairman of CCF, a medium-sized French retail bank recently acquired by HSBC of the UK, he had once been *chef de cabinet* when Edouard Balladur was finance minister. Messier was fully behind the candidacy of his former boss at the finance ministry. It would be a way of keeping a foot in the door and, at the very least, of smoothing the unpleasant negotiations over the financial terms of his departure. However, Claude Bébéar and Edgar Brofman Jr. opposed de Croisset's nomination. "His demands in return for accepting the job were enormous," Bébéar would later say.

Amid the exploding flashguns that signaled the departure of Jean-Marie Messier, Moody's dropped its bombshell, downgrading the group's debt to junk status. Messier announced the bad news to the board, blaming them for wasting time over the weekend in quibbling over the terms of his departure when they should have been negotiating with the banks. "They would soon find out that having started so many fires to blow them out with a single breath would be complicated," he commented.[1]

In panic, Edgar Bronfman Jr. went straight to Guillaume Hannezo's office to demand the full picture: "Within less than two hours it was clear to me that we were dead at the end of the following week. I called Claude that night. I couldn't risk Fourtou turning up on Wednesday, seeing how bad things were, and walking right out again. That would have cost us thirty-six hours. We did not have that time. I needed to ask Bébéar, 'Are you guys in or out?'"

The chairman of AXA had decided, in order to prove his distance from Vivendi Universal, not to join the board. For good measure, he went big-game hunting in Africa, meaning to be far away from Paris at the moment power was transferred to Jean-René Fourtou. His plans were soon disrupted. The board members had hardly sat down on July 3 when they demanded that Bébéar should join the board. The AXA chairman was coopted in his absence.

Hannezo briefed Fourtou on the cash position and on the status of negotiations with the banks, who were queuing up to tell him that they were withdrawing all credit from the group. "I understood nothing, but I concluded that if someone as brilliant as Hannezo couldn't explain what was going on, then things had to be really serious," Fourtou said.

He managed to reach Bébéar in Botswana.

"I've killed a buffalo," the AXA chairman said. "Have you killed yours?"

"You're a board member, you're chairman of the finance committee of Vivendi Universal, and you're coming back straightaway. I need you. The banks have cut all credit lines. I'm not sure Vivendi Universal will last the week," replied the new chairman, still not managing to believe that the world's second biggest media group, with turnover of €28 billion, could have contrived to put itself in this fragile position.

A few weeks later, Fourtou would tell the French parliament: "If Jean-Marie Messier had stayed at the head of Vivendi Universal, the company would have filed for bankruptcy within ten days. Without my credibility as the former boss of Rhône-Poulenc and without that of Claude Bébéar, we would never have succeeded in raising the necessary funds to save the group from bankruptcy."

❧

✦

In a last letter to Vivendi Universal's 380,000 employees, Messier exhorted his successor to preserve his vision for the transatlantic media group: "Mistakes have been made, but they can all be corrected; and that's what I had started to do. However, in my mind, the only mistake that could never be corrected, one from which there could be no return, would be to break up the company's core business. Vivendi Universal's vision deserves to succeed and it can succeed if everyone wants it to."

However, over the next six months, Jean-René Fourtou and Claude Bébéar, assisted by Henri Lachmann, who was appointed head of strategy, systematically dismantled the Messier empire. France was once again forced to abandon its ambitions to build a champion in the media industry.

Within six months of Messier's departure, Fourtou, under pressure from the banks, which had grudgingly extended a €1 billion lifeline to allow him time to undertake a fire sale of assets, rapidly disposed of over €7 billion worth of assets, and promised to raise another €16 billion from further sales by the end of 2004. The severity of the financial crisis left him no room for sentimentality.

Every branch of the sprawling conglomerate was either hacked off or cut back. Vivendi Universal ceased to claim that it was a coherent entity or that the whole was worth more than the sum of the parts. Fourtou denied there were any worthwhile synergies between media and mobile telecommunications and casually referred to Vivendi Universal as a holding company. The breakup was swift and professional.

It started with the long tail of indefensible assets. Messier was given until the end of the year to vacate his Park Avenue apartment, which, ironically, in view of the damage it had done to his image, was one of the only assets bought during his reign that kept most of its value. The baubles of empire—the half-dozen aircraft, the Seagram art collection, the soccer clubs, the château outside Paris—were all slated for sale.

The purge continued with the loss-making divisions: the Internet and Canal Plus. Vivendi Universal's 50-percent stake in Vizzavi, the Internet start-up that had been valued at €30 billion two years earlier, was sold to Vodafone for just €143 million. Canal Plus abandoned its ambitions to dominate the European pay-television industry. Its loss-making European operations were sold, with Rupert Murdoch picking up Telepiu in Italy for just €873 million, just over half of the originally agreed-upon price. French media groups such as Lagardère were expected to buy the residual French rump of Canal Plus, which was otherwise set to be sold off via a stock market listing.

The purge extended well beyond the loss-making businesses. Vivendi Universal's publishing arm—which Messier had once boasted would be the world number one—was broken up. The European publishing houses that had been part of Havas were sold to Lagardère, and the U.S. arm, Houghton Mifflin, was sold to private equity houses for 25 percent less than the $2.2 billion Messier had paid in the summer of 2001. French investors bought the remaining 40-percent stake in Vivendi Environnement for €4 billion. The 10-percent stake in Echostar, acquired in December 2001 for $1.5 billion, was sold for $1 billion a year later.

By the start of 2003, Vivendi Universal, as conceived by Messier, had ceased to exist.

The publishing, international pay-TV, and Internet arms of the sprawling conglomerate had been sacrificed. Moreover, Fourtou felt no compunction in admitting that he had "next to zero credibility" as a manager of Vivendi Universal's U.S. entertainment assets. Within days of his arrival in July, it became clear that Vivendi Universal's U.S. entertainment assets—Universal Music, Universal Studios, and USA Networks—would soon return to American ownership, either through an outright sale or an initial public offering.

John Malone, chairman of Liberty Media; Sumner Redstone, chairman of Viacom; and Marvin Davis, a former chief executive of Paramount, all made no attempt to disguise their hopes of picking up prime U.S. media assets cheaply. However, by April 2003, Fourtou was held in an armlock by Barry Diller, who had resigned his position as chairman of Vivendi Universal Entertainment to maximize the value of all the rights he had negotiated from Messier at the moment of his sale of USA Networks to Vivendi Universal. Bankers close to Diller claimed he would be entitled to up to $2.5 billion of compensation from Vivendi Universal if the sale of USA Networks triggered any tax liabilities for its original owners.

However, few expected Vivendi Universal would delay the sale of the U.S. entertainment business once it had paid off Barry Diller, who was also waiting for an opportunistic bid. The only asset of any size that appeared to have even a short term future within the rapidly disappearing group was Vivendi Universal's stake in Cegetel, France's second largest mobile telephone operator.[1] Analysts were convinced, however, that even this solitary asset would sit more naturally in the hands of Vodafone, for whom France represented the missing piece in its coverage of the European market.

Vivendi Universal swiftly became an embarrassingly grandiose name for the reality of the shrunken group. The financial collapse and fire-sale breakup of the group wiped out the investments of more than 1 million individual shareholders: Vivendi Universal's shares at the end of the year were worth little more than €12–€13, compared to €150 in March 2000. Messier had promised to make his shareholders rich. They lost their shirts. In March 2003, Vivendi Universal announced its 2002 results amid a sea of red ink. For the second year running, the media group claimed the record for the largest loss in French corporate history. Its loss reached an astounding €23.3 billion in 2002, after Fourtou was obliged to record further massive write-offs to the book value of Messier's acquisitions.

A strong nationalism colored the rescue of Vivendi Universal. Politicians of all shades intervened relentlessly to demand that French businesses stay French. Laurent Fabius, the finance minister, likened Vivendi Universal's story to "a bad Hollywood film which also finishes very badly." Vivendi Environnement was sold to a core group of French institutions, with the state-owned Electricité de France becoming its largest shareholder. Vodafone, the giant UK mobile telephone group, was repulsed in its attempts to gain control of Cegetel.

Its French publishing assets—which included the country's

best-known dictionaries and reference books within the Larousse and Robert imprints—were barred from falling into foreign hands. The fact that Vivendi Universal had itself bought Houghton Mifflin, owner of the *American Heritage Dictionary*, was conveniently forgotten. All memories of "la France qui gagne" faded as the country struggled to keep control of its own schoolbooks.

Nowhere was this nationalism more evident than in relation to the Hollywood assets. Many in Paris seemed obsessed with the idea, initially planted by Messier, that "the Americans" planned to regain control of their company on the cheap. "There is an anti-American tinge to the desire to keep the Hollywood assets," noted Edgar Bronfman Jr. "It's odd there's no similar sentiment in France about selling Vivendi Environnement at knock-down prices or selling Houghton Mifflin cheaply or Canal Plus or Telepiu. It's the fact that Hollywood is Jewish, that the Bronfmans are a Jewish family. It's a fear not just of selling it back to the Americans, but of selling it to Jews. I feel this undercurrent of anti-Semitism. It's in the water. That Hollywood is a Jewish town has a lot to do with all this."

As Peter Bart, editor of *Variety*, put it on *Charlie Rose* the day of Messier's coup d'état: "He modeled himself as the most American of all the European executives. What we learned, though, was that that part of the role model he most venerated was the rainmaker. He talked a nice soft-spoken game but he thought big, he thought outrageously big. I think he thought far beyond the boundaries of what anyone could possibly achieve."

Messier's stress on the importance of the wireless device was "ten years if not a generation ahead of its time," Bart said. No one seriously doubted that the mobile distribution platform would one day be very important for media companies. But as Edgar Bronfman Jr. put it, the trouble was that Vivendi Universal suffered from two gigantic failures, when one alone would have been fatal: "First, we were early, way too early, and that's the same as being wrong. Second, value creation is all about execution, and we did not execute the merger."

It is hard to execute an idea that is ahead of its time. More than any other chief executive during the bubble years, Messier worshiped the false god of synergy. He believed that the cross-promotion of products throughout the divisions of his vast conglomerate would justify all the complexity that conglomerate entailed. Academic and consultant Mark Sirower had revealed the hole in acquisition logic based on synergy as early as 1997, in his book *The Synergy Trap*. He observed that "for most acquisitions, achieving significant synergy is not likely."

But for Messier, who was attempting to create a world-leading media company ex nihilo and was therefore unable to benefit from more humdrum cost savings and economies of scale, synergy was an indispensable crutch. It acted as handmaiden at the creation of Vivendi Universal and then the numerous deals that extended the empire. Without being able to claim that the new mobile Internet technologies would create €400 million of additional profit, he would never have been able to justify the price he paid for a Hollywood giant.

The assumptions turned out, of course, to be wildly optimistic. Messier had flashed a hand he did not hold. His bluff was called. Vivendi Universal's failure further undermines the case for other media conglomerates, such as AOL Time Warner and Disney, whose shape is also in large part justified by supposed synergies: "AOL Time Warner arguably does not work. Disney arguably does not work. Vivendi Universal arguably didn't work," Bart argued. "One wonders whether the Balkanization of Vivendi Universal is going to signal a similar trend throughout the universe of companies of this sort."

Nonetheless, the Messier affair had a devastating impact on French capitalism. According to a poll published by Sofres in February 2003, the crisis of corporate governance at Vivendi Universal is in large part responsible for the astonishing fact that 93 percent of people now think companies are primarily being run for the benefit of self-serving executives. It found that 54 percent of all French people no longer trust the chief executives of France's leading public companies, compared to 25 percent in 1985.

"These results reflect the shock people felt at the revelation of how Jean-Marie Messier ran Vivendi Universal," said Muriel

Humberjean, deputy managing director of Sofres. "The idea that he could be negotiating a golden parachute after he promised never to do so in his book, after he had just driven the company close to bankruptcy, and after he destroyed the savings of millions of shareholders and employees was shocking."

Many in the French business establishment would like to pretend the Vivendi Universal debacle never happened. In time, it will become clear whether this attitude extends to the public authorities charged with maintaining confidence in France's stock market. An investigation by the COB is expected to conclude during the first half of 2003. Its findings will be measurable against those of the under-resourced SEC in the U.S., which is also conducting an investigation.

The COB findings could have an impact on the class-action suit gathering steam in New York and the criminal investigations on both sides of the Atlantic. At the start of 2003, insiders at the COB said it was "certain" that the watchdog would move to a "sanction procedure" against Vivendi Universal and its previous management team. Whether this indeed happens and how serious any criticism might be remains to be seen.

In the spring of 2003, however, several pieces of news whetted the appetites of the lawyers probing the fallen media company. Of particular interest was the revelation of hitherto undisclosed share dealing by several members of Messier's Dream Team. A handful of executives close to Messier exercised options and sold stock days before the huge share placement sent the stock crashing in the first weeks of 2002. Guillaume Hannezo, for example, booked a profit of €1.3 million ($1.4 million) on December 28, 2001.

A week later, on January 7, 2002, Vivendi Universal sold 55 million shares to Deutsche Bank and Goldman Sachs, who had been discussing the placement since December 22. "This is material information," said one banker involved in the transaction. Both banks are now awaiting the COB's report before deciding whether they have a strong enough case to recover the money they lost through the courts. In late March 2003, Liberty Media decided it had a strong enough case to sue Vivendi Universal for allegedly inflating its share price at the time of the USA Networks transaction. John Malone's company alleged that Vivendi Universal had disguised its financial crisis at the time it exchanged its own shares for Liberty's stake in USA Networks. "At the time of the merger agreement, Vivendi Universal faced a massive and crippling liquidity crisis, but through straightforward representation and concealment hid the material facts from Liberty Media," the complaint filed on March 30, 2003, stated.

Messier himself admited taking out a loan of €5.3 million from Société Générale and investing all his savings to exercise options at €50 at a time when the shares were around €60. But he strenuously denies selling any of the acquired shares in the run-up to the disastrous €3.3 billion placement in January 2002. Catherine Gros, Messier's head of communications, and Micheline Clerc, his personal assistant, were also found to have exercised options in December 2001. An internal legal report that was also seized during the raids suggested the new management team was aware these share dealings might arouse the suspicion of investigations looking for evidence of any insider trading: "Certain people could ask whether J.M.M, G.H., Catherine Gros, and J.M.M.'s personal assistant were not all in possession of privileged information (in particular because they were the only ones to know the real financial situation of the company) when they bought at €50 [shares] that could still at that point be resold at €60, knowing that the shares would likely rapidly be worth much less. We note that at least three people [Messier, Hannezo, and Micheline Clerc] exercised options on the same day [December 28, 2001]: is this a coincidence?" the internal report asked.

In April 2003, however, doubts over Messier's share dealings dramatically intensified after Vivendi Universal published its 2002 annual report. Extraordinarily, this showed that his holdings in the company's stock had fallen by some 231,000 shares in the first half of that year, despite all his denials of ever having sold shares.

For an entire week after the first news story broke, Messier continued to deny that he had sold any shares. After a week of such obfuscation, however, on April 8, 2003, Messier attempted to clarify the discrepancy. He admitted that he had, in fact, sold €15.4 million worth of Vivendi Universal shares, but stressed that he had passed the sale order in late December 2001, which enabled him to claim that he had not lied about selling shares in 2002. The fault lay with bureaucracy, he stated.

The official response was severe. Jean-René Fourtou was un-amused. On April 10, Vivendi Universal released an ominous statement outlining their discovery and confirming that they "imme-diately transmitted this information to the COB and the SEC." For the class action lawyers in the U.S., the news of Messier's secretive share dealings and the widening rift between Vivendi Universal and the former chief executive was a godsend. On April 11, lawyers from Abbey Gardy, the law firm leading the class action suit, filed a motion to the Southern District court in Manhattan claiming that "Messier concealed his [share] trading for more than a year."

The internal legal report also suggested Messier misled in-vestors by disguising the extent of the liquidity crisis in the last few weeks of his time as chief executive. It said two statements released on June 18 and June 25 without the formal approval of the board appeared to have misrepresented the real state of the company's indebtedness by as much as €5 billion to €7 billion: "These two in-complete or false statements to the market could without doubt fall under the heading of article L.465-1 du Code Monétaire et Fi-nancier, for 'false information.' According to Guillaume Hannezo, Jean-Marie Messier's communiques were abnormally 'reassuring.' Two professors of law are now working on this issue."

These questions coincided with a shake-up at one of Vivendi Universal's auditors, Salustro Reydel, a small French firm that de-rived 10 percent of its €136 million turnover from the media group. Bernard Cattenoz, the accountant responsible for Vivendi Universal's audits for more than a decade, has been asked to relin-quish that responsibility. This is one of several preliminary recom-mendations put forward by Christian Blanc, the mediator charged by the accounting profession with resolving a feud between Jean-Claude Reydel, chief executive, and Edouard Salustro, chairman of the supervisory board.

Blanc's final report is expected to call for both Reydel and Salustro to step back from day-to-day running of the company. Salustro Reydel maintains Blanc's recommendations are not linked to the COB investigation, which has seized the e-mails between Messier and the accounting firm that suggest it was subject to pressure to agree to a favorable treatment of the BSkyB transaction in the 2001 results. Once again, many questions would appear to remain unanswered.

Suspicion of Vivendi Universal's accounts, as of all large, aggressive, and acquisitive companies, has been aroused by the collapses of Enron and WorldCom. Yet the chances that investigators will discover any Enron-style fraud are slim. Since its collapse over the summer, Vivendi Universal has been one of the most audited companies in the world.

On September 25, Jacques Espinasse, Vivendi Universal's new finance director, told a press conference that he had found no evidence of any accounting irregularity or intentional misrepresentation of the group's financial situation. Jean-Marie Messier has repeatedly insisted that he and his fellow executives never did anything wrong, never defrauded the company or wrongfully enriched themselves. "It was a problem of debt and not of fraud."[2]

Vivendi Universal showed how quickly a breakdown of trust between investors and a chief executive can paralyze a company. Midway in his odyssey, Messier lost his credibility. An all-powerful chairman and chief executive with an insatiable appetite for complex multibillion-dollar deals, financial risk, and celebrity interviews, he personified the crisis of capitalism as it swept from Wall Street into Europe.

Caught in the crossfire of worsening Franco-American relations and cursed with an uncanny ability to irritate the French establishment, Messier was soon isolated. But unlike other chief executives, he refused to hunker down until the storm of suspicion passed. Even the most revered executive in U.S. corporate history, Jack Welch of General Electric, came under fire. The presumption of innocence no longer applied to anyone. It certainly had ceased to apply to Messier, who experienced the hysterical opprobrium that often succeeds extreme celebrity.

It would be wrong to blame the near collapse of France's largest private-sector employer on the hubris of just one man. An entire system of corporate governance failed. In the end, it took a complete outsider, Claude Bébéar, in alliance with the Bronfmans, who were protecting their interests as shareholders, to step in and avert disaster. Calls for increased stewardship by big shareholders and board members have always been a feature of stock market crashes.

John Kenneth Galbraith, almost fifty years ago, in his account of the 1929 crash, observed that in the good times the amount of shareholder money squandered or siphoned from the system—the "bezzle"—rises sharply because everyone feels good and nobody notices. "In depression all this is reversed. Money is watched with a narrow, suspicious eye. The man who handles it is assumed to be dishonest until he proves himself otherwise. Audits are penetrating and meticulous. Commercial morality is enormously improved. The bezzle shrinks."

At the end of 2002, Jean-Marie Messier started a boutique investment bank called Messier Partners. "I failed. I start again from zero. I take my hat and my cane and go and see clients," he told a press conference at the launch of his second book, *Mon Vrai Journal*. Edgar Bronfman Jr. is less kind about the Frenchman's prospects, the anger at his betrayal by Messier all too evident: "What future? It's just a name on a door." But Messier is still a young man: he turned forty-six in December 2002, the day after the police raided his Paris apartment and country home.

He says that after six years with Balladur and six years with Michel David-Weill at Lazard, he wants to work for himself now. That is just as well, for it is unlikely that Jean-Marie Messier is inundated with invitations to run large public companies. The breakdown in his relations with the financial community was almost total by his last weeks in power. In large part, his own future is now in the hands of the investigators, whose work was still in progress at the start of 2003.

If there was any wrongdoing at Vivendi Universal that is punishable by law, the numerous investigations will presumably uncover it. If not, the probes will slowly uncover the hubris and self-delusion, described in this book, that ended up destroying around $100 billion of shareholder wealth in a little over two years. As Michael Wolff, media pundit for *New York Magazine,* would succintly put it, the question really boils down to whether Jean-Marie Messier was not "one of the greatest knuckleheads of the age."

That conclusion will be little consolation to the Bronfmans. A lot of people lost money in the new economy bubble, but the Bronfmans lost more than most, and they also lost their family company, Seagram. By the time Edgar Bronfman Jr. presided over the early-July board meeting that sealed Messier's fate, the value of the Bronfmans' holding had plunged 75 percent—wiping out more than $2 billion of the family fortune in the previous six months alone.

"I'm not going down in history as the one Bronfman who pissed away the family fortune," Edgar Bronfman Jr. famously once said. He has time to rebuild his reputation. Strangely, his credibility has not suffered as much as many might imagine. It is actually only thanks to Edgar Bronfman Jr., Samuel Minzberg, and Claude Bébéar that Vivendi Universal did not go bankrupt over the summer. As Barry Diller would later say, "Edgar is the real unsung hero of this story." That is likely to be some consolation to Edgar Bronfman Jr. as he starts a new life making small investments in the luxury goods sector through his private investment company, Lexa Partners. He recently took a small stake in the Asprey & Garrard jewelry company, adding to an interest in the Four Seasons restaurant on the ground floor of the Seagram Building.

He remains, however, anxious to rebuild his own reputation in the eyes of his family and investors. The Bronfmans' investment in Vivendi Universal is now worth a little more than $1 billion, down from some $7 billion at the time the merger was announced—the decline is in part due to stock sales, notably of $1.3 billion in May 2001. But even so, a fortune built up since the 1920s vanished in eighteen months.

Messier turned out to be "less than we thought," Edgar Bronfman Sr. would later say. "Not to pooh-pooh the money, but that's not the real disaster. The real disaster is bad judgment. [We] took something my father had built and my son converted into something which was really dynamic, and put it in with these guys to get the kind of size we needed. And suddenly it blew up in our faces."[3]

Vivendi Universal's misadventures in the new economy are over. Whatever the ultimate findings of the many legal investigations, it is a clear that the company was an extraordinary creation of an extraordinary man. It was a noble vision to create a French and European champion in the media and entertainment industry. Only a man as self-confident—some would say foolhardy or reckless—as Jean-Marie Messier would ever have dared to attempt it.

That it ended in failure cannot be in the least surprising. The odds were stacked against Vivendi Universal from the start. What is extraordinary is that so many people believed for so long in Jean-Marie Messier and the likelihood of his success. In the end, he and his empire fell. Their like will not be seen again.

# ACKNOWLEDGMENTS

The authors would like to thank the hundreds of people they have interviewed. Too numerous to mention individually, collectively they made this book possible. The authors are also grateful to their respective newspaper editors, Andrew Gowers of the *Financial Times* and Jean-Marie Colombani of *Le Monde*, for backing the collaboration and giving them time to step back from the demands of their daily newspapers. At *Le Monde* and the *Financial Times*, the authors would like to thank Laurent Mauduit, Edwy Plenel, Will Lewis, Lionel Barber, and James Harding. Many thanks also to Leo Hollis and Adrian Zackheim, our incisive editors at Penguin, and to John Makinson for suggesting the book. Caroline Dawnay of PFD in London and Michael Carlisle of Carlisle & Co. in New York were everything that two first-time authors could dream of finding in their agents. Nicki Kennedy of International Literary Agency, Alexandre Wickham of Albin Michel in Paris, and Robert Tobin helped us reduce the logistical difficulties of simultaneously producing a French and an English text so that the *entente* remained at all times more than *cordiale*. Robert Graham, Charlotte Johnson, Leo Johnson, and Amelia Gentleman all made valuable comments on different drafts of the book. And lastly, a big thank-you from Martine to Jérôme and to Raphaël.

# NOTES

Throughout the book the authors have drawn on innumerable private interviews and conversations with interested parties, as well as publically available material which have not been specifically annotated. The quotations from Jean-Marie Messier's own books, *j6m.com* and *Mon Vrai Journal,* were translated by Jo Johnson.

## Introduction

1. Richard Lambert, "A master of political naivety," *The Times,* November 30, 2002.
2. Jean-Marie Messier with Yves Messarovitch, *Mon vrai journal* (Editions Balland, Paris, 2002), p. 82.
3. Jean-Marie Messier made this comment at a breakfast at the *Financial Times* on May 14, 2002, attended by one of the authors.
4. See Messier, *Mon vrai journal,* Chapter 5.
5. Ibid., p. 87.

## Chapter 1: A Perfect Frenchman

1. "The man who blew €72bn," *Le Point,* July 5, 2002.
2. Jean-Marie Messier, *j6m.com* (Hachette Littératures, Paris, 2000), p.16.
3. Ibid., p. 88.
4. David Owen, "A new-style networker with a radical edge: Jean-Marie Messier, chief executive of Vivendi," *Financial Times,* June 7, 1999.
5. Ibid.

## Chapter 2: *In Medias Res*

1. Jean-Marie Messier, *Mon vrai journal* (Editions Balland, Paris, 2002), p. 208.
2. "I failed, I start from zero," *Libération,* November 14, 2002.
3. Jean-Marie Messier, *j6m.com* (Hachette Littératures, Paris, 2000), p. 33.
4. Guillaume Hannezo, submission to the Commission des Opérations de Bourse investigation, October 2002.
5. Messier, *j6m.com,* p. 33.
6. Ibid., p. 38.
7. Ibid.
8. Messier announced that he would sue Esser for implying that he had acted in bad faith, but nothing more was ever heard about it. Esser's comment was made in an interview in the *Financial Times* by Bertrand Benoit, published on April 4, 2001. Messier withdrew an offer to publish all correspondence between him and Esser.
9. Guillaume Hannezo, submission to the Commission des Opérations de Bourse investigation, October 2002.
10. Quoted in Frank Rose, "Vivendi's high wireless act," *Wired,* December 2000.
11. Messier, *j6m.com,* p. 20.
12. Quoted in Rose, "Vivendi's high wireless act."
13. Messier, *j6m.com,* p. 43.
14. Ibid.
15. Interview by Bertrand Benoit, *Financial Times,* April 4, 2001.
16. Quoted in Carole Matlack, "Vivendi: going Hollywood," *Business Week,* July 3, 2000.
17. Ibid.
18. Quoted in Vizzavi marketing material.
19. Guillaume Hannezo, submission to the Commission des Opérations de Bourse investigation, October 2002.

## Chapter 3: *Hurry Up Please, It's Time*

1. Edgar M. Bronfman, *Good Spirits: The Making of a Businessman* (Putnam, New York, 1998), p. 48
2. Ibid., p. 48.
3. Quoted in Anthony Bianco, "Deal time at Seagram," *Business Week,* June 26, 2000.
4. Bronfman, *Good Spirits,* p. 187.
5. Quoted in Ken Auletta, "No longer the son of," *The New Yorker,* June 6, 1994.
6. Bronfman, *Good Spirits,* pp. 185ff.
7. Ibid.
8. Ibid.
9. Ibid., *Good Spirits,* p. 214.

10. Jean-Marie Messier, *j6m.com* (Hachette Littératures, Paris, 2000), p. 64.
11. Ibid., p. 55.
12. Ibid.

## Chapter 4: Bonjour, Hollywood!

1. Guillaume Hannezo, submission to the Commission des Opérations de Bourse investigation, October 2002.
2. Quoted in Frank Rose, "Vivendi's high wireless act," *Wired,* December 2000.

## Chapter 5: *Maître du Monde*

1. Peter Bart, *Variety,* June 19, 2000.
2. Erik Israelewicz, "Has France become big-headed?" *Les Echos,* July 5, 2000.
3. Philip H. Gordon and Sophie Meunier, *The French Challenge: Adapting to Globalization* (Brookings Institution Press, Washington, 2001), p. 43.
4. Films either wholly or mostly funded by French investment. All figures on the French and international film industries have been taken from the Centre Nationale de Cinématographie 2001 annual report, p. 39.
5. Other books critical of the shareholder movement to appear that summer include Philippe Labarde and Bernard Maris, *La Bourse ou la vie* (Albin Michel, Paris, 2000).
6. Jean-Marie Messier, *j6m.com* (Hachette Littératures, Paris, 2000), p. 191.

## Chapter 6: Vivendi Frères

1. Guillaume Hannezo, submission to the Commission des Opérations de Bourse investigation, October 2002.
2. Michael Wolff, "Meet Barry Buffett," *New York Magazine,* September 30, 2002.
3. See Vicky Ward, "Inside the Vivendi Universal meltdown," *Vanity Fair,* October 2002.
4. Edgar M. Bronfman, *Good Spirits: The Making of a Businessman* (Putnam, New York, 1998), p. 140.
5. Messier was speaking at Manhattan's 92nd Street Y on June 13, 2002 on a platform with *Business Week* editor-in-chief, Stephen B. Shepard.
6. See Vivendi Universal, 2002 half-year financial information, p. 7.

## Chapter 7: The French Exception

1. Canal Plus SA, 2001 annual report, p. 10.
2. Philip H. Gordon, "Liberté, fraternité, anxieté," *Financial Times,* January 19, 2002.

3. Interviewed by the *Financial Times* in January 2002.
4. Robin Pogrebin, "New York philanthropy embraces a charismatic French executive," *New York Times,* May 28, 2002.
5. Michael Wolff, "The big fix," *New York Magazine,* May 13, 2002.
6. "Becoming a New Yorker in a hurry." *New York Times,* December 4, 2001.

## Chapter 8: Speeding Up

1. Jean-Marie Messier, *Mon vrai journal* (Editions Balland, Paris, 2002), p. 162.
2. Quoted in *Toronto Globe and Mail* magazine, August 30, 2002.

## Chapter 9: Claude and the Boys

1. Jean-Marie Messier, *Mon vrai journal* (Editions Balland, Paris, 2002), p. 60.
2. Barry Diller was interviewed by Brenda Buttner on Fox News, April 24, 2002.
3. Messier, *Mon vrai journal,* p. 68.

## Chapter 10: Vivendi vs. Universal

1. Money makes life so fluid. . . . Little by little you risk isolating yourself, as in the stretch limousines, those all-white or all-black centipedes, that you see sliding along the streets of New York protected by tinted windows and bulletproof doors. . . . So why am I so afraid of developing the limousine syndrome? Because I know that in the end it is fatal. It anesthetizes you against reality." (Jean-Marie Messier, *j6m.com* [Hachette Littératures, Paris, 2000], p. 15).
2. Jean-Marie Messier, *Mon vrai journal* (Editions Balland, Paris, 2002), p. 70.
3. Ibid.
4. Ibid., p. 82.
5. Ibid.
6. Ibid., p. 78.
7. Ibid.
8. Ibid.

## Chapter 11: The Last Days of J6M

1. Jean-Marie Messier, *Mon vrai journal* (Editions Balland, Paris, 2002), p. 178.

## Epilogue

1. Jean-Marie Messier, *Mon vrai journal* (Editions Balland, Paris, 2002), p. 27.
2. Messier, *Mon vrai journal,* p. 184.
3. Brian Milner, "Edgar's blues," *Globe and Mail,* August 30, 2002.

# INDEX

Abbey Gardy, 244
ABC, 60
Accor, 223
Adam, 192, 208
Adecco, 165, 206
Aéro Services, 172
Aerospatiale, 42
Afghanistan, 136, 137
Airbus, xv, 42, 93
  of Messier, 134, 170–73, 176
Air France, 169, 204
Albright, Madeleine, 49, 68
Alcatel, ix, 7, 82, 113, 164, 222
Alcock, Clarissa, 4, 54
Allen, Herb, 116
Altuzarra, Philippe, 108, 156, 219, 220,
  221
Amazon, 95
Amoco, 93
AOL (America Online), 38, 95, 107
AOL France, 151
AOL Time Warner, xi, 10, 44, 72–74,
  126, 134, 158, 159, 241
  merger of, 2, 34, 37–39, 40, 43, 50,
    64, 80n, 90–91
  sales of, 80
Arnault, Bernard, ix, 7, 20, 31, 48, 108,
  111, 113, 173, 189, 194, 207
  Messier criticized by, 227–28

resignation of, from Vivendi board,
  165, 217–18, 220, 227–28
shareholder dividend and, 188–89,
  200
Arthur Andersen, 110, 146, 160–61, 162
AT&T, 150
A3E (Association pour l'etude des
  Expériences Etrangères), 15
Auletta, Ken, 53
Aventis, 42, 113n, 169, 226
AXA, xv, 169, 173, 174, 175, 197, 199
AXA-UAP, 113, 175

Badinter, Elisabeth, 206
Balladur, Edouard, 13, 15, 16, 17, 20,
  23, 235
  Messier as adviser to, 11, 15, 103,
    229, 246
  Messier's Générale des Eaux post and,
    23–24
Barbizet, Patricia, 19, 195
Barclays Bank, 225
Bart, Peter, 61–62, 78, 91, 240, 241
Bayerische Landesbank, 225
Bazire, Nicolas, 10, 15
Beaumont, Count Jean de, 175
Bébéar, Claude, 113n, 169–70, 173–76,
  187–88, 197–99, 202, 209, 227,
  247

Bébéar, Claude (*cont.*)
  on buybacks, 147
  career of, 174–75
  Fourtou and, 235, 236
  and liability of board members for
    damages, 205–6
  Messier criticized by, 173
  Messier's attempts to discredit, xv,
    174
  Messier's ouster and, 224, 226, 229,
    237, 246
  radio interview of, 198
  Vivendi board seat offered to, 187
Beffa, Jean-Louis, 10, 48, 113, 122,
  164–65, 189, 192, 193, 227, 234
  resignation of, 206, 227
Belgacom, 150
Berger, Alex, 38
Berlusconi, Silvio, 103
Bernheim, Antoine, 20
Bernis, Valérie, 195
Bertelsmann, 31, 33, 37, 39, 67, 80
Blair, Tony, 136
Blanc, Christian, 169, 244–45
Blondet, François, 144
BNP (Banque Nationale de Paris), 10,
  20, 31, 165, 173
BNP Paribas, 15, 17, 113, 164, 165–66,
  173, 193, 220, 225
Boeing, 42, 93
Bolloré, Vincent, 10, 234–35
Bono, 142
Boonstra, Cor, 62
Bordas, 33
Boston Consulting Group (BCG), 153
Bourges, Hervé, 168
Bouton, Daniel, 225
Bouygues conglomerate, 32, 133
Bouygues, Martin, 133
Bové, José, xiii, 93, 101, 102, 173
Breton, Thierry, 169, 187, 197
Brewer, Sherry, 53–54
British Petroleum, 93
British Telecommunications, 29, 44
Bronfman, Ann Loeb, 51
Bronfman, Charles, 2, 3, 51, 54, 55, 57,
  59, 62, 64, 67, 86, 163–64

  Vivendi Universal shares sold by,
    145–46
Bronfman, Clarissa Alcock, 4, 54
Bronfman, Edgar, Jr. ("Efer"), 2, 51–64,
  112, 114, 115, 116, 126, 137, 155,
  164, 181, 189, 190, 210, 219–23,
  228
  Bronfmans' share sale and, 117
  Diller and, 76
  ebitda and, 85
  *Financial Times* and, 203
  on French-American culture clash, 77
  French nationalism and, 240
  Goldman Sachs analysis solicited by,
    218–19, 220–22
  on governance committee, 208
  Houghton Mifflin deal and, 110, 117
  on integration of Vivendi acquisitions,
    153
  Maroc Telecom deal and, 106
  on Messier's deceptions, 163, 224
  on Messier's future, 246
  and Messier's ouster and replacement,
    219, 224, 226, 232, 233, 235–36,
    247
  Messier's relationship with, 116,
    117–18, 119, 172
  Minzberg's attacks and, 207, 208
  on Murray, 208
  music industry and, 86
  reputation and future of, 247
  resignation of, 117–18, 119
  in Seagram/Vivendi merger deal, 2,
    3–5, 39–41, 47–50, 48, 49–50,
    64–69, 71, 72, 73, 86, 91
  Universal and, 73, 79, 80
  Vivendi Universal collapse and, x, 247
Bronfman, Edgar, Sr., 1–2, 3, 50–55, 57,
  58, 59, 86, 116, 164, 219
  Hannezo and, 210
  on Vivendi Universal collapse, 247–48
  Vivendi Universal shares sold by,
    145–46
Bronfman, Holly, 51
Bronfman, Phyllis (Phyllis Lambert),
  116, 118, 196
Bronfman, Samuel, 2, 50–51, 119

Bronfman, Samuel, II, 51, 52, 54, 86
Bronfman, Sherry Brewer, 53–54
Bronfman family, 1–5, 39, 50–55, 66,
    67, 69, 86, 118, 196, 203
  Goldman Sachs and, 221
  Vivendi Universal collapse and, 218,
    222, 246, 247
  Vivendi Universal shares sold by,
    116–17
Brown, Richard, 219, 221
Brown, Tina, 60
Browne, John, 31
BSkyB (British Sky Broadcasting), 29,
    32, 33, 45, 82, 100, 121, 150, 156,
    161, 245
BT Group, 209–10
Bujon de l'Estang, François, 92
Bush, George W., 136–37, 223
Business Week, 10, 146

Cabana, Camille, 16
Calvet, Jacques, 24, 31
Camus, Philippe, xv
Canal Plus, 3, 39, 48, 81, 84, 97–100,
    116, 123, 138–39, 176–85, 189,
    193
  Carolco and, 75, 78
  Echostar deal and, 120
  French cinema subsidized by, 97–98,
    99–100, 127–28, 130–31, 132,
    181, 184
  Générale des Eaux and, 22–23
  Guignols show on, 100, 104, 183,
    189
  identity and valuation of, 81, 145
  Lescure dismissed from, 181–82, 183,
    184, 185, 186, 187, 188, 189, 191,
    201, 216
  losses of, 151, 177–78, 179, 181,
    182–83
  in merger with Vivendi and Seagram,
    65, 68, 70, 77, 78–79, 81, 84, 86,
    90, 105, 106, 128, 150, 154
  Messier's difficulties with, 176–85
  NetHold acquired by, 29–30, 32, 65
  rebellion against Vivendi Universal,
    178–79, 183–84, 189
  sale of, in Vivendi Universal breakup,
    238, 240
  Telepiu and, 30, 158, 177–78, 179,
    210, 238
  Vivendi losses blamed on, 177, 181,
    182–83
  Vivendi's ownership of, 32, 45, 65,
    68, 70, 88, 103–4
  Vivendi Universal as viewed by, 100,
    103–4
  Vivendi Universal breakup and, 209
  Vizzavi and, 44
Can't Wait for Sunday, 103
Cap Gemini, 169
Carolco, 75, 78
Case, Steve, 38, 39, 80
Castries, Henri de, 175
Cattenoz, Bernard, 161, 162, 244
CBS, 90, 113–14
CCF, 15, 235
Cegetel, 3, 27, 29, 36, 45, 82, 83, 133n,
    152, 209–10
  valuation of, 145
  Vivendi Universal breakup and, 209,
    239
Chaisemartin, Yves de, 205
Char, René, 21
Charlie Rose Show, The, 146, 240
Château Cheval Blanc, 194
Chevènement, Jean-Pierre, 136
Chirac, Jacques, 8, 13, 16, 18, 20, 22,
    91–92, 94, 131, 184
  Messier's Airbus and, 171
  Messier's resignation and, 228, 229,
    230
  Vivendi Environnement sale and,
    186–87
Chrysler, 93
Cinven, 150
Citigroup, 218
Clerc, Micheline, 243
Club Med, 108–9, 150
Club of 40, 19, 27–28, 199
COB (Commission des Opérations de
    Bourse), x, 121, 160, 161, 162,
    224, 242, 244–45
Coca-Cola, 57, 58, 78

Colombani, Jean-Marie, xv, 182
Columbia Pictures, 56, 57, 58
Comcast, 150
Compaq, 190
Concorde, 151
Coutts, Eric, 219
Couture, Xavier, 181–82, 183
Creative Artists Associates, 59
Crédit Agricole, 193
Crédit Lyonnais, x, 15, 22, 56, 75, 78,
    89, 162–63, 166–68, 200
    Pathé and, 74–75
Croisset, Charles de, 15, 235
cultural exception, French, xiii, 96–98,
    99, 100, 125, 127, 128–32, 139,
    140, 176, 184, 186

Daimler-Benz, 31, 93
Danjou, Philippe, 160–61
Darrois, Jean-Michel, 9
David-Weill, Michel, 18, 20, 246
Davis, Marvin, 238
Davos World Economic Forum, 141–42
Dead Sea, 26
De Gaulle, Charles, 12, 33
Dejouany, Guy, 22–25, 28, 90, 122
Deneuve, Catherine, 138
Deutsche Aerospace, 42
Deutsche Bank, 150, 156–57, 211, 213,
    225
    Vivendi's sale of shares to, 242
Diageo, 49, 61, 105, 121
Diller, Barry, 59–62, 72, 76, 112–15,
    118–20, 178, 179, 181, 184, 185,
    224, 247
    Lescure replaced by, 179–80
    stock options and, 149
    Vivendi appointment of, 122–23, 124,
    125–27, 139
    Vivendi Universal breakup and,
    238–39
DirecTV, 30, 81, 112
Disney, 39, 56, 66, 67, 72, 80, 82, 90,
    107, 126, 159, 241
Dixon, Christopher, 76
dot-coms, see Internet
Dubos, Jean-François, 192

Ducasse, Alain, 227
Duet, 108
Du Pont, 55, 57, 58–59, 67, 82

EADS (European Aeronautic Defence
    and Space Company), 42, 94
Earle, Glenn, 219
ebitda, 83, 85, 153, 160
Echos, Les, 88–89, 92, 176
Echostar, 81, 112, 120, 150, 154, 158,
    163
    sale of, in Vivendi Universal breakup,
    238
Ecole Polytechnique, 12, 174
education, 84, 108, 109–10
Eisner, Michael, 60, 61, 126
Electricité de France, 239
Elf, 20
Elf Aquitaine, 232
EMI, 73
ENA (Ecole Nationale d'Administra-
    tion), 12–14, 19, 235
énarques, 13, 103
Enron, 110–11, 113, 146, 151, 154,
    155, 160, 162, 176, 211, 216, 245
Enterprise et Cité, 175, 199
E Plus, 34
Equitable, 175
Espalioux, Jean-Marc, 19, 111, 124,
    197, 207, 223, 227, 234, 235
Espinasse, Jacques, 245
Esser, Klaus, 35–36, 37, 40, 41–42, 43
Europ@web, 108
Eurosport, 151
Express, L', xv, 182

Fabius, Laurent, 133, 186, 239
Ferrero, Dominique, 168, 200
Ferry, Luc, 136
Figaro, Le, 19, 205
film industry, 60, 78, 88, 96–97
    Carolco, 75
    European, 96–97, 128, 130
    French, 96–98, 99–100, 125, 127–32,
    140, 181, 184
    Hollywood, see Hollywood
    Pathé, 74–75

*Financial Times (FT)*, xiv, xv, xvi,
34–35, 78, 85, 103, 176, 181,
185*n*, 203, 213
"Lex" column in, 30–31, 85, 193–94
*Forbes*, 198
Forgeard, Noël, 171
Foriel-Destezet, Philippe, 165, 206
Forrester, Viviane, 101
*Fortune*, 10, 54, 127
Fouquet, Nicolas, 171
Fourtou, Jean-René, 20, 113*n*, 169, 175
as Messier's successor, x, 226–27,
235, 236, 237, 238, 239, 244
Vivendi breakup under, 237–40
Fox network, 61, 113–14, 126, 137
Fox News, 185
France:
cultural exception in, xiii, 96–98, 99,
100, 125, 127, 128–32, 139, 140,
176, 184, 186
economy of, 11, 15, 16–17
election campaigns in, 184–86
ENA in, 12–13
film industry in, 96–98, 99–100, 125,
127–32, 140, 181, 184
finance ministry of, 16–18, 128, 133,
235
as *la France qui gagne*, 91–93
globalization and, xiii, 11, 49,
92–104, 129–30, 184, 185
left in, 15, 18, 23, 96
nationalism in, Vivendi and, 90–91,
93–94, 95–96, 239–40
nationalization in, 14–15, 18
*noyaux durs* in, 16–17, 201
privatization in, 11, 16, 17, 18, 20
right in, 16, 18, 20, 23, 186
U.S. relations with, xiii, 95, 136–37
Vivendi/Seagram merger and, 90–91,
93–94, 95–96
France Loisirs, 151
France Telecom, 45, 204
French-American Business Council, 49
Frère, Albert, 194
Friedmann, Jacques, 15–16, 113, 124,
207, 227–29, 235
Fukuyama, Francis, 136

Gaccio, Bruno, 103–4, 189
Galbraith, John Kenneth, 246
Générale des Eaux, 18, 19, 81, 89, 92,
99, 111, 122, 139–40, 144, 163,
173
Canal Plus and, 22–23
history of, 21
investigation of, 22, 25
Messier at, 20, 22–25, 26–27, 28, 31,
166
power and influence of, 21–22,
186
refashioned as Vivendi, 27, 31
share price of, 215
General Electric (GE), 76, 84–85, 114,
153, 245
General Motors, 81
Gent, Chris, 31–32, 34, 36–37, 42–43,
44, 45
Georgeson Shareholder, 190
Germond, Philippe, 3, 19, 27, 137, 139,
195, 206, 217
Gibert, Dominique, 151, 161, 200
Giscard d'Estaing, Henri, 109
Giscard d'Estaing, Valéry, 175, 226
globalization, xiii, 11, 49, 92–104,
129–30, 144, 184, 185, 196
Goldman Sachs, 120, 156–57, 220–21
analysis of Vivendi Universal by,
218–19, 220–22, 224
Vivendi's sale of shares to, 242
Gordon, Philip H., 94–95, 129–30
Gros, Catherine, 127, 139, 176, 195,
243
Guardian Royal Exchange, 175
Gucci, 173
*Guignols, Les,* 100, 104, 183, 189

Haberer, Jean-Yves, 14–15, 22, 89
Hachette, 19, 27
Hannezo, Guillaume, 27, 139, 176,
191, 195, 213, 215–17, 225,
244
assets sold by, 210
buybacks and, 147
credit rating agencies and, 120, 143,
154, 156, 199

Hannezo, Guillaume (*cont.*)
  Internet investments and, 107
  Mannesmann/Vodafone negotiations
    and, 36, 37
  Messier's deal making and, 120–21,
    150
  Messier's financial risks and, 143,
    147, 151, 154
  Messier's relationship with, 162
  Messier's replacement and, 235–36
  USA Networks deal and, 120
  on Vivendi's accounting methods,
    159–60
  on Vivendi's debt, 121–22
  Vivendi/Seagram merger and, 3, 48,
    65, 87–88, 120
  Vivendi's growing financial problems
    and, 156, 158, 199, 200, 215–16,
    219
  on Vivendi's strategy, 33–34, 45,
    87–88, 120–22
  Vivendi stock sold by, 242, 243
Havas, 23, 32–33, 45, 81, 82, 238
Henri-Lévy, Bernard, 93
Hewlett-Packard, 19, 27, 190
Hoechst, 42
Hoenn, Dominique, 166, 220, 227
Hollywood, xi, 56–62, 65–66, 73,
    74–75, 78–79, 116, 129, 179, 240
  Europe and, 91, 97
  Messier's resignation and, 229
  Universal Pictures, 1, 39, 56, 58, 66,
    72, 75–77, 84, 85, 112; *see also*
    Universal Studios
Home Shopping Network, 114
*Horreur économique, L'* (Forrester), 101
Houghton Mifflin, 109–10, 112, 117,
    120, 150, 240
  sale of titles of, 150–51
  Vivendi Universal breakup and, 209,
    238
Hughes, 81
Humberjean, Muriel, 241–42
Huntington, Samuel, 136

Intel, 95
Internet, 2, 72, 110

AOL Time Warner merger and, 38–39
  music industry and, 64, 67, 73–74,
    86, 108
  and U.S. power, 95–96
  Vivendi and, xii, 2, 35, 37–38, 40, 69,
    72, 76, 107–8, 151–52; *see also*
    Vizzavi
Ishihara, Shintaro, 56*n*
Israelewicz, Erik, 88–89, 92, 93, 101–2

Jaffré, Philippe, 232
Jahanchahi, Amir, 197, 198
Japan, 56, 79, 116
Johnson, Jo, xv, 203
Jospin, Lionel, 13, 92, 94, 96, 131–32,
    137, 184, 186
*j6m.com* (Messier), xiv, 100–101, 102,
    195, 232
Juppé, Alain, 13, 16
Justice Department, U.S., x, 74–75,
    134*n*

Kampf, Serge, 169
Kassar, Mario, 75
Keller, Hubert, 156
Kerkorian, Kirk, 56, 75
Kessler, David, 130
Kohler, Horst, 173
Koplowitz, Esther, 207, 211–12
Kozlowski, Dennis, 134, 204
KPN, 34
Kravis, Henry, 219
Kravis, Marie-Josée, 219

Lachmann, Henri, 48, 169, 197, 207,
    227–31, 237
Ladd, Alan, Jr., 74
Lagardère conglomerate, 209, 238
Lagardère, Jean-Luc, 20, 209
Lamaze, Ariane de, 146–47
Lambert, Phyllis Bronfman, 116, 118,
    196
Lambert, Richard, xiv
Larousse, 30, 33, 240
Lazard Frères, 141
  Messier at, 11, 18–20, 246
  Vivendi and, 48

*Legionnaire* (Murray), 208
Legion of Honor, 7–10, 136
Lehman Brothers, 81–82
Lellouche, Pierre, 103
Le Pen, Jean-Marie, 184, 186
Lescure, Pierre, 23, 77, 79, 98–99, 111,
    127, 128, 131, 138–39, 154,
    176–82, 190, 203
  Diller's appointment and, 139
  Diller's replacing of, 179–80
  dismissal of, 181–82, 183, 184, 185,
    186, 187, 188, 189, 191, 201, 216
  Henri-Lévy on, 93
  Hollywood and, 116
  Lévy's advertising campaign and, 140
  NetHold acquisition and, 29–30
  Rousselet and, 23, 99
  Universal Studios and, 153, 179–80
  Vivendi/Seagram merger and, 3, 4, 40,
    64, 65–66, 98–99, 128, 139
Levin, Gerald, 38, 39, 57, 61, 80, 126,
    134
Lévy, Maurice, 120, 139–40, 176, 186,
    195, 205, 206
Lévy-Lang, André, 88
Lexa Partners, 247
Lhotelian, Hubert Dupont, 143–44
*Libération*, 127, 132, 184
Liberty Media, 242–43
Licoys, Eric, 2–3, 27–29, 139, 150,
    153–54, 176, 195, 201, 207*n*,
    215–16, 233
Loeb, John, Sr., 51
L'Oréal, 204
*Los Angeles Times*, 78
Louis XIV, 171
LVMH (Moët Hennessy–Louis Vuitton),
    ix, 7, 10, 15, 48, 94, 113, 164, 165,
    194, 204, 228
Lycos, 114
Lyonnaise des Eaux, 22

McDonald's, xiii, 101
McGraw-Hill, 109
Madelin, Alain, 130*n*, 184
Malone, John, 114, 124, 148, 238, 243
Mandelson, Peter, 195

Mannesmann, 29, 144
  Vivendi's negotiations with, 35–37,
    39, 40–42, 43–44, 64
  Vodafone's negotiations with, 31–32,
    33, 34–35, 36, 42–43
Marceau, Sophie, 140
Marconi, 111
Maris, Erik, 48
Maroc Telecom, 106–7, 110, 150, 158
Marsaud, Alain, x–xi
Martin, Laura, 146
Matsushita, 2, 56, 58, 59–60, 62–63,
    78, 79, 116
Maxwell, Robert, 201
MCA, 56–58, 62–63, 110, 116
  Seagram's acquisition of, 57–60, 61,
    62–63
media industries, 64
  AOL Time Warner and, 2, 38–39
  Vivendi and, 31, 32, 33, 35, 40, 44,
    45, 82
  Vivendi/Mannesmann merger and, 35
  Vizzavi and, 44
Messier, Antoinette Fleisch, 7, 14, 134,
    231
Messier, Jeanine, 11
Messier, Jean-Marie:
  acquisitiveness of, xi, 107–10, 111–12,
    114, 120–21, 145, 150, 158
  Airbus of, 134, 170–73, 176
  background and career of, 10–25
  Bronfman's relationship with, 116,
    117–18, 119, 172
  Bronfman's resignation and,
    117–18, 119
  Bronfman's talks with, about Seagram
    merger, 39–41, 47, 48, 49–50
  brooch worn by, 135–36
  cartoon depicting, 182
  celebrity status of, 102–4
  and changes in corporate climate,
    111, 146
  childhood of, 11
  Club of 40 and, 19, 27–28, 199
  credibility lost by, 158, 163–64, 167,
    172–73, 176, 188, 195, 214, 216,
    224, 245

Messier, Jean-Marie (*cont.*)
  cultural exception and, 97–98, 100,
    125, 127, 128–29, 130–32, 139,
    140, 176, 184, 186
  at Davos World Economic Forum,
    141–42
  Dream Team of, 139, 195
  education of, 11–12
  election campaigns and, 184–86
  at ENA, 12–14
  "exotic little country" remarks of,
    100, 139
  extravagance of, 170–72, 203–4
  farewell address of, 233–34
  at finance ministry, 16–18
  future of, 246
  Gaccio on, 103–4
  at Générale des Eaux, 20, 22–25,
    26–27, 28, 31, 166
  as godfather of French capitalism, 173
  image of, 28–29, 102–3
  as incarnation of *la France qui gagne,*
    91–93
  as *inspecteur des finances,* 14–16
  isolation of, 195–96, 245
  *j6m.com,* xiv, 100–101, 102, 195, 232
  last letter of, to Vivendi employees,
    237
  at Lazard Frères, 11, 18–20
  as Legion of Honor member, 7–10,
    136
  Lévy's advertising campaign for, 140
  Louvre speech of, 90–91
  Mannesmann/Vivendi negotiations
    and, 35–37, 39, 40–42, 43–44, 64
  media attention courted by, 102–3,
    173, 176
  Messier Partners bank of, 246
  mobile telephone license fees and,
    128, 133
  *Mon vrai journal (My True Diary),*
    xiv–xvi, 170*n*, 172, 188, 203, 246
  networking of, 18–19
  New York apartment of, xiii, 116,
    203–4, 237
  New York move of, 7–10, 133–35,
    137–38, 140, 146, 185, 196

  overpaying by, for acquisitions, 27,
    72, 73, 106, 120, 122, 241
  paranoia of, xiv, 182, 193, 194,
    202–3, 229–30
  in *Paris Match,* 102–3, 140–41, 172,
    176
  personality of, xi, 10, 28–29, 102
  physical appearance of, 133
  political speculation about, 103
  public reaction to revelations about,
    241–42
  question of dismissal or resignation
    of, 166–67, 168, 176, 182, 187,
    198, 204–5, 206–9, 213–14, 215,
    218, 219, 222–32
  resignation of, 228–29, 231–32,
    233–34, 235, 237
  salary and bonuses of, 102, 209, 232
  in Seagram/Vivendi merger, xi, 1–5,
    39–40, 47–50, 64–69, 70–80,
    82–89; *see also* Seagram
  severance package for, 232, 233,
    242
  as sole leader of Vivendi Universal,
    137, 141
  Tétreau and, 167–68
  Vivendi Universal shares purchased
    by, 143–44, 145–46, 149, 155
  Vivendi Universal shares sold by,
    155–58, 243–44
  in Vodafone/Vivendi negotiations,
    36–38, 40, 42–44
  Wolff on, 135
  *see also* Vivendi; Vivendi Universal
Messier Partners, 246
Meyer, Ron, 66, 77, 79, 84, 123, 124,
  178
MGM (Metro-Goldwyn-Mayer), 15,
  56, 75
Michelin, 94, 204
Microsoft, 95
  MSN, 44, 84
Middelhoff, Thomas, 31, 37, 39, 67
Minc, Alain, 9, 14, 205, 225
Minzberg, Samuel, 163–64, 188, 190,
  203, 209, 212–13, 219, 220, 228,
  229, 247

hostility of, at board meeting, 207–8, 209
Messier's ouster and, 226
Mital, Christine, 100
Mitterrand, François, 15, 18, 23, 27, 99, 136
Moët Hennessy–Louis Vuitton, *see* LVMH
*Monde, Le,* 23, 99, 103, 133, 136, 170*n*, 185*n*, 189, 201–2, 203
cartoon in, 182
Messier's allegations against, xv–xvi, 201
Monod, Jérôme, 22
Montrone, Paul, 135
*Mon vrai journal (My True Diary)* (Messier), xiv–xvi, 170*n*, 172, 188, 203, 246
Moody's, 120, 154, 156, 199, 226, 230–31, 235
Morishita, Yoichi, 57
Morita, Akio, 56*n*
Morris, Doug, 63, 77
Moussaoui, Zaccarias, 136
MP3.com, 108, 148, 150
Mulligan, Brian, 47, 48, 65
Murdoch, Rupert, xvi, 39, 44, 56, 61, 78, 80, 90, 120, 137, 145
BSkyB and, 29, 32, 100
Echostar purchase and, 112
Telepiu and, 177–78, 179, 210, 238
Murray, Simon, 207–8, 212–13, 219, 222, 228
music industry, 63–64, 67, 73–74
Duet and, 108
French cultural exception and, 96
Internet and, 64, 67, 73–74, 86, 108
*see also* Universal Music

Nathan, 30, 33
NBC, 76, 114, 137
NetHold, 29–30, 32, 65
Neuville, Colette, 192, 202, 208
Newmark, Evan, 44
News Corporation, 39, 67, 72, 80, 90, 107, 159

New York:
Davos World Economic Forum in, 141–42
Messier's apartment in, xiii, 116, 203–4, 237
Messier's move to, 7–10, 133–35, 137–38, 140, 146, 185, 196
September 11 attacks on, 109, 135–37, 141, 146, 147, 155, 199
*New Yorker,* 53
*New York Magazine,* 135, 247
New York Stock Exchange, 134
*New York Times,* 117, 134–35, 138
Normandy, 178
*Nouvel Observateur, Le,* 100
*noyaux durs,* 16–17, 201

Olivennes, Denis, 77, 84–85, 99, 127, 128, 138, 153, 176–80, 216
Lévy's advertising campaign and, 140
resignation of, 180
One Hundred Club, 227
Orange, 34, 41
Orange, Martine, xv–xvi, 201
Osaka, 116
Ossard, Claudie, 129
Ovitz, Michael, 57, 59

Paper, Xavier, 161–62, 168
Paramount, 56, 60, 113, 126
Paribas, 17, 88, 173
*see also* BNP Paribas
*Paris Match,* 102–3, 116, 140–41, 172, 176
Parmentier, Guillaume, 98
Parretti, Giancarlo, 15, 56, 74, 78, 79
Parsons, Dick, 126
Pathé, 74–75
peace canal proposal, 26
Pearson, 110
Pébéreau, Michel, 165–66, 225
Peres, Shimon, 26
Pernod Ricard, 105, 121
Peyrelevade, Jean, 168
Philips Electronics, 2, 62, 86
Pinault, François, 19, 116, 173
Pinault Printemps Redoute, 19

Pineau-Valencienne, Didier, 19, 20–21
Pioneer Electronics, 75
Plantu, 182
Plon, 33
Polygram, 2, 62–64, 71, 73, 80, 86, 153
Prat, Jean-Francois, 48
Proglio, Henri, 27, 153, 154, 201, 211, 212
Prot, Baudouin, 15, 166
Publicis, 120, 139–40, 186, 195, 206
publishing, 30, 32–33, 45, 58, 65, 81, 84, 106–7, 109–10, 238, 239–40
  Houghton Mifflin, see Houghton Mifflin
Putnam, 58
Putnam Berkley, 110
Puttnam, David, 53

Raffarin, Jean-Pierre, 13
Ralli, Georges, 48, 141, 176, 206
Ravary, Eric, 166, 167
Redstone, Sumner, 50, 61, 113, 238
Reid, Richard, 136
Renault, 204
Reydel, Jean-Claude, 162, 244
Rheims, Bettina, 8, 9
Rhône-Poulenc, 20, 42, 226, 227, 236
Richemont, 30
Rives, Jean-Pierre, 169–70
Robert imprint, 30, 33, 240
Rogard, Pascal, 129
Rohatyn, Felix, 49, 68, 196
Rondor Music, 149, 209
Rothko, Mark, 1, 116
Rousselet, André, 23, 99, 138
Roux, Ambroise, 20, 22, 23, 24, 173, 174, 175, 199
Ruiz, Raoul, 129
Rupert, Johann, 30
Rushdie, Salman, 136
RWE, 81

Sagittarius Productions, 53
Sahut d'Izarn, André, 174
Saint-Gobain, 17, 48, 82, 113, 164, 192, 193
Salustro, Edouard, 244

Salustro Reydel, 160–62, 168, 244–45
Schneider Electric, 19, 21, 48, 169, 173
Schrempp, Jurgen, 31
Sci-Fi channel, 59, 114
Scoot.com, 108
Seagram, 1, 39–40, 49–69, 78, 79, 85
  Bronfmans' decision to sell, 64
  debt of, 68, 71, 121
  Du Pont and, 55, 57, 58–59
  Goldman Sachs and, 221
  MCA acquired by, 57–60, 61, 62–63
  origins of, 50
  Polygram acquired by, 2, 62–64, 71, 73, 80, 153
  price of Vivendi's acquisition of, 68, 70–72, 73
  profit of, 85
  shareholders' approval of merger of Vivendi, Canal Plus and, 86–87, 105
  share price of, 47, 64, 68
  Universal subsidiary of, see Universal Music; Universal Studios
  USA Networks percentage held by, 60, 71–72, 76, 114, 115
  USA Networks sold by, 59–60, 114, 119, 122, 126
  Vivendi's acquisition of, xi, 1–5, 39–40, 47–50, 64–69, 70–89, 90, 100, 105, 106, 149–50, 159
  Vivendi Universal disaster and, 247
  Vivendi Universal's sale of drinks business, 71, 82, 85, 105, 121, 151
Seagram Building, 1, 116, 118, 204, 247
SEC (Securities and Exchange Commission), x, 204, 242, 244
September 11 terrorist attacks, 109, 135–37, 141, 146, 147, 155, 199
SFR, 29, 31, 74, 133n
Sheinberg, Sidney, 57, 59
Sirower, Mark, 241
Six Nations tournament, 169, 197
Smith, Terry, 78, 85, 86, 159
Snider, Stacey, 66, 75, 79, 123, 124
Snook, Hans, 41, 42, 44
Société Générale, ix, 7, 17, 23, 31, 113, 173, 193, 225, 243

Sofres, 241–42
Sony, 39, 56, 57, 78
Duet and, 108
Spielberg, Steven, 57, 117
Square D, 19–20
Standard & Poor's, 154
Stern, Edouard, 20
Stewart, Collins, 159
Stewart, Martha, 134
Stream, 158, 177–78
*Synergy Trap, The* (Sirower), 241

Tasca, Catherine, 127, 130–31, 180
Tchuruk, Serge, ix, 7, 113, 207*n*, 222, 227
telecommunications, 64, 145
Maroc Telecom, 106–7, 110, 150, 158
mobile, xii, 2, 44, 64, 84, 95–96, 128, 133, 237, 240, 241
Vivendi and, xii, 29, 31–35, 37–38, 40, 43, 44, 45, 81, 82, 87, 106–7, 237; *see also* Cegetel
Vivendi/Mannesmann merger and, 35
Vizzavi and, 44
Telepiu, 30, 158, 177–78, 179, 210, 238, 240
television, 2, 35, 58, 60, 81, 99
BSkyB, 29, 32, 33, 45, 82, 100, 121, 150, 156, 161, 245
Canal Plus, *see* Canal Plus
DirecTV, 30, 81, 112
Echostar, 81, 112, 120, 150, 154, 158, 163, 238
Fox, 61
French cultural exception and, 96
NetHold, 29–30, 32
Telepiu, 30, 158, 177–78, 179, 210, 238, 240
Universal, 59, 61
USA Networks, *see* USA Networks
Vivendi and, 32, 33, 44, 45, 65, 87; *see also* Canal Plus
Vizzavi and, 44
Tétreau, Edouard, 166–68, 200
Thatcher, Margaret, 15
Thomas, René, 10, 31, 113, 165, 206

Thomson Multimedia, 169
*Time*, 104
Time Warner, 52, 56, 57, 67, 77
*see also* AOL Time Warner
TotalFinaElf, 45, 94
Touraine, Agnès, 19, 27, 137, 139, 140, 176, 195, 206, 217, 231
TPS, 30
*Tribune, La,* 177
Trichet, Jean-Claude, 92–93
Twentieth Century–Fox, 56, 60–61, 78
Tyco, 154, 204

UAP, 113, 175
UMTS, 34
United Kingdom, 15
Universal Mobiles, 84
Universal Music, xi, 1, 9, 69, 73–74, 84, 85–86
Davos World Economic Forum and, 141–42
Maroc Telecom and, 107
Seagram's acquisition of, 2, 71
Vivendi merger and, xi, 1–5, 50, 72, 73–74, 87
Vivendi Universal breakup and, 238
Universal Pictures, 1, 39, 56, 58, 66, 72, 75–77, 84, 85
Echostar purchase and, 112
Universal Studios, xi, 61, 65–66, 67, 76–77, 119
contract renegotiations at, 123–24
Diller's replacement of Lescure at, 179–80
education and, 110
Lescure and, 153, 179–80
Sci-Fi channel, 59, 114
Seagram's acquisition of, 2, 71
television channels, 59, 61
theme parks, 85, 108–9, 116
USA Networks, *see* USA Networks
Vivendi merger and, xi, 1–5, 50, 79–80, 87; *see also* Vivendi Universal
Vivendi Universal breakup and, 238
Uproar, 108
USA Interactive, 126

USA Networks, 148, 210
  Liberty suit and, 243
  Seagram's sale of, 59–60, 114, 119,
    122, 126
  Seagram's stake in, 60, 71–72, 76,
    114, 115
  Vivendi's acquisition of, 112, 115,
    119–24, 125–27, 139, 143, 150,
    156, 158, 163, 200
  Vivendi Universal breakup and,
    238–39
U.S. Department of Justice, x, 74–75,
    134n
U.S. Filter, 27

Valenti, Jack, 129
Vanity Fair, 58
Variety, 61, 66, 78, 91, 183
Védrine, Hubert, 94, 95, 137
Veronis, John J., 135
Viacom, 50, 56, 72, 80, 90, 107, 113, 159
Viénot, Marc, ix, 7, 31, 113, 164, 190,
    198, 207n
  on governance committee, 208
  Messier's ouster and, 213–14, 222,
    227, 232, 233, 235
Villin, Philippe, 19, 197
Vinci, 27, 193, 230
Virgin Records, 56
Vivendi:
  acquisitions of, 30–31, 32–34
  BSkyB and, 32, 45, 82, 100
  Canal Plus owned by, 32, 45, 65–66,
    68, 70, 88; see also Canal Plus
  Club of 40 and, 27–30
  creation and early days of, 27–46
  Générale des Eaux renamed as, 27, 31
  Internet services and, 35, 37–38, 40,
    44, 69, 72; see also Vizzavi
  lack of focus in, 32–34, 45, 65, 87
  Lazard Frères and, 48
  Mannesmann's negotiations with,
    35–37, 39, 40–42, 43–44, 64
  media products of, 31, 32, 33, 35, 40,
    44, 45
  price of Seagram deal with, 68,
    70–72, 73

publishing businesses of, 30, 32–33,
    45, 65
Seagram acquired by, xi, 1–5, 39–40,
    47–50, 64–69, 70–89, 90, 100,
    105, 106, 149–50, 159
shareholders' approval of merger of
    Seagram, Canal Plus and, 86–87,
    105
share price of, 30, 34, 43, 45–46,
    64–65, 66, 68, 70–71, 72, 86, 87
telecommunications interests of, 29,
    31–32, 33–34, 35, 37–38, 40, 43,
    44, 45, 87
television interests of, 32, 33, 44, 45,
    65, 87; see also Canal Plus
Vodafone's alliance with, 36–38, 40,
    42–44, 66
water operations of, xii, 2, 27, 33, 45,
    65; see also Vivendi Environnement
see also Vivendi Universal
Vivendi Environnement, 27, 33, 45, 80,
    81, 121, 150, 154, 206
  debt of, 105, 121, 163
  flotation of, 81, 82
  Koplowitz and, 211–12
  lockup agreement and, 226
  Maroc Telecom and, 107
  RWE offer and, 81
  sale of, 186–87, 196, 199, 200–201,
    206, 210–12, 216, 218, 226, 238,
    239, 240
  U.S. Filter acquired by, 27
  Vivendi Universal breakup and, 209,
    238
Vivendi Universal:
  accounting methods of, 159–60, 163
  acquisitions and assets of, xii–xiii,
    80–82, 107–10, 111–12, 120–21,
    145, 148–50, 152–54, 158, 241
  Airbus and, 170–73
  annual report of (2002), 243
  assets sold by, 210
  auditors of, 160–62, 244–45
  bankruptcy crisis of, xv, 222, 236,
    242, 247
  banks' refusal to extend loans to,
    225–26, 236, 237

board members of, *see* Vivendi
Universal, board of
breakup of, 209, 237–40
Bronfman family's sale of shares of,
116–17
BSkyB and, 100, 121, 150, 156, 161,
245
Canal Plus and, *see* Canal Plus
claw-back clauses and, 148–49,
209
climate of fear at, 201–2
Club of 40 and, 19
complexity of, as hindrance to
understanding value, 80–83
convergence and synergies in, 72–74,
83–85, 87, 107, 110, 152–54, 178,
237, 240–41
corporate scandals and, 111, 113,
146, 151, 154, 155, 160, 162, 176,
211, 216, 223–24
creation of, xi, 1–5, 42, 50, 68–69,
70–71, 80, 86–88, 90, 100, 105
credit downgrade threat and, 120,
143, 154–57
credit downgrading of, 199–200, 226,
230–31, 235
debt of, 105, 121–22, 146–47, 150,
152, 155, 161, 163
Duet and, 108
ebitda measure of, 83, 85, 153, 160
extravagance at, 151
financial problems and collapse of,
ix–xvi, 151–67, 199–201, 209, 213,
215–26, 230–31, 234, 236–37,
239, 242–48
Fourtou as Messier's successor at, x,
226–27, 235, 236, 237, 238, 239
French-American culture clash in,
77–78
French nationalism and, 90–91,
93–94, 95–96, 239–40
globalization and, 92–104
Goldman Sachs' analysis of, 218–19,
220–22, 224
identity of, 81–82, 87, 105, 106, 107
Internet sector and, xii, 2, 76, 107–8,
151–52; *see also* Vizzavi

investigations of, ix–xi, 156, 242,
243, 244–45, 246–47, 248
junk status of, 231, 235
Liberty Media's suit against, 242–43
liquidity crisis at, 199–200, 213, 215,
217, 218–19, 220–22, 222–24,
243, 244
losses of, 162–63, 166, 209, 239
Maroc Telecom and, 106–7, 110, 150,
158
Messier's letter to employees of, 237
Messier's purchase of shares of,
143–44, 145–46, 149, 155
Messier's resignation from, 228–29,
231–32, 233–34, 235, 237
Messier's salary, bonuses, and
severance package from, 102,
209, 232, 233, 242
Messier's sale of shares of, 155–58,
243–44
mobile telephone licenses of, 128, 133
operational skill lacking in, 153
Paris office of, 137–38
philanthropic patronage of, 134–35,
196
profits of, 82–84, 85
publishing interests of, 81, 84, 106–7,
109–10, 238, 239–40; *see also*
Houghton Mifflin
reasons for failure of, 240–41,
245–48
sale of drinks business in, 71, 82, 85,
105, 121, 151
share buybacks at, 147–48, 149
share creation and, 148
shareholder dividends and, 188–89,
200
share price of, 87, 140, 144–49,
156–58, 167, 185, 188–89,
199–200, 206, 208, 209, 213, 215,
217–19, 234, 239, 242–43
size and sales of, 80, 90–91
stock option programs at, 124*n*, 149,
185, 188, 191–92, 194
telecommunications sector of, xii, 81,
82, 106–7, 237; *see also* Cegetel
television market and, 76

Vivendi Universal (*cont.*)
Universal wing of, *see* Universal
Music; Universal Studios
USA Networks purchased by, 112,
115, 119–24, 125–27, 139, 143,
150, 156, 158, 163
U.S. shareholders in, 132
valuation of, 80–83, 159
water business of, xii, 2; *see also*
Vivendi Environnement
*see also* Messier, Jean-Marie; Vivendi
Vivendi Universal, board of, ix, 7, 48,
163–66, 196–97, 204–9
bank refusals and, 225
damage liability feared by, 205–6
financial details unknown to, 205
Goldman Sachs' analysis and,
218–19, 220–22, 224
governance committee and, 208
meetings of, 178, 188–94, 205,
206–8, 209, 210, 212–13, 218,
219–22, 223, 226, 227–28,
231–32, 233
Messier's attempts to replace members
of, 206
Messier's dividing of U.S. and French
members of, 196
Messier's replacement and, 234–35,
236
Messier's resignation and, 228–29,
231–32, 233
Messier's severance package and, 232,
233
and question of Messier's dismissal or
resignation, 166–67, 168, 198,
204–5, 206–9, 213–14, 215, 218,
219, 222–32
refusals to join, 165–66
resignations from, 164–65, 206,
217–18
rules of governance and, 204–5
stock option proposal and, 188,
191–92, 194
support for Messier's resolutions on,
189–94
WorldCom scandal and, 223–24

Vivendi Universal Entertainment (VUE),
122–23, 126
Viventures 2, 107–8
Vizzavi, xii, 3, 42, 43–46, 47, 74, 84,
87, 88, 95–96, 121, 210
hyping of, 45, 66
launch of, 65
problems with, 84–85, 86
valuation of, 145
in Vivendi Universal breakup, 238
Vodafone, 82, 84, 210
Mannesmann and, 31–32, 33, 34–35,
36, 42–43
Vivendi's alliance with, 36–38, 40,
42–44, 66
Vivendi Universal breakup and, 238,
239
Vizzavi and, 44, 238

*Wall Street Journal,* 58
*Wall Street Journal Europe,* 70, 193
Walt Disney, 39, 56, 66, 67, 72, 80, 82,
90, 107, 126, 159, 241
Warner Music, 73
*Washington Post,* 126
Wasserman, Lew, 56–57, 59, 116
water business, xii, 2, 27, 33, 45, 65
*see also* Générale des Eaux; Vivendi
Environnement
Weinberg, John, 39
Welch, Jack, 245
Wintel, 95
Wolff, Michael, 114, 135, 247
WorldCom, 155, 176, 223–24, 245
World Economic Forum, 26
*World Is Not for Sale, The* (Bové), 101
World Trade Organization, 96
Wright, Bob, 4
*www.capitalisme.fr* (Minc), 225

Yahoo!, 37, 39, 67, 84, 95, 150
Messier and, 108
Vizzavi and, 44

Zacharias, Antoine, 27, 193
Zidane, Zinedine, 92